The Vital Tradition

THE CATHOLIC NOVEL IN A PERIOD OF CONVERGENCE

Gene Kellogg

LOYOLA UNIVERSITY PRESS

Chicago, 1970

© 1970

LOYOLA UNIVERSITY PRESS

Printed in the United States of America

Library of Congress Catalog Card Number: 74-108375

ISBN 0-8294-0192-X

CONTENTS

---

v

In the physical world whatever has life is characterized by growth, so that in no respect to grow is to cease to live. It grows by taking into its own substance external materials; and this absorption or assimilation is completed when the materials appropriated come to belong to it or enter into its unity. Two things cannot become one, except there be a power of assimilation in one or the other. Sometimes assimilation is effected only with an effort; it is possible to die of repletion, and there are animals who lie torpid for a time under the contest between the foreign substance and the assimilating power. . . .

This analogy may be taken to illustrate certain peculiarities in the growth or development of ideas. . . . It is otherwise with mathematical and other abstract creations, which, like the soul itself, are solitary and self-dependent; but doctrines and views which relate to man are not placed in a void, but in the crowded world, and make way for themselves by interpenetration, and develop by absorption.

John Henry Cardinal Newman
An Essay on the Development of Christian Doctrine, III

What is a Catholic novel? By some people it is assumed that any novel written by a Roman Catholic qualifies for inclusion in what has been widely acknowledged as a distinct literary movement. Others have the impression that any novel about Roman Catholics or addressed to Roman Catholics must be similarly recognized.

This essay applies the term "Catholic novel" more strictly. Only a novel whose mainspring of dramatic action depends upon Roman Catholic theology, or upon the history of thought within one of the world's large Roman Catholic communities, or upon "development" of Roman Catholic "ideas" in Newman's sense, is regarded as contributing to the flowering of major literary achievement which began when the isolation of the world's Roman Catholic communities started to break down in the nineteenth century, and which tapered off—perhaps ended—when Roman Catholics, in the phrase so widely used at the present writing, "joined the modern world" after the Second Vatican Council. To discover how this flowering of the Catholic novel began, what it achieved, and how it ended is the purpose of the chapters that follow.

Three Roman Catholic communities are examined, French, English, and American. Each section consists of two parts. In

1

the first, the community is described so as to emphasize the historical characteristics that made it what it was, to show as large a part as possible of its internal dynamic and its relation to the surrounding environment, and to note the first signs of its creative activity. The second part then examines the work of the community's major Catholic novelists: in France, François Mauriac and Georges Bernanos; in England, Evelyn Waugh and Graham Greene; and in the United States, J. F. Powers and Flannery O'Connor.

An effort is made to point out that the Catholic novels of the three communities, while "Catholic" in the sense we have defined—that is, in depending for the mainspring of dramatic action upon Roman Catholic theology, the thought of the Roman Catholic community, or "development" of ideas in Newman's meaning—are different from one another. Catholic novels written in France differ from those written in England, for instance, and much of the difference depends upon background differences between the two communities. These differences are not enumerated one by one or labored over at length—the treatment would become impossibly detailed and ponderous. It is expected that by absorbing the description of the community in its relevant aspects and then reading the analyses of the major Catholic novels produced within it, the significant correspondences will be seen, and the contribution of religious and cultural dynamic to creative activity, which often in turn reacted upon subsequent cultural and religious development, will be understood. It is taken for granted that readers are sufficiently sophisticated to allow for differences caused simply by the fact that authors are individuals and no two are alike.

To get any meaningful picture of the Catholic novel, rather long periods of time and a substantial number of novels must be examined. Intense compression, particularly in the background chapters, has therefore been necessary. Yet it is hoped that the reader will feel the "flow" of what is being described—that he may see, for example, how opposing currents in the intellectual and political life of France came to a typical confluence in the quarrel between the secularist Gide and the Catholic Claudel, and how the dispute illustrated the way French Catholic literature grew out of the strenuous divisions of French life after 1789. The reader should not feel pressed to see from the beginning relationships between the novels and the backgrounds, anticipating equations as he goes along, but rather should read for enjoyment (I hope this is possible) and absorb gradually an overall understanding of relationships which are complex but which he will soon find it impossible not to comprehend. In every discussion of a major novel the emphasis is on its quality as an artistic achievement, and it is believed that in these discussions the reader will discover how the cultural and religious problems to be settled within the Roman Catholic milieu related to the creative "intensity" that in the Catholic novels produced so many works of outstanding literary excellence. The dynamics of cultural and religious growth "entered," so to speak, into the thought of the writers, who passed on their intellectual and emotional tensions as fiction, often with superb and, I believe, lasting dramatic effects. The chapters on the backgrounds will, I hope, be interesting in themselves, but each should be regarded as a patient preparation for the understanding of the novels that follow, rather than as a separate essay. At the end, the reader who has had sufficient patience with the preparatory work will, I believe, arrive at some stimulating conclusions about artistic creativity as it relates to cultural surroundings, and may even be moved to develop a new insight into some of the problems posed by the present state of literary criticism. If such is the case, the modest contribution this study hoped to make will have been achieved.

PART I

Revolutionary France

French Catholics after 1789

From the time of the French Revolution of 1789 the people of France were divided. On the one hand, were the idealists of liberty, who not infrequently indulged in distinctly unlibertarian coercion, in 1789 relying on the guillotine, in 1848 on mob action, and in 1871 on summary firing squads. On the other hand, were the idealists of "order," who were often to be found supporting suppression of every opinion differing from that of the authorities. The diminishing number of French Catholics belonged in general to the idealists of order, although small but growing groups adhered to the ideal of liberty. But, too frequently, idealists on both sides were primarily faithful to the darker aspects of their beliefs, a fact that gave each party occasion to sneer at the other and establish a basis for retaliation and polemic.

For example, in 1814 after the defeat of Napoleon and the restoration of the Bourbons, it was impossible for the many dissenting idealists of liberty not to observe what good use the returning Royalists made of the Church. The great nobles, often skeptics or deists before the Revolution, now began, in large numbers to resume the practice of Catholicism.[1] Under the Gallican Monsignor Frayssinous, almoner to Louis XVIII, grand master of the University and minister of public instruction, twenty of the twenty-five rectors named to supervise French education were ecclesiastics. At the University, Frayssinous suppressed Guizot's history course, suspended Cousin's course in philosophy, and eliminated all other teachers considered dangerous. The Medical School and the École Normale were centers for freethinkers; Frayssinous dissolved the one and suspended the other, thus taking a major step in initiating the long struggle for control of the right to teach.[2]

The first move in this direction, however, had been made long before—by Napoleon after the Concordat of 1801. The first consul encouraged the return of monks to the elementary schools, with the aim of having the consulate's newest citizens leave behind as quickly as possible the ideas of the Revolution. Later, for the Empire, Portalis and Caprara prepared a *Catechism* for the children of France. Napoleon was the "Lord's Anointed," raised up to restore order to the nation. To love him, to pay his taxes, and to answer the call of military conscriptions were obligations to be fulfilled under pain of hellfire.[3] Napoleon's long duel with the pope, who broke with him after 1808, did little to alter conditions for the people. As conscription became more and more unpopular, he had the bulletins of the Grand Armée read from the pulpit.

Although the Church was thus used by both governments after the Revolution, nevertheless the Catholics of France meanwhile achieved a remarkable renaissance of devotion. In the early years the return of the upper class to the faith of their fathers may have been prompted primarily by the need to establish order and by the romantic revival that saw Catholicism as the historical source of beauty, chivalry, and honor, as depicted by Chateaubriand's *Génie du Christianisme* at the turn of the century. But the next generation was genuinely devout, educated by the religious orders returning from exile[4] and served by the simple, fervent priests recruited among the people by Saint Sulpice. And although the bourgeoisie—lawyers, industrialists, shopkeepers, and the rest—remained for three more decades in the grip of deism, even this was altered by the fall of the "bourgeois king," Philippe Égalité in 1848, when tentative efforts toward more representative government dissolved as republican mobs took to the streets. Their excesses frightened the middle class almost as much as the guillotine had frightened the nobles. Reaction suddenly became a middle-class virtue, and the bourgeoisie in their turn sought the Church as an ally of morality and order.

While the bourgeoisie thus strengthened the Catholicism of the right, a different sort of Catholicism was forming on the left. More flexible and less motivated by self-interest, this movement is the one that most appeals to liberal Catholic historians, who often forget to emphasize that it depended upon an idealistic minority, whose power was never to equal its aspirations, though its ideas remained as a foundation for the Catholicism of the future. In 1848, at the fall of Louis Philippe, a little band of Catholic Republicans gathered around the young priest Lacordaire, already noted for his gifts as a preacher. These men understood the steady de-Christianization of the working class, whose conditions of exploitation were upheld by successive political regimes using the moral authority of the Church to support the economic *status quo*. Hopes of Catholic Republicans had been raised by the death in 1846 of Gregory XVI, the pope who had condemned the brilliant journalist-priest Lamennais. With Lacordaire, the Comte de Montalembert, who was a gifted politician, and the social theorist de Coux, Lamennais in his famous paper *L'Avenir* had pressed for an alliance of papacy and peoples, a universal franchise, legislation to protect labor, and regional decentralization to limit the power of nationalism. Lamennais' aberrations (such as his belief that the chief witness to the truth of Catholicism was the majority's having always accepted it) help to explain but do not mitigate the loss to the Church of its foremost Republican idealist when in the 1830s Lamennais' apostasy followed his condemnation by Gregory XVI. The apostasy of Lamennais weakened Catholic Republicanism as much as it strengthened the forces of the right.

A decade later, however, the dream of Catholic libertarianism seemed to revive. The new pope, Pius IX, in 1846 granted the Roman people freedom of the press and an advisory house of representatives.[5] But this tenuous spirit of freedom could not survive the fear aroused by the mobs of 1848. On the one side the new pope saw the orderly middle and upper classes; on the other, a growing epidemic of violence. In Rome his own minister, Rossi, was assassinated as he prepared to present a reform program to the new chamber,[6] and in Paris Archbishop Affre, a supporter of Lacordaire and a Republican, was shot down while appealing for peace between the barricades.[7] The pope's revulsion was deep and bitter, and in Rome libertarianism was dead.

In France it died as swiftly as it could be decently interred. The new hero of the bourgeoisie, the Prince President Louis Napoleon, made a few gestures toward ruling by plebiscite, and then the presidency turned into the Second Empire, and the Church became for it the same ally of authority that it had been for earlier governments. Louis Napoleon, himself uncertain in the field of religion, married the beautiful and devout Spanish Countess Eugénie de Teba, and under her influence going to Mass became the fashion.

Nevertheless, if many of the bourgeoisie who by 1850 formed the new ruling class became Catholic out of fear and because of fashion, great numbers of their sons and daughters repeated the process of 1814. Like the nobility before them, they received Catholic educations and became genuinely devout. But the notion of Daniel-Rops that France after her age of revolutions entered a period of rising religious renewal from 1800 to the 1870s is more than a little mistaken.[8] In fact, from 1800 to 1876 the hold of the Church on the French people was steadily weakening. In countless parishes the peasants were drifting off to the cities, and by 1850 they formed vast masses not only unchurched but totally ignorant of religious and even moral teaching. Added to the hard core of the professional class and that element of the middle class who were not part of the ruling bourgeoisie, and for most of whom Voltaire and Rousseau continued to be patron saints and anticlericalism an article of Republican faith, they made a growing and ever more powerful antireligious underground, which needed only the enlargement of the franchise to make its power felt.

There were some who understood what was happening and tried to stem the tide. Attempts were made by the liberal Catholics on the left to found workers' religious study circles, cooperatives, and factory councils that could ensure both Christian alleviation of exploitation, and mitigation of the steadily spreading moral disintegration. In 1871 Albert de Mun founded his Workers' Circles.[9] Earlier Léon Harmel at Val des Bois had established a model spinning mill.[10] Efforts to lighten the hardships of industrialization dated from the 1830s with Ozanam and the Society of Saint Vincent de Paul,[11] and the attempts of *L'Avenir* to make priests the people's natural protectors.[12] Such efforts were to continue with *Sillon* in 1899, the cooperatives of the period after the First World War, and the worker-priest movement after the Second. Although the majority of the hierarchy was conservative and almost always unsympathetic, the enterprizes went stubbornly on. Most of the early ones were paternalistic and under the direction of liberal members of the upper and middle classes; but Harmel, the most influential of the pioneers, insisted that Workers' Councils were not worthy of the name if they did not actually govern.[13] And although it is estimated that by 1900 no more than two percent of French laborers had ever been directly affected,[14] the thinking had begun that would climax in the social encyclicals *Rerum Novarum* in 1893, *Quadragesimo Anno* in 1933, and *Mater et Magistra* in 1961. Thus there came about in the first half of the nineteenth century a division in the development of French Catholicism. Although political Catholicism remained within the rightist authoritarianism of the period, the most vital thinking and much of the most fervent action within Catholic intellectual circles was taking an opposite direction, and it was this liberal minority that would carry the future—not, however, until nearly a century had passed and incalculable damage had been done by the Catholic political right.

In the 1860s the focus of official preoccupation in Rome began to center on atheism, statism, and the nineteenth century's dominant philosophies. In 1864 Pius IX issued the *Syllabus of Errors*.[15] It condemned a broad range of beliefs, all of them widespread and cherished by the period: pantheism, which said that God is in nature and changes as nature changes; naturalism, which claimed that not God but natural forces made the world; immanentism, which saw the world as making itself;[16] indifferentism, which contended that it made no difference what a man believed;[17] statism, which asserted the state's unlimited rights;[18] nationalism, which held that "any wicked or flagitious action . . . is altogether lawful and worthy of the highest praise when done through love of country";[19] materialism, which held that "no other forces are to be recognized except those which reside in matter";[20] profitism, which declared that "all the rectitude and excellence of morality ought to be placed in the accumulation of riches";[21] and most other popular philosophies of the dominant bourgeoisie.

The *Syllabus* raised a storm of indignation—a tempest that was and still is misunderstood. It was not the unlibertarian aspects of the *Syllabus* that outraged the spirit of the times—the assertion of the indissolubility of marriage[22] or the territorial claims of the papacy[23] or even the denunciation of religious liberalism[24]—these were matters of only antiquarian interest to the majority of secularists. The outrage lay in the attack upon all the major secular projects of the era. Adherents of these projects refused to recognize them as the *Syllabus* depicted them— "progress"[25] by which the nineteenth century believed it was directing the twentieth into the millenium, "civilization"[26] in whose name the countries of Europe were taking over the destinies of those with darker complexions or different noses, and the whole "light of reason"[27] under whose guidance it was believed the human race would enter a period of endless peace and prosperity.

The *Syllabus* was thus a manifesto of Catholic separatism from the whole orientation of the nineteenth-century secular world. That world was not slow to feel the need to strike back, especially when six years later, in 1870, fuel was added by the First Vatican Council's proclamation of papal infallibility in matters of faith and doctrine, a proclamation as heartily exaggerated by delighted Catholic conservatives as by their exacerbated enemies. That same year in France the Empire fell in the wake of the Franco-Prussian War. The excesses of the Paris Commune, with its brutal execution of hostages—among them Monsignor Darboy, archbishop of Paris, wearing to his death the same pectoral cross that had belonged to Monsignor Affre— caused a reaction that confirmed the Catholicism of the ruling bourgeoisie, barely missed restoring the monarchy, and gave Catholics their greatest freedom in education to date, the permission to open colleges.[28]

Meanwhile the alarm of secular Republicans had been rising. When the 1876 elections returned the first Republican majority, preparations began at once for the secularization of education. In 1880 came the expulsion first of the Jesuits and then of most of the other teaching orders.[29] With occasional lapses into leniency, educational freedom was gradually abolished, until by 1904 all members of religious orders were forbidden to teach. Crosses were removed from courtrooms, public prayers were prohibited, diplomatic relations with Rome were broken off, and the separation of Church and state passed into the law of the French nation.

The Republic, which under a stormy succession of contending ministries was to carry on a sort of government by factions right up to 1940, took science as its philosophic prop and used it in somewhat the same manner as the Empire had used the Church. Where the alliance of throne and altar had once reinforced the subservience of the individual to the imperial state as a reflection of proper subservience to God, so now the subordination of the individual to the secularist programs of the new rulers reflected the subordination which the popular science of the time taught was the natural relationship between human beings and their environment. Evolutionism developed into the overriding determinism of Taine, according to which not only events but even literature was said to be molded by nation and race. At the University, whose cast of mind, now that the party of religious teaching was silenced, penetrated every corner of France, social thinking was under the influence of Durkheim, according to whom society was a deterministic force, shaping individuals to its needs.

These beliefs, and the "naturalism" of an endless stream of novels intended to demonstrate the mechanistic determinism of human behavior according to the new biological and sociological laws, led to a feeling of helplessness, and a craving to assert the freedom of personality. Under the Republic men felt less free in spirit and action than in any other period. Emotionally the Republic bore an odd crop: not a bright daylight flowering of confidence in progress but night-blooming superstition, metaphysical despair, and a longing to demonstrate liberty by every conceivable excess. The result was the "decadence" of the period eventually to be known as the "fin de siecle," a period which by curiously convoluted processes ended by giving way to a revival of Catholicism in France.

CHAPTER II

Aestheticians and Precursors

The fever for liberty which was the nineteenth century's reaction to the attempted binding of the individual into the systems of scientific determinism gave rise to strange aberrations. "Satanism," "dandyism," and esoteric sensualism developed as assertions of freedom of action in the face of the rigid mental and spiritual authoritarianism of the era's popular philosophies. The passionate visions of the last romantics, the "decadents," took shape in the powerful poetry of Baudelaire, Verlaine, and Rimbaud. In the novel *Against the Grain*, Joris-Karl Huysmans drew as his protagonist, des Esseintes, a connoisseur of voluptuousness who sought to enjoy every possible sensation. Des Esseintes was a freehand likeness of the notorious Comte de Montesquiou, who was later to serve Proust as the model for the pederast, Baron Charlus. The conversion of Huysmans to Catholicism marked the failure of the secular philosophies to account for the strange passions they were arousing. There was a tendency to turn to other explanations, and to ideas of the past: the natural sinfulness of man, the necessity of religion, the need for God's grace in controlling the passions. A rising tide of crime was affecting the cities, swarming with the de-Christianized masses, while beneath the smooth surfaces of bourgeois and upper-class society there was corruption of every kind. Barbey

15

d'Aurevilly, another convert to Catholicism, was actually, in his stories of hidden evil behind impeccable facades, a symbolist. In his story, "The Other Side of the Cards" (1850), he told of a countess and her daughter enamored of the same lover. During the games of whist that whiled away time in this circle, the Countess habitually wore a corsage of flowers grown in the jardinere in her bedroom, in which was buried the murdered infant engendered by the Countess' lover—an infant to whom her daughter had given secret birth.[1]

There is no light of hope or redemption in Barbey d'Aurevilly's fantasies. They are unrelieved landscapes of nightmare, with little or no analysis of motives except what the reader can supply. The mode is reminiscent of de Maupassant. Barbey d'Aurevilly's stories on one hand scandalized the Church, and, on the other, brought down the condemnation of Republican censors. Nevertheless, he insisted on the duty of the Catholic artist, who is "Catholiquement au dessous des Ascètes," to treat crime as well as virtue.[2] There is no doubt that in a sinister way his fantasies managed to say something essentially true about the spirit of his age. But critics saw him simply as one more example of romantic extremism,[3] and their verdict largely obscured the full meaning of his work, which, like the poetry of Baudelaire, sought to explore the mystery of evil.

During the era of the "decadents," the average French Catholic's sense of separation between Catholicism and the secular environment was acute. At the same time convergence was beginning. A curiosity about Catholicism, so long despised by the secular world, was growing within that world. Ironically, the victory of secularism had carried in its results—determinism, license, aspirituality—the seeds of a Catholic renaissance. This renaissance would affect not only the secular world from which such converts as Huysmans came, but have an even more powerful effect on the isolated Catholic community, whose isolation would finally dissolve in a fever of creative expression, ad-

dressed both to the secular environment and to Catholics themselves, as the two communities approached on what amounted to
a collision course of mutual recognition. The Catholic generation of 1876 was growing up, and without its own schools the
Catholic community could no longer maintain its young in insulated apartness. Young Catholics were thrown into the secular
environment, and the secular environment had to receive them.
Péguy noted how little awareness children in this period had of
the separatism cherished by their elders. During five days of the
week the state school taught reading, writing, arithmetic, and patriotism—much emphasized in France after the defeat of 1870.
On Thursdays and Saturdays the curé taught the catechism and
allegiance to God. Little Catholics like Péguy never felt they
were passing from one world to another between the idealistic
schoolmaster and the religious curé. It was a harmonious division of ideals that seemed naturally complementary. We have
Péguy's word for it: "We loved the Republic and we loved the
Church, at one and the same time. . . . We believed absolutely
and equally, and with the same faith, in the grammar we were
taught . . . and in everything the catechism contained." Nevertheless, there was the fact that "the Republic and the Church
gave us educations which were diametrically opposed to each
other."[4] Clearly, the Catholic generation of 1876 was in that
state of transition between separatism and assimilation that
marks the beginning of intense convergence.

At the same time, the aspects we have noted in the secular
environment were pushing many people out of that environment
and into Catholicism. Catholic orthodoxy had strong attractions:
a clearly defined faith, an eschatology that gave each person a
sense of purpose and direction, and an insistence on the individual's responsible freedom for his own fate. But there can be
no doubt that a powerful auxiliary attraction in France was Jansenism. To trace Jansenism's history is beyond our scope. We
must be content to recall that the beliefs of Pascal and Port

Royal did not die with the passing of the eighteenth century, and many French Catholics held to a certain Jansenist orientation long after Jansenism no longer officially existed. Such people believed that human nature was naturally depraved and that human beings were more vulnerable to forces of darkness than responsive to forces of light. They held that men had little freedom of the will but were utterly dependent on God's grace, which was overwhelming and could not be resisted except where God himself predestined the sinner to resist. These beliefs were not so much dogmatic formulas as implicit assumptions that lingered on from Jansenism's past as a Catholic parallel to Protestant Calvinism. Frequently converts with backgrounds of decadence or satanism were unconsciously being attracted by Jansenism as an explanation of their world when they thought they were being attracted by traditional Catholicism. Certainly this was true of Barbey d'Aurevilly, who believed strongly in natural depravity and in the infirmity of the will when confronted by evil. And whatever one may think of the truth or falsity of his orientation, no one can deny that it furnished him with compelling dramatic themes—as it would do later for a more talented writer, François Mauriac.

Huysmans' early view of Catholicism seems to have been much like Barbey d'Aurevilly's. In his first Catholic novel, *Là-bas*, which followed his portrait of des Esseintes in 1884, he recorded his initial steps toward religious belief. *Là-bas*, written in 1891, was a melodramatic procession of black masses and sorcerer priests, but, for all of its Jansenist darkness, it was a compelling story in the mode popularized by Barbey d'Aurevilly and it went on to develop an important principle. The hero, Durtal, is writing a novel about Gilles de Rais. He says, " 'The novel . . . ought to be divided into two parts, that of the soul and that of the body—which should be welded together, or rather intermingled, as they are in life.' "[5] This is the first mention of a fiction to be based on study of internal, spiritual states. As we shall see, the development of such fiction was a central concern of the later Catholic aestheticians, Maritain and Claudel, and became the basis of the work of Mauriac and Bernanos.

Huysmans had early lost his faith and become a libertine, actually witnessing some of the practices he ascribes to his characters in *Là-bas*. Among his acquaintances was a lapsed priest who celebrated satanic rituals, and on at least one occasion— unknown to Huysmans until years later—such a ritual ended with the murder of a child.[6] Satanism, as Huysmans realized even without specific knowledge of this crime, was a monstrous and quite serious manifestation of the disease of decadence. His portrayals of it were the more vivid for readers of the time because, when he described the dark experiments of the satanists, he gave up the highly colored romanticism with which he had depicted des Esseintes and returned to the flatly matter-of-fact prose of his early naturalistic novel, *Marthe* (1876). As a result, *Là-bas*, published the year before his conversion, makes use of meticulous factual description in treating aberrations of the spirit, a technique which he developed in his next novel, *En Route*, in 1895. This development, too, was to become important in later Catholic novels.

A decade before *En Route*, in 1885, the Vicomte de Voguë, a Republican Catholic, had contended in a widely read work, *Le Roman Russe*, that the triumph in France of a fiction that eliminated all consideration of spiritual forces could fatally erode the novel. In 1889 Paul Bourget, sympathetic to Catholicism as a source of moral order but not yet a practicing Catholic, published *Le Disciple*, a book whose sensational success had not been paralleled since Renan's *Vie de Jesus* thirty years earlier. In the intellectual world everyone discussed the theme. A young man, a fervent disciple of a philosopher who taught the sole authority of the laws of science (a figure modeled on Taine), seduces a girl whom he drives to suicide. In rudimentary form it is a "psychological" novel, but one which probes not only the mind but the spirit. It is a forecast of Huysmans' concern with a fiction dealing with internal, spiritual states.

In *En Route* Huysmans veers away from the Jansenist orientation of *Là-bas* and adopts the same "psychology" of the soul that Bourget pioneered in *Le Disciple*. While the satanic priests of *Là-bas* were weak-willed, "possessed" by the demonic forces to which they surrendered, the monks of *En Route* freely cooperate with God's grace. It would seem that Huysmans, penetrating further into Catholicism, became more orthodox as he left the darkness of the decadents behind. *En Route* was a totally new departure in fiction, and it had enormous influence. Huysmans was inundated by letters from people trying to explain their own spiritual despair and desire for grace. The story has a minimum of action and, artistically, is not an unqualified success, but the student of the development of Catholic fiction will look closely at the theme. It expresses the idea of substitution, by which people who suffer may follow the pattern of Christ and offer their lives to redeem others. Huysmans does not use the theme as a basis for the plot, as it was later to be used by Bernanos and Mauriac, but the characters in the novel discuss it at length, and it was at the center of Huysmans' thinking. And the extraordinary personal endurance with which he bore the torment of his last illness in 1907 dispelled the fable that the spectacular convert from decadence had merely been enjoying one more "sensation."

Converts among the gifted abounded before and after the turn of the century. A name that should be remembered is that of Léon Bloy. As Barbey d'Aurevilly's friend and secretary, he fell under his influence, but the decadence which Barbey d'Aurevilly saw as a chronic and static condition in which satanic forces gripped the world, Bloy saw as a dynamic of advancing evil leading humanity to a swiftly approaching end. To Bloy, only the humility and sufferings of the poor atoned for the moral degeneracy of society and suspended God's vengeance.

Bloy's finest novel is *La Femme pauvre*, published in 1890. He, too, emphasizes the theme of atonement and free human choice, and, in spite of his dark view of the world, he may therefore be regarded as more orthodox and less under Jansenist influence than his master, Barbey d'Aurevilly; but his work is somber and shows no such radical newness as *Le Disciple*, *Là-bas*, or *En Route*. Bloy's chief contribution to the Catholic novel was the depiction of poverty as at once an evil and a source of sanctification and redemption, a theme forecasting that of Bernanos' later novel, *The Diary of a Country Priest*, which in the mid-1930s was regarded as an archetype of Catholic thinking about poverty and its spiritual relationship to the redemption of a morally degenerating society.

Bloy expected the Apocalypse in his own time, and his death came in 1917, in the middle of the war that introduced the modern era. Quite a different view of the world was taken by Bloy's younger acquaintance, Charles Péguy, who was killed in that war three years earlier. Péguy, always financially straitened in his career as a largely self-financed socialist editor, and conscious of his working-class origins, was temperamentally an antibourgeois Catholic of the left. At the same time he was a patriot and gave his allegiance to the bourgeois-ruled Republican state. He reached an intellectual crisis during the Dreyfus affair in 1894. To Péguy the issue was clear: which was more important, the patriotism of people who would rather see their country lie than admit a mistake, or the spiritual integrity of people who chose to see their nation risk war rather than condemn an innocent man.[7] Péguy was in no way under the shadow of Jansenism. To him all people were morally responsible, and obligated to choose truth in a universe where the forces of light were as spiritually strong as the forces of darkness—men having been created free.

The choice Péguy saw in the Dreyfus case was imperative, particularly as it affected Catholics. In the complex twofold development we noted earlier, the great majority of French Catholics had remained conservative in this first quarter-century of the Republic, and in the Dreyfus affair their natural loyalty was to the army, whose conservative officer corps had sentenced Dreyfus. The role of anti-Semitism should not be underestimated. To French Catholic conservatives, whether of the nobility or of the "old" bourgeoisie who had made their fortunes in earlier generations, Jews were the source of what they regarded as decadence and growing commercial amorality. Many such conservatives believed that Jews belonged to no country and would do anything for profit, even spy for the Germans. Most of those who accepted the guilt of Dreyfus, therefore, tended to be conservative Catholics of the right who repudiated Pope Leo XIII's reversal of the separatism of Pius IX and the attempted *ralliement* to the Republic; while most of those who believed in Dreyfus' innocence tended to be Republicans of the left, liberals who rejected the prevailing anti-Semitism. There was a deeper level, however, on which the Dreyfus case involved a choice of loyalties. On the one hand was loyalty to truth; on the other, was loyalty to country, which in the atmosphere that followed 1870 aroused the keenest emotions. In opting for truth Péguy and the little group of liberal French Catholics who split off from the main body of their coreligionists were actually making a decision as to the primacy of a spiritual over an emotional affirmation. But Péguy and his friends were isolated. In later years, though calling himself a convert, and in his marvelous verse proving himself Catholic to the bone, Péguy never adhered formally to the Church. God, Christ, and the saints of France had been in his view silent allies of the innocent accused, but most Catholics belonged to the right and gave their allegiance to the opposite side. Péguy acted accordingly. His commitment was always to the "invisible" Church of the communion of saints, not the "visible" Church in the world. It is a deep irony that this most orthodox of French Catholic writers, whom Jansenism never darkened and who was to have so much influence on the development of the Catholicism of the future, was in his own period technically "outside" the Church.

Péguy was not unnaturally regarded with suspicion by most Catholics during his lifetime, but after his death the reverence accorded him became an inspiration to the spirit of renewal that marked the Church after the war. A terrible honesty seemed to follow that holocaust: at all costs the truth against appearances, against all other Catholics, if need be. It was a spirit that naturally added to acerbity between Catholics of the right and left. In 1900 the work of *Sillon* in overcoming class conflict gave evidence of an increase of vitality on the Catholic left. But *Sillon* fell into idolatrous demagoguery under its founder, Marc Sangnier, and the pope condemned the movement. In the first quarter of the new century the growth of *Action française* showed increased vitality on the Catholic right. Many Catholics, including Maritain and Bernanos,[8] rallied to its leader, Charles Maurras, who, although not a practicing Catholic, held the idealism historically adhered to by Catholic conservatives. Catholics, monarchists, and conservatives were now thoroughly blended with the bourgeois ruling class, most of whose members believed that the way to progress was to accumulate profits. According to the ideas of the ruling bourgeoisie, profits at the top would eventually bring material benefits to all, and since material benefits were the source of every human contentment, the key to universal happiness was in hand. In this orientation, belief that the unselfish virtues were necessary to man's survival was vanishing more with each generation. The sense of honor, chivalry, and devotion, which had held so large a measure of Catholic allegiance ever since Chateaubriand, seemed to be steadily disappearing. It is easy now to see that *Action française* was merely the first of the fascist movements, exploiting the hungers aroused by the spiritual starvation of the nineteenth and twentieth centuries. Such movements lend themselves to demagoguery, whose goal readily becomes the murderous obliteration of all who disagree. But this fact was not so visible in the early years of the century. The pope condemned *Action française* in 1926, and many conservative Catholics were aghast. The one force of idealism in modern France seemed to them to have been renounced.[9]

At the condemnation of *Sillon* twenty-five years earlier it had seemed normal to ardent Catholics when one of *Sillon's* members copied out the decree on his knees. But in 1926 there was a different spirit. The Catholic right was deeply attached to its idealism. Obedience came hard. It came, nevertheless. And, meanwhile, on the left, emerging from their long eclipse as a sort of Catholic underground, the labor unions, the *Jeunesse ouvrière chrétienne* (JOC) and the *Jeunesse agricole chrétienne* (JAC), made steady progress in a dedication and solidarity that had none of the dangers of *Action française*. After the Second World War the JAC held much of the countryside; its cooperatives flourished; and, although sections of rural France still automatically voted Communist, it was in the same spirit of habitual dissent that some of America's rural areas vote Republican.[10] It is estimated that in 1959 some 4,000 rural mayors were veterans of JAC.[11] In the cities after the second war, the priest-worker movement, in which priests lived as laborers in the poorest sections, was an effort to mitigate the blindness of society. Unfortunately, when in opposition to the government the movement began to lose followers and even some priests to Stalinist Communism, the pope was forced to suspend it.

The Church's course in this period reminds one of Chesterton's description of a chariot hurtling through history, swerving to avoid rocks on the left, escaping by inches a wreck on the right, swerving again to miss cliffs on the other side.[12] Mauriac, of the Catholic left, depicted in his early novel *L'Enfant chargé de chaines*, the pernicious idolatry around Marc Sangnier. Bernanos, an intellectual of the right, recorded undying revulsion against fascism's masquerade as "honor and chivalry" when he described the brutality of Franco's forces in Majorca in his burning essay, *Les grands Cimetières sous la lune.* Both books are studies in the post-Dreyfus obsession among Catholics, an obsession with honesty that in the search for truth could turn against even an author's own convictions.

In these years of convergence the reason for the Catholic oscillation between left and right was the effort of the Catholic community to join hands, first on one side and then on the other, with the modern world. The real forward progress, meanwhile, was in the spirit of belief. Catholics were seeing their own ideas in a new light. The Dreyfus case had brought the Catholic community into searing confrontation with the secular environment and caused bitter internal reassessment. While the early Catholic novelists, Huysmans, Bourget, and Barbey d'Aurevilly, criticized the pagans, lapsed Catholics, and scientific secularists of the non-Catholic environment, the later novelists, Mauriac and Bernanos, criticized the Catholic community itself, particularly its corruptions of belief. The transitional figure between the two attitudes was Péguy. It was Péguy who drew the distinction between the clerks of the spirit, who considered it unimportant if the people starved as long as they got to heaven, and the clerks of materialism, who believed that if they took care of the body and educated the mind they need trouble themselves no further. A process of ongoing redefinition, what Newman called "development," had begun within the Catholic community. It was also Péguy who made Jeanne d'Arc declare that she would accept damnation herself rather than see a single other soul damned,[13] a passionate statement widely at variance with the usual Catholic contemporary belief that each person's duty toward God was to seek first of all his own salvation. After his death Péguy was so widely read that he became a legend, and his insights are met decades later as sources of drama in Catholic fiction, not only in France but in England and even America, where the clerks of materialism became a favorite target in the years after the Second World War for the biting ironies of the gifted young writer, Flannery O'Connor.

In 1908 there was founded a periodical which was to become a major source of French intellectual controversy, the *Nouvelle Revue Française.* From the beginning it represented a generation that reversed the stand of La Parnasse:[14] detachment was not to be its characteristic. It soon developed an intense polarity around the commitments of its two most distinguished contributors, André Gide and the Catholic convert, Paul Claudel. In the early years it was felt that Gide was merely a man who was reacting against his conventional Protestant family: he stood for self-fulfillment, for freedom, for the release of every vital force affected by nineteenth-century French Calvinist puritanism. But later Gide was regarded somewhat more seriously. In 1914, in *Les Caves du Vatican,* he showed his protagonist, Lafcadio, pushing a man off a train—to prove to the reader (and to Gide) that, in killing for no reason someone whom he did not even know, Lafcadio could illustrate an ultimate in the perfection of human freedom, the famous "acte gratuit." Gide then seemed somewhat more sinister than in the early days of *L'Immoralist* back in 1902. But Gide at first appeared merely as a disarming apostle of self-understanding and self-fulfillment. Claudel, on the other hand, from the beginning stood for uncompromising self-transcendence, in which the love of God evoked the sacrifice, chivalry, and nobility he infused into his poetic symbolism. Claudel's plays, particularly *L'Otage* in 1911, appealed to the best and most unselfish elements in human nature, an appeal that was characteristic of the Catholic tradition stemming from Chateaubriand. Claudel also, like Péguy, believed in God-given freedom of human choice. He represented all that was most attractive in Catholic orthodoxy. Thus the generation that read the NRF, which frequently was the initial publisher in serial form of the works of both Gide and Claudel, was drawn in two directions. As Mauriac was to write, "What Christian of twenty was not torn between opposing temptations: that of the God of Claudel with His exacting love, and that of the delightful world of Gide where 'everything is allowed'?"[15]

This conflict in ideals brought on direct collision between Gide and Claudel, who at first had been such close friends that Claudel hoped to convert Gide, as he had already converted the poet Francis Jammes. The hope ended spectacularly when a passage in Gide's *Les Caves du Vatican* seemed to hint that the writer was a homosexual. When Claudel and Jammes wrote to Gide, he replied passionately in a letter to Claudel that he was as he was, and he would not submit to "lying conventions."[16] But, even apart from this issue, Claudel's whole background was radically different from Gide's. Although in his youth Claudel had slipped away from the Catholicism of his family, he had been drawn back into the Church by the great protest of the nineteenth century, antiscientism. It first touched him when, in reading Rimbaud's *Saison en Enfer*, he felt that there must exist realities of the spirit for which the "laws of nature" could not account. "Nature" for Gide and "nature" for Claudel were thus two different things. To Gide, "nature" emancipated from God was the fountainhead of instinct, in response to whose promptings everything was permitted. To Claudel, Godless "nature" appeared from his earliest years as the philosophic prop for the deterministic dogmas of popular secularism, the dogmas he most despised. Claudel was a climax in the procession of the great converts to Catholicism. Behind him one sees the shadow of Péguy, going to listen week after week to Bergson's lectures on the free human person, liberated from mechanistic determinism by the "durée," which applies to the dynamism of personality as it exists from birth, and which because it is a quality is exempt from the quantitative analytic measurements of positivistic science. Bergson's "durée" was

the first widespread philosophic denial of the social environ-
mentalism of Durkheim and the historical determinism of Taine.

One cannot think of Bergson, or of Claudel, without remembering also young Jacques and Raïssa Maritain. As students, before their marriage, they had decided that if there was no order
in the world but mechanistic determinism, and no absolute truth
accessible to man, they would not consent to live in such a world
but would commit suicide. Then they heard of Bergson and began to attend his courses at the Collège de France. There, the
teaching that human decisions could be free, and, later, that intuition, if not intelligence, could arrive at truth,[17] gave Jacques
and Raïssa hope. This hope grew when they came to know Léon
Bloy, a man whose life devoted to faith and oblivious to material advantage was even stronger evidence of the human ability
to make decisions free of the environment.[18]

Bloy became Jacques Maritain's godfather, and Maritain,
followed by Gilson, was to make his life's work the uncovering
in Thomism of its original vitality. The official philosophy of the
Church since Leo XIII's encyclical *Aeterni Patris* in 1879,
Thomism had been taught chiefly by direct quotation. Saint
Thomas' thinking thus had been buried in its form, and to students it inevitably seemed a dead system, something belonging
to the Middle Ages. But Maritain wrote in 1921, "in the great
Thomists the thought of the master does not petrify but develops, becomes a living being more perfect, more highly
evolved,"[19] and he made his life's work the application of Thomism as a living philosophy to the problems of the twentieth
century. In spite of Maritain's later rejection of Bergson over
the issue of intellectual access to truth (an access Bergson believed was the province of the instincts not of the mind), it is
undoubtedly to Bergson's lectures and their effect on such thinkers as Maritain and Gilson in their youth that Catholic thought
owed much of its new emphasis on the continuously creative.
The idea of the ongoing and never-ceasing creativity of the uni-

verse became the center of Catholic aesthetics as well as of the
Thomistic renewal. Claudel wrote in *Art and Poetry* in 1907,
"With each breath we draw, the world is as new as when the
earliest man first filled his throat." Every creature is in continual re-creation and depends upon creative community with every
other creature.[20]

Long before there was an open break, the difference in ideas
between Gide and Claudel became a contest whose focus was
young Jacques Rivière, in later life to become NRF's greatest
editor, holding that post from 1919 to his death in 1925.
Rivière, moved by Claudel's plays but at twenty still under the
spell of Gide's affirmation of life as a flow of endless novelty
and beauty, wrote to Claudel in 1907, and Claudel replied.
After assuring the young man of his interest and sympathy, he
said, "God is everywhere as the Creator who sustains and contains. We are witnesses to a continuous process of creation."[21]

By 1912 Rivière had renounced Gide. He came to believe
that the Gidean "disponibilité," the readiness to give oneself to
every attractive idea, every passing sensation, was actually a
way of giving oneself to nothing. Gide was like Proteus. Whenever one tried to grasp his infinite complexity, he presented a
new and bewildering side. Gide was so complex and so opposed
to absolutes that he could not really give himself, nor yet could
he withhold himself. The relativism of nineteenth- and twentieth-
century secularism reaches a climax in Gide, while the sense of
decision, commitment, and dedication that marks Catholics at
this time defines itself as opposition. The chief characteristic of
Gide's position is its "disponibilité," often resulting in amorality and lack of direction, which Bernanos in the late 1930s
was to make the target of his novel *Monsieur Ouine* (Mr. Yes-
No). The characteristic of the Catholic position, on the other
hand, is a tendency to deal in the blacks and whites of absolute
right and absolute wrong. Whatever may be said about the shortcomings of the Catholic position in regard to tolerance, it lends

itself to strong drama, and we should keep the early Gide-Claudel-Rivière discussion in mind when we look at the quality of later Catholic fiction. Rivière's decision was absolute. In a long essay, "De la Foi," published in the NRF in 1912, Rivière said that in true "sincerity" (always a watchword of Gide himself) he felt there was no middle way between religion and atheism and he threw in his lot with Pascal.[22]

The aesthetic that Claudel set forth in *Art and Poetry* was oriented toward creativity in being—an ontological, not a technical orientation. The other major work of Catholic aesthetics, Maritain's *Art and Scholasticism*, completed in 1920,[23] takes up this trend in going on to examine the functioning of artistic and poetic inspiration as it penetrates being to draw from its interiority the sustenance of the creative act. There is penetration not only ontological but psychological, from which the poet or artist distills the beauty that consists in imposing order, proportion, and form upon his insights.[24] The artist not only draws from the "immense treasure-house of created things," he also draws from "the world of souls"[25]—a type of artistic approach we have already seen beginning to be practiced in elementary form by Bourget and developed by Huysmans.

Like Claudel, Maritain is almost as notable for what he does not say as for what he says. Neither he nor Claudel divides art into schools. "Parnassian," "Naturalist"—such words almost never occur. Technique as part of the artist's *habitus* in seeking beauty is important but is not central. Maritain says, ". . . the feverish acceleration which modern individualism . . . imposes on the succession of art forms, abortive schools, and puerile fashions is the symptom of wide-spread intellectual and social poverty."[26] For both Claudel and Maritain what is essential is the artist's entry into being. His strength of spirit is, therefore, all important. In a note on the novel Maritain declares, "only a Christian, nay more, a mystic, because he has some idea of *what is in man*, can be a complete novelist (not without risk, for he needs *experiential knowledge* of the creature; and this knowledge can come from only two sources, the old tree of the knowledge of evil, and the gift of Understanding, which the soul receives with the other gifts of grace)."[27] Later Maritain in the Mellon lectures, published as *Creative Intuition in Art and Poetry*, was to speak of the artist's intuition as forming "on the verge of the spiritual preconscious,"[28] and one is reminded of Bernanos' references to his states of creativity as "dreams."

To those familiar with Bernanos in literature and Rouault in painting, these observations do not now seem startling. But in 1920 it was revolutionary to suppose that there could be artists who did not depend for identity on belonging to some technical school but relied upon entry into being by processes said to be akin to mysticism. For generations, French intellectual life had been compartmentalized by its "schools." "Realists" fought the "Romanticists"; manifestos flooded art galleries and literary periodicals. But now not the least of the annoyances inflicted by Catholic novelists on their critics was uncertainty as to classification, an uncertainty that began very early. Was Barbey d'Aurevilly really a "romantic," or was he a metaphysical visionary who could symbolically draw up subsurface corruption? Was Huysmans a "naturalist"? What could be said of a naturalist who insisted on portraying the supernatural? Was Bernanos a romantic? A symbolist? A realist? It depended on which book you were reading. Was Mauriac a realist? Or should he be called, and to what degree, a neoclassicist? What Bernanos and Mauriac had in common, however, could not be disputed: it was their belief that they were immersed in the interiority of being and had access to a spiritual dynamic that had not previously entered into the novel. With Mauriac the portrayals are primarily psychological, and his books are first of all stories of shifting states of soul; with Bernanos the inner dynamic of each story is ontological, and his books are dramas of the warfare between cosmic forces of evil and powers of grace, forces of which his priests, his countesses, his little peasant girls, his poachers, his horse traders, his criminals are sometimes the symbols and always the carriers. And always the sense of keen definition between good and evil, right and wrong, permeates each novel.

When, as in certain essays of Mauriac's, there are comments on literary art, observations center on *what* is portrayed, the subjects, not on *how* the portrayals are carried out, the techniques. In 1925, three years after the publication of *Le Baiser au lépreux* made him famous, seven years before his election to the French Academy, and nearly three decades before his reputation reached its height and he was awarded the Nobel Prize,[29] Mauriac already understood the order of his goals. Taking over from Marcel as drama critic for the NRF, he wrote of his contempt for Ibsen. With few exceptions, Ibsen's personages, he said, are stock characters: Hedda Gabler's husband, the stupid mate of a spirited woman; Eylist, the sublime drunkard; Madame Elvsted, the angelic female as savior: all these are leftovers from an exhausted gallery of stereotypes. On another occasion Mauriac similarly condemned Sacha Guitry. Instead of "individuals" taken out of stock, Guitry should portray universal interiority of character: the "eternal Tartuffe, the eternal Harpagon"[30]—types which, as the modern reader of Catholic fiction will recognize, were to be the mainstay of Mauriac's own vivid and sometimes virulent writing.

All this can of course be taken as neoclassical protest, part of the current of antiromantic intellectualism around Rivière at the NRF,[31] part of the postwar preference for the precise geometry of Nijinsky's dancing of the brilliant and novel *Sacre du printemps* in place of the long-used themes and tired nostalgia of *Lac des cygnes*. The precision of the Cubists in art was a similar reaction against the vagueness of Impressionism. But this reaction alone will not account for Mauriac's insistence that the modern writer must reach "the deepest levels in ourselves."[32] Although Proust, Joyce, and the stream-of-consciousness writers

were also explorers of "deepest levels," their type of probing
into mental processes is only faintly related to what Mauriac has
in mind. He says, "I invest a metaphysical dimension in all my
characters. . . ."[33] The "metaphysical dimension," the drama of
a world that is part of eternity, becomes in the fullest sense the
medium of the later Catholic novelists of whatever community.

Mauriac's view of the "world that is part of eternity" has a
special aspect. He says, "I make the Catholic universe of evil
palpable, tangible, pungent. The theologians offer us an abstract
idea of the sinner; I present him in flesh and blood."[34] Sin is an
obsession with Mauriac. It never occurs to him to question
whether the examination of sin is the most important goal of fiction. As we will see, his share in the Jansenist heritage is strong,
and the freedom of his characters often seems impaired. "Sin,"
Mauriac declared when at the peak of his reputation he was ex-
plaining his art, "is the writer's element."[35]

Bernanos, who, with his usual bluntness, said of Mauriac that
his art "smelled of the water closet," objected so intensely to
this aspect of Mauriac's work that even the very real regard between the two men could not dissolve their disagreement.[36]
Bernanos belonged to the line of Péguy, Claudel, and Maritain;
while Mauriac stemmed from Huysmans and Barbey d'Aurevilly. Bernanos' world is as dark as any Jansenist could wish,
but darkness never has the final victory. Speaking of his beloved
Artois, Bernanos said that he belonged to a race of "people who
never despair, for whom despair is a word that makes no sense.
. . ."[37] Bernanos created characters who freely received or freely
rejected grace; he wrote about invisible human solidarity—not
sinners only, but souls of all kinds as they exist in the community of each with all. "We shall learn from God, someday when
the time has come," he said, "what mysterious ties link the
great sinners to the great saints. . . ."[38] This theme, central to
Claudel in his dramas and in *Art and Poetry*, infused the major
themes of dramatic action in Bernanos' work, from the time of

his first famous novel, *Sous le Soleil de Satan* in 1925 to *Dialogues des Carmélites* in 1948, the last year of his life.

Bernanos' "dreams," as he often calls his stories, center on figures who form a sort of knighthood of the spirit.[39] Honor, unselfishness, chivalry, humility—all the idealism that had been so long cherished by French Royalist Catholics as being slowly extinguished in the French modern world—are found by Bernanos to be living on in a sort of noble underground whose invisible strength has the endurance of Artois traditionalism.[40] He says, "my dreams—I wanted them to be past all measure— if not, what good is it to dream? . . . I dreamed of saints and heroes, neglecting the intermediate forms of our species, and I realized that these intermediate people barely exist that only saints and heroes count."[41] The passage is deceptive. Saints and heroes seem superhuman—unreal and gigantic. But, in Bernanos, they are usually the humble and unnoticed—a shabby little priest, a peasant child, a frail young bourgeoise. But his figures are drawn with conviction and authority. When Bernanos said of himself that he belonged to that "race of people who never despair," he added, "And it is we who are right!" In the defiant last sentence we can sense what we have already seen to be characteristic of Catholics in this period: namely, their tendency to define their positions by opposition. The Catholic novelists are always "in opposition"—whether it is opposition to the secular environment, or to the entire modern world, or, as with the later novelists, to corruptions within their own Catholic community. The time is out of joint. Resolutely they set themselves against it.

Before we go on to examine the fiction of Mauriac and Bernanos, therefore, we should take one more glance at the historical background. The attempted *ralliement* in 1892 of Leo XIII to the Republic did not for any majority succeed in arousing either the enthusiasm of Republicans for Catholics or of Catholics for Republicans, whose regime most Catholics regarded as

incurably hostile. This hostility was confirmed by the cancella-
tion of freedom of education, the expulsion of the religious
orders, and the separation of Church and state. Materially and
politically after 1905 very little remained to French Catholics,
and the more peaceful relations with the Church after the war
were simply the Republic's tolerance of an enemy felt now to
be so weak that there was nothing to fear. Spiritually the great
majority of French Catholics began to suffer an inertness and
acedia more dangerous than any amount of political loss. The
Catholic upper class was largely Royalist and grew so senti-
mentally attached to the creed of throne and altar that it became
hard in most cases to distinguish between moldering nostalgia
and real religion. Among the ruling bourgeoisie, all too frequently desire for respectability became the source of superficial religiosity, while moneymaking was the underlying
passion, a chronic blasphemy that would furnish much material
to Mauriac. Below the bourgeoisie was the populace, the great
bulk of it de-Christianized for three quarters of a century, although occasionally by habit some of its members called upon
the diminishing number of priests for a baptism, confirmation,
or burial. These "dead parishes," as Bernanos was to call them,
were the rule rather than the exception. He makes them the typical setting for some of his most moving stories.

But, in spite of the "death" of so many parishes, Catholicism gained enormously in spiritual and intellectual resources.
Knowledge of their isolation deepened the devotion of loyal and
sensitive Catholics until they developed the intensity of a gar-
rison under siege. Conversions among intellectuals continued,
and the zeal of the converts became legendary. When Gide said
that Claudel in his youth looked like a nail and in his maturity
like a steam hammer,[42] he was expressing a psychological truth.
Claudel, Maritain, Bernanos, and Mauriac did not regard themselves as Catholics writing only for a Catholic public. They felt
that their mission was worldwide, and that their orientation was

universal. Indeed, they believed that only Catholic writers, in portraying "souls" instead of "characters," could either fully understand the ills of the times or completely fulfill the possibilities of the novel. Maritain drew his distinction between the "individual," who is a citizen and member of society, and the "person," who is rooted in eternity. In his view, "individuals" who forget or do not know that they are "persons" corrupt the world in which they live.

If non-Catholic or agnostic readers are to enjoy plots involving "persons" in this sense, the Catholic novelist must be able to induce a suspension of the state of disbelief in which such readers normally live. The popularity of Mauriac and even Bernanos with non-Catholic readers during the period from the 1920s to the 1950s indicates that for many years they induced this suspension of disbelief with remarkable success. Undoubtedly they were helped by the spiritual hunger of the era that had lost confidence in the scientism of Durkheim and Taine and was looking for faith. People who were rejecting the determinism that had prevailed in the nineteenth century found Catholics stimulating, and sometimes even convincing. As early as Huysmans, Catholic novels had brought about conversions. This process continued. Many readers, however, were simply attracted by descriptions of a world so different from their own.

There are of course limits to how much suspension of disbelief secular readers will exercise in order to enjoy fiction. The same reader, for example, who would have no trouble accepting the Greek pantheon as a poetic background to Homer, would—to take an illustration first used by Wayne Booth—absolutely refuse to accept in the days after the second war a protagonist who happened to be a Nazi. Did not many readers, particularly in France, have an antagonism to Catholicism nearly as deep as anti-Nazism in the 1940s? Was there not a bigotry unbearable to any fair-minded person in the spectacle of a Church whose conservative members considered that they and their fellow be-

lievers had special passports to heaven? Was not the whole
aspect of the French Church hopelessly unappealing? Many of
its parishes were spiritually dead or dying. Its creed was popularly held to include such beliefs as automatic damnation for
those unfortunate enough to be driven to suicide. Its bourgeoisie
was notoriously pharisaical. Its upper class was often corrupt.
Its more wealthy members frequently seemed to believe that the
sufferings of the poor scarcely mattered since they would be
compensated in heaven. What one must observe is that these
very corruptions of Catholicism were the most frequent material
of the later Catholic writers. As we noted, while the early novelists defined their positions by opposition to the secular environment, the later novelists found their themes by opposing the
habits and modes of thought that had corrupted their own Catholic community.

Yet one must not forget that while the later novelists made
criticism of the Catholic community the focus of their work, they
were still part of the older rebellion against secularism. To the
theory that blind forces governed the world, they opposed their
belief in the providence of a personal God. The novels of Balzac
and Zola were answered by the novels of Mauriac and Bernanos.
The Catholic novelists were engaged in a rebuttal of the nineteenth century's most cherished convictions just at the time when
nearly every thinking person was beginning to question those
convictions. It is no wonder that they found an audience outside
the area of their Catholic cobelievers.

The work of the Catholic novelists was both a symptom and
a cause of the fact that since Péguy's schooldays in the 1880s
the breaking of the isolation that had once characterized the
Catholic community was a steadily accelerating process. Since
the publication of the first works of Barbey d'Aurevilly, Catholics had been scrutinizing their non-Catholic neighbors with
heightened awareness and seeking to communicate what they
saw. By the time Mauriac brought out his somber attack on the

Catholic Marc Sangnier in *L'Enfant chargé de chaines* in 1913, they were also scrutinizing themselves. The artistic base that made the depth of such scrutiny possible was the aesthetic developed by Maritain and Claudel, and thus the pioneers in bringing to birth the new school of Catholic fiction were the French. But the English were to add notable variations, evolved by the need to assess the situation in England and the points of view of Englishmen. The Americans followed, with their own traditions, their own perceptions, and their own modes of expression. In all three communities creativity rose as isolation diminished.

Then in the 1960s the Catholic communities "joined the modern world." A spirit of accord with the non-Catholic environment replaced the old spirit of opposition. Many of the trends that brought about the new orientation in which Pope John could address an encyclical to "all men of good will" had been furthered by the Catholic novelists. On the one hand, the extremes of secularism and, on the other, the separatism and many of the corruptions of Catholicism had been worn away. Altered recognitions characterized thinking people on both sides. After the Second Vatican Council the convergence of the Catholic and secular communities became, for many practical, purposes, a confluence. In this period, for reasons we cannot attempt to diagnose until the conclusion of this essay, the appearance of Catholic fiction of high quality virtually ceases. It is, therefore, a good time to look back and take stock of a movement that is for the moment, if not ended, at least quiescent. J. F. Powers and Flannery O'Connor were the major Catholic novelists in America. Graham Greene and Evelyn Waugh were the climax of a tradition that in England began with Rolfe, Belloc, and Chesterton. But the leaders were the French, whose two most important Catholic writers of fiction, Bernanos and Mauriac, are the subjects of the two concluding portions of this section on the country whose ferment gave birth to the most influential tradition in developing the later Catholic novel.

CHAPTER III

François Mauriac

François Mauriac is the first of the French Catholic writers to define his position of opposition at least as much as opposition to corruptions in the Catholic community as to abuses in the secular environment. A powerful early story typical of his writing in the period after the First World War is *The Kiss for the Leper*, published in 1922. It depicts the martyrdom of a pious and beautiful young girl married to an unattractive but rich young man. The marriage had been accepted for financial reasons by the woman's grasping Catholic bourgeois family, but the suffering of her young husband is scarcely less than her own. It is characteristic of Mauriac at this time that neither protagonist seems in any way a free agent. The man is driven by his sexual desires. The woman is the victim of hopeless repulsion. Neither resists the expectations of their families nor pious convention, one of whose demands is that when the young woman is finally released by being widowed she must not remarry. Another bitter story is *Genitrix* in 1923. An aging woman from the Catholic middle class has such a strong property sense that her possessiveness fastens upon the people around her as if they were extensions of herself. She is obsessed by jealous attachment to her son and persuades herself that her dying daughter-in-law does not need care. Again, one has no sense of free choice. The murderous mother-in-law is as if demonically overcome by her unhealthy fixation. Nor does either book show any touch of redeeming grace. Both are portraits of victims and their executioners. They are indictments of bourgeois possessiveness, greed, false religiosity, and hypocrisy. But, while Mauriac's attitude is marked by the Catholic liberal's hatred of the profit system and of the decadent Catholicism which has been used to cloak it, the underlying spirit is that of Jansenist fatalism before a tide of natural depravity.

The outrage of the Catholic bourgeoisie at these portrayals was predictable, and Mauriac was not greatly troubled by it. Less easily dismissable, however, were the claims of those Catholic critics who said that, in his exposure of hidden sins and vices, Mauriac was more apt to draw his readers into voyeurism and sadism than into aversion. The hostility of Catholic publications made Mauriac decide to cease writing as a specifically Catholic novelist.[1] Much had been made of the piety of the martyred young woman in *The Kiss for the Leper* and of the self-deceiving devoutness of the family in *Genitrix*. Mauriac determined that he would dispense with such overtly religious sequences. Apparently he believed that his books could not then be called "Catholic novels." But, paradoxically, the first work of Mauriac's new period, *The Desert of Love* in 1925, is a "Catholic novel" in a far more essential way than his earlier works. Explicitly religious background has duly been excised, but the principles behind the action have a moral and theological depth greater than any he had previously explored. *The Desert of Love* shows more than creatures overcome by greed or possessiveness. It depicts them drawn by a blind longing for good, which they cannot understand and which they distort, but which also touches them inescapably. *The Desert of Love* expresses a different side of Mauriac's Jansenism: emphasis on supernatural grace.

The story opens with Raymond, a man of thirty-five, sitting in a Paris bar. He has spent his life in a series of affairs which he has conducted in such a way as to avenge the traumatic scorn that met his first attempt to make love as a youth of eighteen. By chance the woman who had scorned him in his youth comes into the bar with her husband. She ignores Raymond, while he stares at her angrily; and the reader is then taken back into the past— to Bordeaux seventeen years earlier and the early life of the remarkable woman known as Maria Cross.

A widow in her mid-twenties with a child to support, Maria Cross had drifted into a position as mistress to a rich man. Her "benefactor" is often away, leaving her alone. She is admired by Dr. Courrèges, who tends her child in a fatal illness, but she is both bored by the doctor's company and oblivious to his devotion. After her little boy's death, she goes each day to the cemetery to visit his grave, and returning by tram she regularly sits opposite a high-school student with a face of angelic beauty. With an urgency she cannot understand Maria has longed blindly for purity in love. She had had an illogical attraction to a young woman, Gaby, which made the doctor—who was hoping to ask her to flee to Algiers with him—wonder if she was a latent lesbian. Now her blind longing for purity is distorted again, into another attraction, this time toward the schoolboy; and the attraction turns into a wonderfully depicted confusion, in which are mingled admiration of innocence, memory of her newly dead son, and half-aware incipient desire. Mauriac depicts Maria as helpless before her feelings, the typical Jansenist view of personality.

The young student, Raymond, notes the attention he has aroused and learns soon after that the lady of the tram is the famous Maria Cross, a "kept woman," the scandal of the town. Raymond, too, is helpless before his emotions. They have been twisted by his environment and by the irresistible urgency of his

adolescent sexual desires. He was already informed about
Maria before he saw her because he is the son of that Dr. Courrèges who secretly loves Maria, and who often speaks of her at
home. The doctor's care of Maria's dying son had distressed
Madame Courrèges—not that the doctor's wife had any idea of
the real nature of the doctor's devotion to Maria Cross, but because, as a conventional and respectable person, Madame Courrèges had a horror of Maria's position and called the death of
Maria's child, "God's justice."[2] As the son of this pharisaical
woman, young Raymond naturally has developed a picture of
the world that has combined with his obsession with sex to lead
him to every kind of fantasy. When Maria asks him to her
house, where she shows him pictures of her little son, he tries
on the second visit to take her by force. Repulsed with horror
and disgust, he experiences the humiliation he never forgets and
spends his life avenging on other women.

The only overtly pious figure in this early part of the book
is Raymond's mother. Religious themes, however, predominate
from the beginning, and any notion Mauriac may have had that
he was not writing a Catholic novel was totally unfounded. By
her name and appearance Maria Cross suggests a madonna.
After the scene in which the doctor comes closest to declaring
his love, he finds himself remembering his mother. Just before
the doctor's son made his attempt at assault, Maria had been
feeling that such a young man might have been her son. Images
of the eternal mother thus cluster thickly about Maria. But
Maria is also Maria *Cross*, representing not only the psychic
structure of the mother-son relationship, but also the love on
which human beings are crucified because the psychological elements of which it is composed are unrealizable. Yet in treating
of love Mauriac does not surrender completely to the deterministic pessimism of most French Catholics under heavy Jansenist
influence. Mauriac has the orthodox Catholic view that sees all
earthly love as a shadow of a metaphysical reality. For Mauriac,

love is a reflection of the eternal creative force. As such it can become a road to peace, a forecasting of true fulfillment—or, as with Raymond, a road to despair, a sort of damnation on earth, in which a soul longs to inflict on all other souls the torment it has suffered.

After Raymond's assault, Maria tries to throw herself from a window—a suicide attempt that like every other attempt of Maria's fails, for the window she hysterically chooses is on too low a floor. Suffering from concussion, she tries to describe in her delirium what she sees as the true object of those lost in the "desert." "Not loves, but one single love."[3] Half asleep she murmurs of a "being whom we can reach, possess—but never in the flesh—by whom we are to be possessed."[4] Later, after Maria goes on to marry her protector—drifting into this stage of her life as she has drifted into every other—she falls under the influence of her generous and deeply religious stepson. This young man opens for Maria a channel of undistorted grace at last, and she comes to see that the longings for love that had filled her earlier life were reflections of a longing for the eternal Love that enfolds the universe. Thus the life of Maria Cross symbolizes the creative principle by which all people are drawn and she herself finally becomes obscurely aware of that principle. The doctor and his son, however, never comprehend what had so moved them. At the end, it is the author who must speak and make the central theme explicit. The doctor and his son had been drawn by Him "Whom unknown to them calls from the deepest part of their being."[5]

There are critics who, like Sartre,[6] object vehemently to this kind of recourse to authorial comment, but often, as in this case, it would be impossible for Mauriac in any other way to set forth clearly the final meaning of his story. And it is hard to claim that in his use of the device there are areas where the effect is jarring. In *The Desert of Love* Mauriac as narrator creates a "narrator personality," who is in direct and continuous communication with the reader so that, when this narrator comments, there is never any sense of illogic or break in flow, which is, after all, the test of a story well told.[7] Graham Greene, as we will see, enlarges this device. It is extremely helpful to a Catholic novelist who must convey to his readers metaphysical themes of which his characters themselves have no recognition.

If Mauriac wanted, as he said, to depict the individual in literature and yet show eternal types, and if he wanted to give his readers a sense of having touched mysteries at the heart of life, he succeeded to some degree in *The Desert of Love*; but the characters, who are driven by their desires or helplessly attracted by grace and who also almost never understand their own condition, have a lack of internal struggle that—regardless of what one thinks of Jansenism—impoverishes the dramatic impact. Nevertheless, Mauriac created a compelling novel, in which the theme of grace related to natural depravity is sufficiently cloaked by surface happenings to avoid arousing the skepticism of nonbelievers. The book, with its evocation of prewar France, found an enthusiastic audience among both Catholics and non-Catholics in the 1920s. The war had blunted the old antagonisms which had developed after 1876 and reached a climax during the separation of Church and state after the turn of the century. Catholic Frenchmen and secular Frenchmen had given their lives together against the common enemy from 1914 to 1918. In the years after the war, a spirit of mutual respect replaced the old bitterness between Catholics and secularists. Convergence entered a new period, one in which there was at least as much mutual curiosity as abrasiveness. The fiction of Mauriac had a tremendous vogue. Not only did his neoclassical tendencies in character portrayal precisely fit the aesthetic proclivities of the period which was to delight in Braque and Picasso but his very Jansenism was neoclassicist in its effect. Even in the very early *Desert of Love*, which does not yet have the universal types of "eternal Tartuffe" and "eternal Harpagon" which later were to be the mainstays of his casts of characters, the Jansenist tradition behind the plot has much the same impact as Greek drama. The protagonists in *The Desert of Love* meet fate—grace or the dark promptings of the flesh—and in their endurance there is a heroism that can be deeply moving and remind one strongly of Sophoclean tragedy.

As we noted, *The Desert of Love* reveals itself as a "Catholic novel" long before the Catholic ending in Maria's conversion, for the whole story depends on the Catholic idea that human beings seek the love of God behind all earthly loves. Nevertheless, *The Desert of Love* is not a depiction of the Catholic community. For most of her life Maria is not a believing and practicing Catholic, and Raymond is never one. *The Desert of Love* falls, therefore, into the older category of Catholic writing practiced by Huysmans, which was characterized primarily by opposition to the non-Catholic environment. But in 1932, when Mauriac began a new novel, *Vipers' Tangle*, and was ready to resume writing as a specifically "Catholic" novelist, he returned to the setting of the Catholic rural community of Les Landes, which had been the background for *Genitrix* and *The Kiss for the Leper*. Mauriac had learned a great deal from such ostensibly non-Catholic books as *The Desert of Love*. In his new novel he once more opposes grace to natural depravity but occasionally emphasizes freedom of choice. He also brings Catholics and non-Catholics into confrontation. Catholics and non-Catholics are equally recipients of grace, which they distort to varying degrees. The result is more powerful drama, in which there is an abundance of struggle, both internally in the mind of the protagonist and externally between the characters. *Vipers' Tangle* is a subtle work, easy to misinterpret, and we should turn again for a look at the background.

Even without the evidence of the novels there can be no doubt of Mauriac's loathing of the Catholic bourgeoisie. In his youth he took refuge in *Sillon*; later he was president of a

Cercle Montalembert—both of which were oriented to helping
the workers while maintaining conscious antagonism to the exploiting class. Even the Catholic Mouvement Républicain Pop-
ulaire (MRP), which ruled France after the Second World War,
stirred Mauriac's ever-ready suspicion of the Catholic middle
class. Neocolonialism, with the pretext of giving peace and civilization to the peoples of Indochina and Algeria, convinced him
that pietist pretense had found yet another guise, and he was
moved to furies of journalistic protest.

Les Landes, the dunes area just outside Bordeaux, was
Mauriac's home in his youth. It was among those sections de-
Christianized in 1789 but gripped thereafter by the so-called
"religious revival," the self-serving ostensible piousness in the
interests of the social stability required for prosperous commercialism. *Vipers' Tangle* is, however, more than an attack on corrupted Catholicism. In this book corruption of man's faith is
depicted as a reflection of a metaphysical corruption at the root
of the world. The land itself is under a shadow. The rain that
should nourish the vines also beats them down. A flaw at the
heart of the universe has estranged it from God, as Catholics
have been estranged from true belief. In this sense, Mauriac's
attack on the degenerate Catholicism of the bourgeoisie of Les
Landes is even more profoundly Jansenist than the theme of *The
Desert of Love.*

There are at least two possible readings of *Vipers' Tangle.*
One is to see Louis, the dying miser, simply as a villain who reforms, a sort of Harpagon who receives grace. Mauriac's neoclassical orientation makes this interpretation tempting, but it
not only overlooks the metaphysical depth of the book but also
destroys its unity. Avarice thus regarded is simply a universal
vice, and the book's attack on the Catholic middle class becomes
alien to the main point. A different reading, which I believe to
be the only correct one, is to see the novel as an exposé of the
Catholic middle class, whose victim is Louis. Shunning Louis

because he is a freethinker, Louis' wife from the first years of their marriage forms a cabal against him with their children. If a child ever climbs into Louis' lap, she is quick to call it away. Denied love by his wife and children, Louis turns to his peasant passion for property as a love-substitute. Louis, therefore, is not so much a villain who reforms as a victim who forgives. In this reading, the book's unity is inviolate. It is a single thrust against the blasphemous false piety Mauriac so detested—and yet (here is the subtlety of this Jansenist drama) this same false piety becomes the source of Louis' redemption. Grace is so powerful that it can use evil itself as a source of light.

There are critics who find the religious language of the later pages of Louis' journal an infringement of realism in their depiction of the reactions of the old freethinker. But the notion that Louis' language in the later pages is improbable vanishes as soon as one remembers that Louis was not only receiving grace —irresistible in Mauriac's Jansenism—but was also surrounded with this kind of language by his wife and children for forty years. While they were used to it and were, so to speak, vaccinated against it by custom, it was to him always vital because it differed so radically from the irreligion of his peasant background, de-Christianized for centuries, and from the principles of his lawyer class, agnostic since the eighteen hundreds. Louis is always shocked by his "Christian" family's easy disregard of the principles they profess. The fact that his wife will give to charity and yet does not hesitate to beat down the prices of the old vegetable woman until the few pennies of profit are gone,[8] moves him to disgusted indignation. Mauriac shows that the pagan Louis is actually a more religious man than most members of the "religious" family whose prey he is.

We first meet Louis as an old man writing his wife a letter to accompany a will disinheriting their children. Louis goes back to the root of his despair, to his youth when he believed that his wife, a "demoiselle Fondaudège,"[9] a daughter of the

Catholic ruling bourgeoisie, really loved him, a peasant boy whose mother had managed to build up her vineyards and forests into a fortune. It is of course the forests and vineyards, not the homely, cold, irreligious young man who is acceptable to the spendthrift Fondaudèges; but Louis is blind to the situation until the night when his young wife, Isa, lying in his arms, confides to him—casually, nostalgically, and certainly without much thought—that preceding him on her scene was a certain Rodolphe, a man who was from her own class but whose parents refused to let him marry her because of a rumor that some of her family had died of tuberculosis. Louis, a brilliant young lawyer, who is beginning to be able to read people almost at will, suddenly realized that he was for the Fondaudèges only a deplorable second choice, and for Isa he is not her beloved but her destiny.

Louis' furious letter written forty years later turns into a vindictive journal. Mauriac develops the account skillfully. As Louis goes back into the past, we see how in depicting the actions of his wife and children he is also forced to depict himself, to explore not merely his hatred for them but his self-hatred. The novel thus advances on two levels: the unfolding of Louis' life as revealed by his exposition of his history, and the progress of Louis in self-knowledge, the progress which will make him ready to receive grace. Louis has always accorded his family only the most minimum support. He won't let Isa even give away old furniture out of the attic. Consequently his descendants await his death with an almost frenzied longing for the inheritance—an inheritance Louis is determined to deny them, as they have denied him their love.

But, slowly, as Louis looks back into himself, the soul they have maimed begins to understand itself. And understanding is a powerful source of healing. Louis realizes that he has not only loved, he has been loved, and sometimes he has even helped his fellow beings. A young seminarian who had excited local scandal by attending an opera, was defended by Louis, and he told Louis, "You are good."[10] Louis' straightforward young nephew, Luc, who was killed in the war and to whom Louis was attracted from the time of Luc's earliest childhood, wrote him a postcard not long before he died, concluding, "Tendresses."[11] Most of all, Louis loved and was loved by his youngest daughter, Marie, who like all the children had been told by their devout mother that she must pray a great deal for her unbelieving father and who, dying of a painful illness, offered her death "for Papa."[12] After the first mention of Marie, Louis' account is haunted by the child. Her generosity, her love for all around her, her way of falling trustingly asleep in his lap recur again and again in his remembering. Here was one child whom Isa could not subvert. All through the story Louis' recollections make us remember Marie, who earned for her father the grace he is receiving. This theme of suffering willingly offered by one human being to earn grace for another goes back to Huysmans' early use of it in *L'Oblat* and *En Route*. The doctrine is of course orthodox and as old as the crucifixion. Huysmans had trouble accommodating it to his novels because the concept as he used it was on too heroic a scale for his fiction. By making a child the earner of grace, Mauriac reduces the scale. Greene brings about a similar reduction in *The Power and the Glory* by making the earner of grace an alcoholic priest, who is fallible and weakly human.

Mauriac develops the account of Louis' response to grace and handles it with a naturalness never achieved by Huysmans. Whenever Louis remembers Marie, he is deeply moved. At last his recollections of the child make him see his own contrasting harshness, and Louis feels that his hatred of his family has made his heart a "tangle of vipers." He begins to believe that Isa's family's God came to earth perhaps not so much for them, the "religious ones," as for those like himself who are irreligious.[13] Louis has always had a sort of natural mysticism. In his youth he had a sense of communion with the forests and vineyards, and once, long ago, driving with Isa when he believed that she loved him, he had a strange feeling as he looked off at the mountains, an "almost physical certainty that another world exists, a reality of which we know only the shadow. . . ."[14] Here, again, is Mauriac's characteristic theme that earthly love, earthly possessiveness, reflect the longing for the love of God, hidden and unrecognized but all-powerful. Under the pressure of his memories, Louis' latent religious sense combines with what he has picked up from Isa's piety and he wonders what would happen if he could get Isa to read what he has written. He wonders what changes might take place in both of them if they could live, even for a moment, before Marie's God of Love.

Louis is about to respond to the grace he has been receiving. We see him evaluate his past and then weigh his decision. He determines to forgive Isa. Despite the memories of Marie which keep us aware that the grace granted Louis has been earned by another, we still see him as a free personality, and the drama is enhanced by our feeling that Louis is engaged in internal conflict. Louis in these pages is as free a figure as we meet anywhere in Mauriac's fiction.

But here the journal suddenly breaks off. When it begins again, Louis is in Bordeaux and once more driven by his hatred. He has left home in a deeper fury against his family than ever before. The long work of grace has been suddenly undone by human depravity, and at this point in the story Mauriac's Jansenist determinism replaces his temporary emphasis on freedom. From a window at night Louis overheard his children planning to have him certified as insane, and Isa letting herself almost be persuaded. For the first time in his life, Louis writes, he felt that he was less evil than those around him:[15] the tangle of vipers was not, as he had thought, inside himself but outside, in his family.[16] He plans now to confer his fortune on his illegitimate son, Robert, and he has come to Bordeaux for that purpose.

But Louis' illegitimate son Robert turns out to be as cow-
ardly, cold, and deficient in vitality as the rest of Louis' children. Robert prefers the certainty of a pension from the family
to what seems to him the too risky hope of receiving the fortune
from Louis in cash, and he betrays his father to the others. Then,
however, Isa dies. And with her dies all of Louis' hatred. Fury
and vindictiveness burn out when death takes their object, Isa.
Louis returns home for her funeral, he settles his fortune on the
children, he makes an allowance to Robert, and he retires to his
country home. There Louis receives the final impetus of the
grace earned for him by Marie. It is revealed only when he dies.
His journal ends just as he is about to write of his love for God,
the only love that can satisfy the human need for love.[17]

This close of Louis' story lacks dramatic power. The processes of the climactic change in him are never dramatized. At
the end we know only that he has seen a priest and that he dies
in the love of God. After he goes to Bordeaux and yields to his
rage, and after Isa's death when he as suddenly surrenders to
grace, the account loses its vigor. As we will see later with Flannery O'Connor, when natural depravity or irresistible grace are
introduced as the causes of human action, there may be not only
what many of us would consider suspect theology but also an
apparent gap in the logic of the story, as it takes a sudden and
invisible turning we cannot account for if we believe that God
works within the limits of human freedom. The recipient of
grace must be shown as free to cooperate or refuse, as Louis was
free in the sections where he was remembering Marie, if the
reader is to feel any sense of continuous conflict. Bernanos
and Graham Greene are experts at sustaining this kind of tension. Mauriac regrettably is not. One must conclude that at most
periods of his life he simply did not believe in it. Mauriac was
typical of French Catholics with strong Jansenist orientations.
All his work reflects the community to which he belonged. The
faults he saw in French Catholicism and opposed so vehemently

ironically never included its Jansenism. Mauriac's Louis crosses over the border into death, after which Mauriac can say no more. One remembers that also in *The Desert of Love* Maria felt that all she believed in as most beautiful was only accessible after death—it was never "in the flesh."[18] The bleakness of Mauriac's work comes not only from his Jansenist view of natural depravity and his antipathy toward a profit-oriented world, but is caused also by his complete separation of the world of God from the world of man and the inaccessibility, even to the author's prose, of the former. Bernanos has an entirely different conception, and uses an entirely different treatment. He presents us, so to speak, with a different universe.

CHAPTER IV

Georges Bernanos

In the work of Bernanos there are two prime characteristics that hold true for all of existence. One is that the physical world is not separated from the metaphysical but enfolded within it. The other is that the eschatological existence beyond time is always present at the same instant as existence in time. In *The Diary of a Country Priest*, for example, the Curé d'Ambricourt tells the rebellious young girl, Chantal:

> The world of sin confronts the world of grace like the reflected picture of a landscape in very still, deep waters. There is not only a communion of saints; there is also a communion of sinners. In their hatred of one another, their contempt, sinners unite, embrace, intermingle, become as one; one day in the eyes of the Eternal God they will be no more than a mass of perpetual slime over which the vast tide of divine love, that sea of living, roaring flame which gave birth to all things, passes vainly.[1]

Like Mauriac, Bernanos focuses on the Catholic community not the secular environment; Chantal belongs to the Catholic gentry. She and her mother and father are bound into a fierce communion of mutual hatred, and their Catholicism is as corrupted as that of Mauriac's bourgeoisie. Bernanos' Catholic gentry, however, are not alone together, as Mauriac's bourgeoisie are usually alone so that one almost has the impression that the Catholic community contains no other class. The corruption of Chantal's family is reflected in the corruption of the village parish. If the Count and Countess hate one another, the villagers also hate each other, and the country priest, symbolically ravaged by an incurable cancer, which is like a physical incarnation of the communion of evil infecting his people, is often in despair, unable even to pray to the Christ who is the center of his life and the object of his love. Yet in the crisis which forms the focal point of the novel, the frail young priest is stronger than the united efforts of the forces that oppose him.

The Countess hates her daughter because the girl survived her brother who died in early childhood. Ever since the boy's death, the Countess has turned away from God. Although she "makes her Easter," fulfills her "religious duties" because not to do so would be, as she says to the priest, "beneath her,"[2] she has never forgiven God for her son's death and carries in her heart a mute rage against all existence. Meanwhile, her daughter Chantal, repelled by her mother, has given all her affection to her father. But her father has a mistress, Chantal's governess, and in Chantal's passion for her father, a man whom she not only can never possess but who is possessed by another, Chantal's hatred of all being is as great as her mother's, who has watched the psychological distortion of her daughter's nature with the same mute acquiescence with which she has nourished her own undying rage at God. Chantal, always difficult since her adolescence, sometimes hysterical, is to be sent to stay with friends in England. If she goes, her mother knows that she will never reenter the house.[3] As the Countess says to the priest, when his dawning awareness of the situation forces him to make his way into the chateau and talk to her in an effort to help Chantal, it is unlikely that Chantal is temperamentally capable of killing herself;[4] she will "merely" be like her mother—forever unable to love.

It is then, in the climax of the interview between the Countess and the Curé, that Bernanos develops his theme that a simultaneity exists between the world of time and the world of eternity, an ontological theme of the type pioneered by Claudel and advocated by Maritain as the most challenging to Catholic writers. The priest tells the Countess that in her corruption of religion she has placed herself and her family in hell; she has made them part of the communion of sinners, the mystical communion of evil which is the denial of love. When the Countess cannot understand this concept, d'Ambricourt says:

> . . . what have you laymen made of hell? A kind of penal servitude for eternity. . . . What proud or reasonable man could stomach such a notion of God's justice? . . . The miracle is that we on earth were ever able to think of such a thing, when scarcely has our sin gone out of us, and one look, a sign, a dumb appeal suffices for grace and pardon to swoop down. . . . Our very hate is resplendent, and the least tormented of fiends would warm himself in our despair, as in a morning of glittering sunshine. Hell is not to love any more, madame . . . suppose this faculty which seems so inseparably ours, of our very essence, should disappear!

And then he warns her not to exile herself from her son forever, not to enter irrevocably into hell: "don't place yourself beyond love's reach."[5] He adds, "There is only God's kingdom and, living or dead, we are all therein."[6] God does not separate the Countess from her dead child, but the Countess herself, who by her actions toward Chantal and her husband is destroying her power to love. Bernanos, who depicts freedom of choice in all his characters, is at his best in this scene. D'Ambricourt is a channel of grace—as was Mauriac's Marie—but we see the Countess' resistance; and it is a resistance of such quality that we know she was able to resist to the end, if she had so decided.

But the Countess' resistance vanishes the moment she understands the Curé's argument that only she herself can permanently separate herself from her dead son. Bernanos' view of psychology here reminds us of the effect on contemporary Catholics of the revival of Thomism. If Bernanos owed his depiction of Chantal's emotions toward her father to Freud's insights into the Oedipus complex, he owes to Saint Thomas this important scene, the conversion of the Countess, on which the plot hinges. First the Countess' affections are aroused, her love for the dead boy; her intelligence then is reached by the priest's exposition of the meaning of hell; and finally her will responds. This is exactly the order of human reactions described by Saint Thomas in the *Summa theologica*.[7] Wrenching at a chain around her neck the Countess hurls into the fire a medallion containing a lock of her son's hair, which she has worn ever since his death. Horrified, the priest burns his hand trying to get it out. He is too late, and he tells the Countess she takes no account of God's mercy. God does not ask so much. But the Countess is, as she says, an "all or nothing" person.[8] Having made her decision, she acts on it as the intransigent descendant of forebears in whom the old chivalric code of total giving of the self in fealty or enmity was part of the feudalism of their medieval heritage. Bernanos here is writing as a typical Catholic idealist of the French right. From the time of Chateaubriand, Frenchmen of this type attempted to preserve the sense of chivalry, honor, and dedication, which they longed to see reborn in the modern world. The Countess' "Thy will be done" is in accord with this centuries-old, traditional ideal.

The Curé d'Ambricourt dies of his cancer, but his life has brought healing to the Countess and her family. He brings grace, too, to the peasant child, Seraphita Dumouchel, whose corruption symbolizes the bestiality of the parish that huddles at the foot of the chateau. He also alters the life of a lapsed priest, a fellow seminarian, who gives up the mistress who has been supporting him. The shabby young Curé d'Ambricourt in his ragged and spotted soutane is a hidden martyr, whose life alters every circumstance he touches.[9] It may be objected that cancer is not martyrdom, but Bernanos makes it clear that the illness is a symbol of the surrounding corruption and, also, that the priest's physical condition is the result of generations of poverty and undernourishment, not only physical but psychic as well. And, until more is known about the relationship between the body's resistance to disease and unconscious processes, who is to say that, even within the framework of strict causality, Bernanos' depiction of this illness is overdrawn? Certainly, as a symbol, the priest's illness is convincing within the supernatural frame-work of the story. D'Ambricourt suffers and dies. The wills of those around him are touched and changed by the force of his example. The "mysterious ties" which Bernanos saw as linking the "great sinners to the great saints," the penetration into more than merely visible existence, which Maritain saw as the mission of the Catholic artist, are the very tissue of this novel. Bernanos wanted to "dream" of a knighthood of the spirit; he wanted his dreams to be "past all measure"—and so they are, but with a simplicity and a humility that, at least in this particular novel, do not seem in any way strident or shockingly unnatural. In nearly all cases, grace in the work of Bernanos seems to operate within the human limits of the personalities affected. The super-natural never seems to be disjoined from the nature of the char-acters, as in Mauriac, who often makes the reader feel as if there were a hidden supernatural stage machinery in the back-ground, through which "grace" evokes responses beyond free will, in an automatic and puppetlike reaction.

An aid to the comprehensible naturalness of *The Diary of a Country Priest* is the fact that the chateau and the village are corollary parts of the same decadent Catholic environment. If the chateau is in the shadow of hypocrisy and evil, so is the vil-lage. Its peasant-farmer class is represented by the Dumouchels, and the corrupt child, Seraphita, who is in love with the Curé d'Ambricourt with the childish hopelessness of such passions, and who spreads rumors of his drunkenness with the furious vindictiveness of such child women in all times (they did not in Bernanos' day have their modern name of "nymphets"). When Seraphita understands and looks back on what she has done, she repents with the blind feverishness and touching immoderation of such personalities. In her, too, the medieval traits of chivalry, honor, and loyalty survive. She is the village parallel to the impassioned and iron-willed Countess.

Just as the chateau is set in complementary and thoroughly believable surroundings, so the Curé d'Ambricourt as a warrior of the spirit is not alone. On either side of him are placed fellow combatants, each worthy to be compared with him, but each entirely different. On one hand is the Curé de Torcy, an older priest of the generation of *Rerum Novarum*. He is a muscular fighter, a sort of overlord in his parish. The doughty battles for social justice of an earlier, simpler era cast into relief the complexities of the spiritual warfare of the 1930s that challenge the Curé d'Ambricourt. On the other side of the Curé d'Ambricourt is de Torcy's great friend, Dr. Delbende. The humane doctor has reduced himself to penury not only by treating the sick poor without remuneration but by paying their debts for them. In the end he surrenders to the temptation of despair and commits suicide, a reminder that the warriors of the spirit can be most bitterly defeated.

The two men, de Torcy and Delbende, are foils for d'Ambricourt. Only d'Ambricourt fills completely Bernanos' mold of the Christian hero, only he is a martyr as well as a warrior. Yet d'Ambricourt entirely lacks what admirers of classical drama would call "magnitude." De Torcy and Dr. Delbende are characters of much more striking stature, de Torcy by sheer energy, Delbende by the passion of his atheism. The Curé d'Ambricourt is a hero of the "little way," and he makes one remember Bernanos' affection for Sainte Thérèse and her *Story of a Soul*. D'Ambricourt's spiritual struggles are not the weighty battles of atheistic despair but the long slow acedia that is much harder to endure. His campaign to reform his parish entails no fiery sermons on social justice but a desperate effort to stem a slow steady erosion of souls by poisons that, far from being spectacular, are largely invisible. And if the Curé d'Ambricourt is a saint, as seems probable, it is a sanctity that is as unostentatious in the world around him as his life.

In the world of Bernanos we are always conscious of the supernatural—as we logically must be, since in Bernanos' novels the natural and supernatural coexist: there "is only God's kingdom and, living or dead, we are all therein." *The Diary of a Country Priest* is Bernanos' finest work, and the handling of the supernatural there is far more subtle than in *Under the Sun of Satan,* his first book, or in such later works as the frequently obscure *Monsieur Ouine.* The country priest, though often fallible, nevertheless sometimes has the gift of reading thoughts, but d'Ambricourt's gifts of understanding are not conferred on him at a miraculous moment in his life as happens to the Abbé Donissan in *Under the Sun of Satan*; he never meets the devil incarnated as a horse trader as does Donissan in that book, nor is he like Donissan tempted by being the subject of a false miracle. D'Ambricourt is surrounded by evidence indicating the malice of a supernatural adversary. He has the same experiences as the Curé of Ars in hearing mysterious sounds. His gate bangs back and forth at night and is found tight shut in the morning nevertheless. But all of these occurrences might be accidental. Similarly, the Curé's incurable cancer is described as an ordinary illness, but we never doubt that it has been caused by the corruption of the Curé's world and that his patient endurance of his suffering is helping to win redemption for that world. *The Diary of a Country Priest* is a moving book, and it is not hard for unbelievers to accept the supernatural in it simply as an aesthetic enhancement of the story's effect, although in some of Bernanos' other novels the supernatural continuously at work within the natural is so stressed or seems so extraordinary that for many non-Catholic readers suspension of disbelief may be at times somewhat difficult.

We have seen how Mauriac's novels reflect the Catholicism characteristic of France. Indeed without some understanding of it, particularly of Jansenism, Mauriac's work loses much of its comprehensibility. Understanding of the background is even more necessary in order to appreciate Bernanos. As Gaëton Picon says, "Bernanos' novels, at the same time as they are a legend of supernatural combat, are a history of French society and the Church at a certain moment of their evolution."[10] Bernanos is not a novelist whose introduction of characters is limited to what they contribute to the plot. Mauriac practices the usual economy of the modern novel; his personages almost invariably exist to advance the action. But the typical Bernanos novel has "action" of at least two kinds: one is what may more strictly be called "plot," the consecutive action that initiates, develops, and arrives at the denouement; the other is what may be called "descriptive action," which sets forth the state of the human community which it is the novel's aim to depict. Such action is "descriptive" because its function is to make the reader aware of conditions that take no direct part in the consecutive plot. There are also "descriptive characters," who represent a whole throng of similar persons, who then are seen as peopling the "world" in which the plot takes shape.

Such a character, used to describe the state of French rural Catholicism (whose history we saw in Chapter I) is the old sacristan, Arsène. He represents the most "faithful" element among d'Ambricourt's peasants, to whom the Church seems as much part of their heritage as the earth they tend. A century and a half after the Revolution, Bernanos' Artois still had such peasants in 1936, and they exist almost unchanged today. In Arsène, Bernanos draws them for us:

"All our folk be church folk. Me granfer was a bell-ringer at Lyons, me poor old ma was in service with M. le Curé de Wilman, an' there b'aint one o'ours passed on without the sacrament. It be in our blood, no gettin' away from it."

"You'll meet them again in heaven," I said.

This time he thought for ages. I was watching him round the corner of my eye, whilst still at my work, having given up all hope of his speaking again, when he pronounced this final oracle, in a frayed and unforgettable voice—a voice which seemed to issue from the dust of ages.

"When you be dead, everythin' be dead."

Such a blasphemy he couldn't really have meant; he was merely expressing his failure to imagine that eternal life. . . . Nevertheless, his words froze me, and suddenly I had lost heart. I said I felt ill and left him, walking home alone, in the wind and rain.[11]

Clearly, here, d'Ambricourt's view of Arsène is shown by Bernanos to be unreliable. Arsène *does* mean what he says, as d'Ambricourt himself feels. Even in such as Arsène the ancient faith is eroded; the very instinct of faith is under attack by a disbelief that has itself become instinctive. As we will remember, Artois was one of the provinces not de-Christianized in 1789. Right up to modern times it was rated as "faithful," a "Catholic" parish. Nevertheless, as Bernanos shows (and he knew his favorite Artois well), Arsène is a disbeliever. Arsène's disbelief is the village counterpart of the rationalist Dr. Delbende's atheism. As Seraphita reflects the Countess, so Arsène reflects Delbende. Arsène is thoroughly individualized, but he "stands for" much more than is usually given to an auxiliary character to represent. Arsène is the parish itself, d'Ambricourt's parish, in which d'Ambricourt rightly feels himself crucified. "The village has nailed me up here on a cross." The priest has not even the consolation that it is "at least watching me die."[12] What seems most likely is that the villagers are both unknowing and indifferent.

Two other characters whose function is to indicate the nature of the Catholic environment are Monsieur and Madame Pamyre, who dun the priest for some elderberry wine, which d'Ambricourt had naïvely supposed was a gift. It is significant that the wine, which is sometimes the only nourishment that d'Ambricourt's still undiagnosed cancer permits him to digest, has to come from the Pamyres. As the country priest's Dean says, the Pamyres belong to "that class of small hard-working thrifty shopkeepers, who are still the backbone and greatness of our dear France." The Dean can remember when they were "guided" by the anti-Catholic press of the liberal left. "But now they can see the fruits of their labor being threatened by the forces of disorder, and they realize the time for such generous illusions is past, and that the social order has no surer prop than our Holy Church. Is not the right of possession set down in the Gospels?"[13] Bernanos' irony is heavy, but it is relevant to his time. People like the Pamyres were the mainstay of the so-called religious revival. They prospered, rose in the world, and eventually some Pamyre might turn up as a student in a seminary. They were indeed the "nourishment" of the Church. Bernanos' meaning is that, like the Curé d'Ambricourt, the Church, too, suffers from centuries of spiritual starvation. The Church, like d'Ambricourt, is ravaged by cancer, and the "wine of the Pamyres" is what is offered her as sustenance in her need.

Another character who exists to illustrate the condition of French Catholicism is Monsieur Olivier, whom we meet at the end of the book. Here, again, the scene is purely descriptive, contributing nothing to the advance of the denouement but completing the novel's "world." It is significant, I believe, that Bernanos saves this portrait for near the end. It is a climax characteristic of Bernanos, who said he was incapable of despair. Monsieur Olivier is the opposite of Monsieur and Madame Pamyre. He brings to the close of the story Bernanos' hope not only for French Catholicism but for the human race.

The first manifestation of the existence of Monsieur Olivier is the sound of a motor. D'Ambricourt, who is walking down a lonely road, hears it growing steadily louder until it is "like a cry—savagely imperious, menacing, desperate."[14] Then, plunging up and down the hills comes a motorcycle. A bare-headed young man is riding it, and he stops by the Curé to invite him to climb up behind. For d'Ambricourt that ride is the great experience of his life.

> . . . the roar of the engine rose continuously higher and higher till it gave out one note only, wonderfully pure. It was like the song of light, it was light itself, and I felt I was watching with my own eyes the huge curve of that stupendous ascent. The countryside did not come toward us, it opened out on all sides, and just beyond the wild skid of the road, seemed to turn majestically on itself, like a door opening to another world.[15]

The "other world," the magnificent transcendence of space and time conveyed by the description, open to the Curé—and to the reader—the double reality that always exists in the universe of Bernanos. The radiant eternity, which d'Ambricourt is so soon to enter, accompanies this life, is parallel to it, and will be fulfilled at the end of it. The passage foreshadows d'Ambricourt's coming transfiguration by death, his entry forever into that "other world" which now he experiences only by mystical intuition, but into which he then will be plunged to the full depth of his longing spirit.

After the ride Monsieur Olivier talks to the Curé. He is a young cousin of the Countess, and is like her one of the "all or nothing" people. He is a soldier, serving at present in the Foreign Legion. The Curé says,

> "I am sure you believe in God."
>
> "Our people," he answered, "never question the matter. We all believe in God, all, even the worst of us—the worst believe in him most, perhaps. I think we must be too proud to sin without taking risks; we have always one witness to face: God."[16]

The modern state and the modern world have all but done away with the function of the kind of man Monsieur Olivier is, but his race still goes on, careless of life, risking it gladly, joyously, with a defiant integrity that is in their blood.[17] In Monsieur Olivier the best of the tradition cherished by French idealists of the right has triumphantly developed and survived. Bernanos seems to promise that Monsieur Olivier and his kind will go on in Catholic France as long as the nation exists.

Monsieur Olivier and the Pamyres are opposite poles. The Pamyres represent the degenerate, profit-oriented present-day world of petty people and petty concerns which the idealists of the right so despised. Madame Pamyre no doubt "makes her Easter" and fulfills her "obligations," while Monsieur Olivier probably falls repeatedly into the category that Monsieur and Madame Pamyre, two of whose sons are priests, would regard as "sinful"; but there can be no doubt which of these two is the more spiritually robust. The Pamyres will never extinguish the Oliviers. Creatures of the Pamyres' species count for little in a world where the Oliviers ever fight on at the dangerous edges of existence. No matter how vile this world becomes, Bernanos seems to say, it will not extinguish this spirit. The roar of Monsieur Olivier's motor takes hill after hill, far into the "reeling horizon."[18]

Unlike Mauriac, Bernanos gives leading roles to people of every kind and class. One of his most moving novels concerns a peasant child of fourteen. *The New Story of Mouchette* is deeply prophetic of the future of Catholic thought. Mouchette is a young girl growing up in a "dead parish," where Christianity is barely more than a memory. Her father is a drunkard who beats his children; her mother is broken by hardship. Mouchette and all who surround her exist in the most abysmal intellectual and moral poverty. The Curé d'Ambricourt grew up in such a background—in what Bernanos calls *misère*, not what is meant by poverty (*pauvreté*) but utter spiritual as well as material deprivation. Though d'Ambricourt was tormented by the deep inner draining Bernanos represents by cancer, at least he escaped the doom of his birth into *misère* by his entry into the priesthood. The story of Mouchette is the story of those for whom there is no escape.

Her story begins one day in a storm as she is on her way back from the village school, where at fourteen she is the oldest pupil, what we euphemistically call a "slow learner," not out of stupidity but out of blindly stubborn resistance to the whole nature of her existence. Soaked by rain, exhausted from battling the elements, Mouchette meets the half-drunk poacher Arsène. It is drink that keeps these people going; gin is the stimulant that enables them to cling to life through hunger, despair, revolt, and disease.

Arsène has in the past admired Mouchette for not crying out under her father's blows, and he goes back into the storm to bring her the galosh that came off in the mire—such a loss being a major catastrophe in Mouchette's barren household. Mouchette and Arsène take refuge together in a hut, where Arsène, after first cauterizing with a live coal a wound in his hand he tells Mouchette he got during a fight with a gamekeeper, falls down in an epileptic seizure. Mouchette, who has seen his endurance of pain during the cauterizing as he has seen hers during her father's beatings, tenderly takes his head in her lap and sings to him softly.

Mouchette's melody is the symbol of her soul, which she opens to Arsène, the only human being who has ever understood her, the only fellow creature who has ever been kind, the only one to whom she has ever felt akin. At school Mouchette refuses to sing; she will not willingly even join the other children in their music lessons, although she has an exquisite voice. Mouchette has been utterly isolated. The I-thou contact for which her soul was made has never been fulfilled. Her own privations and the spiritual aridity of her companions have robbed her of the greatest of all human birthrights. Now, though, she sits cradling Arsène and crooning gently. Then Arsène wakes. In his drunkenness, out of the brutality into which he has been bred, and out of the desperation of his own spiritual starvation Arsène seeks the most violent possible expression of union, the one response to love he knows. He violates her.

Mouchette flees and reaches home. There Bernanos' gift of creating descriptive characters and descriptive action makes a sort of interlude in which we see Mouchette's world and its pressures upon her. Mouchette's mother, numbed by drink and privation, and with little more consciousness of herself and those around her than an exhausted beast of burden, is old and dying. The youngest child, an infant, is barely alive. The old woman and the baby symbolize the beginning and the end of life for such as Mouchette. Beyond them one imagines hovel after hovel, where from one end of the world to the other the same ancient drama is being played. It stretches back into history; it seems to threaten to stretch on into eternity. Mouchette's story, her hovel, her family, is the story of an endless throng peopling the globe. Bernanos' indignation, white-hot with anger yet full of realism, is in the best French Catholic tradition: it is a culmination of the protest that began with Ozanam, Lamennais, and Albert de Mun, and which in the midst of the world depression reaching France moved Bernanos to an anguish of comprehension of the lot of suffering masses everywhere, whose fate and whose character he understood with a clarity far in advance of his time.

Mouchette goes to the village. The monstrousness of its citizens, more prosperous and looking down on the ragged folk of the countryside, overwhelms her, particularly the cruelty of a sadistic old woman, whose sole pleasure is watching over the dying. She has heard that Mouchette's mother has just died, and so is interested in exploring the girl's feelings. A vampire of emotion, a veritable spirit of death, she tells Mouchette how she once watched a "demoiselle," a young lady, die; and she offers Mouchette one of the dead girl's dresses.

The dress in her arms, Mouchette flees the village and wanders to a pond. She fingers the dress, sees her coarse strong hand through the fine material. Her flesh fills her with disgust. A peasant comes along the road. He passes without a glance, a symbol of the self-centeredness, callousness, and spiritual isolation of the "dead parishes." One feels that had he spoken, had he said even, "Bonjour, petite," Mouchette's fate might even then have been deflected. But he is a man of that nightmare countryside, and he goes his way unseeing. As soon as he is out of sight, Mouchette drowns herself. Her suicide is the most complete rejection of her environment of which she is capable. Mouchette's death is an assertion of spiritual integrity, on a level so primitive that no other act could have sufficed.

Catholics have been slow to penetrate the depths of this perfectly written story. Perhaps until recent years they have not had the sensitivities needed to understand it. In 1954 Albert Béguin remarked, "one has the impression that the poor child is saved, in spite of her suicide."[19] Ten years later Henri Debluë observed that Béguin was wrong to say "in spite of"; Debluë's diagnosis was that this virtual murder by despair of a child who had no refuge makes forever impossible the world's self-justification before its poor and ignorant.[20] This is surely closer to the truth, but would not many modern Catholics feel today that after her death Mouchette would wake to the compassion of Christ? With the second Mouchette Bernanos was approaching an idea new to Catholicism in the 1930s—that even the most spiritually impoverished of human beings may be children of God, and the most desperate acts be innocent. In his insights Bernanos was decades ahead of his own era, but his story shows how early and how vigorously the leaven of the altered thinking that was to result in the spirit of the Second Vatican Council was at work in France. The view that animates the story of the second Mouchette can be recognized today as profoundly "Catholic," but one must realize that it approached views that for some time had been prevalent in the secular and Protestant world and that no doubt Bernanos owed much to them. *The New Story of Mouchette* was addressed to all people. It concerned all people, Catholic and non-Catholic, for the Mouchettes of the modern world are everywhere. *The New Story of Mouchette* is "Catholic" in the sense of that word's oldest meaning of "universal."

After reading *The New Story of Mouchette*, it is interesting to turn back to Bernanos' early flawed masterpiece written in 1925, whose heroine is the "first Mouchette." *Under the Sun of Satan* is a difficult book; the story comes forth in great chunks, and it has few of the purely descriptive interludes that in Bernanos' subsequent works create his symbolism of each novel's "world." It is cluttered with melodramatic episodes and violent, ungovernable emotions.

Under the Sun of Satan opens with the story of the first Mouchette. This Mouchette, too, is a victim of a de-Christianized environment, but in a different way. She comes from the petty bourgeoisie, her father is a brewer, a member of a class that unlike the ruling bourgeoisie had made anticlericalism and anti-Catholicism an article of faith in progress, whose meaning to them was largely economic fluidity and rebellion against the resistant rigidity of French class structure. Detesting her avaricious father and despising her browbeaten mother, Mouchette longs for some way—any way—to surpass the limits of her ugly world. She becomes pregnant by a dissolute petty nobleman. But when she finds in him the same insufferable mediocrity she abhors in her own environment, she shoots him. The murder is thought to be an accident, and this drama with its consequences —among them Mouchette's miscarriage, her insanity, and her confinement in an asylum from which she emerges "cured"— form the book's first block, called "The Story of Mouchette."

The smooth narrative flow Bernanos later achieved in *The Diary of a Country Priest* is lacking in *Under the Sun of Satan.* Not only is the story divided into three distinct blocks, but every paragraph strikes like a separate hammer blow. The novel's second part, "The Temptation of Despair," concerns a heroic young curate, Abbé Donissan—a name that with a little imagination becomes Father Give-His-Blood. Donissan is frankly patterned on the Curé of Ars. He scourges himself mercilessly for his sins and those of mankind; he offers even his salvation (one remembers Péguy). It seems to Donissan that his parish is drowning in malice, indifference, and evildoing. One misty evening, as he walks across the hills at nightfall, the twilit countryside becomes mysteriously dreamlike. He is so lost that he has to feel the dark ground with his hands. Then, suddenly, by his side is an agile little man, a horse trader he says at first; but then he tells the exhausted priest that he, the Abbé Donissan, is the "nursling of his heart," that he has "hunted" the Abbé all his life, that the Abbé "loves" him, and will "love" him better. The priest realizes with horror that he is either with the devil or is dreaming of the devil, and, just as this discovery bursts on him, a "foul mouth" is pressed to his in an obscene kiss. The devil says that today a "grace" has been given to the Abbé but that the Abbé has paid for it and will go on paying.[21]

Lying on the ground unconscious, Abbé Donissan is rescued by a compassionate quarryman, and is guided to the village, where he encounters Mouchette. Donissan finds that he has indeed received a "grace"; he can read souls, and he knows the history of Mouchette's crime even though he has never met her. He talks to her of what she has done, he tells her that she is struggling in God's hand[22] and that in her ignorance of the true nature of murder she has "scarcely offended God more than do the animals."[23] Mouchette then seems to see passing in review her ancestors, "the Malorthys, the Brissauts, . . . traders beyond reproach, careful housekeepers, loving their own goods, never deceased intestate, the glory of chambers of commerce and attorneys' offices,[24] and with them come the "slanderous lies, hatreds long cherished, shameful loves, calculated crimes of avarice and hate," all gradually taking shape in her "just as, when you are awakening, takes shape some cruel image of your dream."[25] She flees the vision of all she has hated in her life and reaches home. She realizes then that she is on the brink of surrender to a force greater than any she has ever known. But Mouchette resists desperately, and Bernanos has shown the reason. Trapped in her petty and hateful environment, Mouchette was from childhood starved with longing for an absolute, a longing which normally would have been satisfied by knowledge of God and mystical intuition of her eternal destiny. But Mouchette's environment has denied her this. Cheated and in a state of baffled rage, she longs for a fate somehow not mediocre but unique, and she has satisfied her longing by doing evil. From being her passport out of mediocrity, doing evil has become the source of Mouchette's very identity. Her being has come to depend upon her unity in mystical communion with what Bernanos calls her "master," Satan.[26] Rather than let this acquired self be obliterated by the forces of grace that Donissan has brought, Mouchette will die—and she cuts her throat. But, as her blood begins to flow, she reverses herself a last time and asks to be taken to the church. Against the protests of her parents, and to the scandal of the villagers, she is carried there in Donissan's arms.

The third block in this impassioned fable is called "The Saint of Lumbres." The Abbé Donissan is seen in his old age. He is famous for his austerities and his power of understanding people before they speak. He spends hours in his confessional receiving penitents who come to him from all over France, just "as though he were another Curé d'Ars."[27] But he is even closer to despair now than in his youth, for he sees that the tide of sin flows from the heart of damaged human nature and is at the core of the world, whose "sun" is Satan's. This vision is not the Jan-

senist one of evil localized in nature or in "the flesh." It is a
depiction of the mysterious and profound spiritual wound that
Bernanos later examined in d'Ambricourt's parish, a wound
that affects not only or chiefly man's passions (as in Mauriac)
but stains the very essence of his soul and brings him under the
sway of a world-embracing malignance that is prehuman and
superhuman.

News is brought to Abbé Donissan of the death of a child.
The Abbé cannot endure the mother's grief, the child's passing,
evidence of death's triumph in God's creation. He takes the body
in his arms, offers his whole life and his salvation for the child's
recovery—before he realizes that in thus storming as if by force
the God who "yields himself only to love,"[28] he allowed a climactic possession of his soul by the devil who has been for so
long his constant companion. The child stirs, then is still—as the
Abbé comprehends the horror of what he has done.

Much of this episode is told by inserting into the narrative
a letter from an unspiritual, uncomprehending fellow priest, the
Pastor of Luzarnes, a former professor at a minor seminary,
writing "long afterward" to a friend. It is an excellent device.
The letter, by presenting the intervening personality of an average man, always astonished, always protesting in the name of
realism and common sense, distances the reader from the miraculous event, whose account might otherwise seem even more incredible and overwhelming than it does.

Returning to his parish, the Abbé Donissan disappears.
Meanwhile, France's foremost novelist, the fashionable cynic
Antoine Saint-Marin (a shadow of Anatole France as Donissan
is a shadow of the Curé of Ars) has arrived at Lumbres with the
notion of refreshing a lifetime of skepticism with a visit to the
famous wonder-worker. But no one can find the old Curé. While
his alarmed parishioners search the woods, Saint-Marin wanders
into the church and, seeing an old pair of shoes under the door
of the confessional, opens it—to find the Curé of Lumbres dead

inside. As Bernanos says in a closing passage set off in italics as containing the "ultimate lament" and "loving reproach" of the Pastor of Lumbres "toward the Judge":

> We are not all those rosy saints with blond beards which good folk see in paintings and whose eloquence and sound health the philosophers themselves would envy. Our portion is not at all what the world conceived. Compared to it, even the compulsion of genius is a frivolous game. Every beautiful life, Lord, testifies for you, but the saint's testimony is as though torn out by iron.[29]

Clearly there is a great deal technically wrong with this novel. The stories of Mouchette hunted down by evil, and of Donissan similarly hunted, and the meeting of the two have rhythm as a pair; but the third part, "The Saint of Lumbres," is virtually another novelette. The character of Donissan is moving rather than convincing. The character of Mouchette is socially a symbol of her kind and class, and metaphysically a symbol of the Catholic belief that unity in evil exists between individual crime and the evil principle at the heart of a fallen world, but as a person Mouchette's reality is nil. To see how far Bernanos was to progress, one need only compare Donissan to the country priest and the first Mouchette to the second Mouchette. Or, one has only to look at the strained, impassioned prose that describes to the reader of *Under the Sun of Satan* the mystical unity of evil, with the country priest's quiet, deliberate exposition to the Countess of the condition of her family, and, beyond that, the whole *Diary's* development of the enclosing corruption of the village. Similarly, the simultaneous existence of the supernatural world of grace and the world of everyday is a matter of page by page record in *The Diary of a Country Priest*, while in *Under the Sun of Satan* the grace that moves Donissan to offer his salvation for souls and to choose the life he leads has none of the psychological background that makes one understand how the Curé d'Ambricourt chose his vocation in the anguish of his youthful poverty that made God his unique recourse.

Nevertheless, thematically, *Under the Sun of Satan* was a brilliant novel, and it was a significant event in Catholic thought and Catholic art. It had an immense sale, and it made Bernanos' reputation. In 1925 no one had yet been able to make convincing drama out of such ideas as the "mystical unity of evil" as opposed to the traditionally Catholic belief in a "communion of saints." Barbey d'Aurevilly and Huysmans had tried to develop the use of such concepts, but their efforts resulted merely in melodrama.

In spite of the early date of *Under the Sun of Satan* and the unavoidable clumsiness with which Bernanos tried to master this entirely new type of Catholic art, one sees the astonishingly integral unity of that art as it was to take shape from this time on. Even the blocklike structure of *Under the Sun of Satan* never results in severance of plot and theme. Didacticism could have been the greatest temptation of Catholic novelists. The tradition of the *roman à thèse* was strong in France, and if Barbey d'Aurevilly never succumbed to it, Huysmans certainly did. But in Mauriac and Bernanos one cannot, except with the greatest artificiality, ever separate theme from plot. The plot *is* the theme and the theme *is* the plot. One can see at once how ridiculous it is to consider any of Bernanos' or Mauriac's works as *romans à thèse* by taking up the book that has the strongest "message" and declaring that *The New Story of Mouchette* has a "theme" of social justice. This is such an understatement as to be ludicrous. *The New Story of Mouchette* cannot be said to "have a theme." The entire story is the theme: the agony of the world's ignorant and deprived.

In France the *roman à thèse* was developed by Gide and Sartre, in novels where action and theme were easily separable, and action illustrated thought, as in *Les Caves du Vatican* or *La Nausée*. With Bernanos and Mauriac, on the contrary, action and thought became one. We can attribute this achievement at least partly to reaction against the type of popular hagiography which, until the major Catholic writers appeared, had been enervating both Catholic art and Catholic thinking by the "rosy saints with blond beards."

Under the Sun of Satan, with its story of the first Mouchette, is a work of Catholic separatism—as one would expect from the early date. The de-Christianized secular world, represented by Saint-Marin and by the Brissauts and Malorthys, is the villain of the piece. The first Mouchette is a misguided wrongdoer who finally repents through the merits and efforts of a noble Catholic Christian able to touch her spirit, the Abbé Donissan. The second Mouchette belongs just as much to the de-Christianized world, but she has her own integrity, and no Donissan has to appear to cause her to repudiate evil. Even the separatist story of the first Mouchette, however, expresses Bernanos' criticism of the Catholic community. The Abbé Donissan is not typical. He is unique, a saint. His fellow priests, who represent the usual *abbés* of the time, misunderstand him in the same way the Curé of Ars was misunderstood. So deep is the corruption of Donissan's Catholic world that he himself is corrupted and succumbs at last to his own particular temptation of the "miracle."

We should note the effect of the radical change in orientation that took place between the time of the early Catholic novelists and the time of Mauriac and Bernanos. Huysmans in *En Route* typifies the distinctions of his time between Catholics and non-Catholics. Catholics are regarded by other Catholics as "better" than people in the secular world. Barbey d'Aurevilly's Catholics who are corrupt or degenerate are Catholics who have "lapsed" from their religion or offended against its rules. The assumption is that "good Catholics" are good people.

The books we have surveyed by Mauriac and Bernanos, on the other hand, adopt a different point of view. As we saw, the murderous mother-in-law in *Genitrix* was a model of orthodox piety, and pious women are a favorite target of Mauriac's. In *Vipers' Tangle*, the devout Isa leads her family in psychological vendetta against her husband. The "good Catholic," Isa, and her "good Catholic" children are the guilty figures in *Vipers' Tangle*, while the protagonist is the pagan Louis.

Bernanos is as harsh in his treatment of "good Catholics" as Mauriac. The Countess who "makes her Easter" and performs her religious "duties" is shown to be carrying mute rage against God in her heart. The pious Madame Pamyre is a hypocrite who has adopted Catholicism as a prop for the social pretensions that go with the Pamyres' acquisition of property, and as a safeguard against the lower class, whom the Pamyres see as clamoring to seize the Pamyres' gains. Meanwhile the peasant, Arsène, with his "faith" that has been handed down by his forebears while each new generation believed less in God, is the representative of the typical "dead" parish. Even the "saint," Donissan, is touched by evil. Only the country priest, dying of cancer and protected by his humility, escapes corruption.

The New Story of Mouchette is an even stronger attack on the Catholic community. The idea that created *The New Story* was the idea of Lamennais and de Coux, an idea that had been crushed in French Catholicism by the rightist and bourgeois majority of French Catholics, who were outraged by the contention that the poor and ignorant had the same feelings and deserved the same rights as the privileged and educated.

Bernanos and Mauriac are critical of secularism, to be sure, and the portraits of the Malorthys and Antoine Saint-Marin in *Under the Sun of Satan* or of Raymond Courrèges in *The Desert of Love* are savagely drawn; but the basic orientation of the two major French Catholic novelists is opposition to corruptions in their own Catholic world. Their work is more powerful for that reason. Catholics are more deeply stirred by evils of their community, of which they themselves are a part, than by the evils of secularism, from which they are relatively detached. The self-assurance of Huysmans and Bloy is lacking in Mauriac and Bernanos. Whatever the corruptions Mauriac and Bernanos disclose, they themselves are not prey to that most basic corruption of all, pride in its favorite disguise as complacency. Their concern for the Catholic community's corruptions represents the self-reflexive power of a living organism, the vital Catholic tradition, of which Catholic writers are the most articulate part. Like every organism, the Church grows. Its growth is often conscious, and self-reflection is the most important element in conscious growth. It also gives rise to superb art as the awareness of each Catholic writer struggles toward more and more piercing insight. Mauriac and Bernanos, writing with the most intense possible effort and commitment, produce work of higher quality than the work of their predecessors. The books of Huysmans and Bourget when reread seem tepid in contrast. And, interestingly, in England much the same difference is found between the work of the early Catholic writers and those who succeeded them—and there is the same contrast in their art. That is a subject we shall take up in our next section.

PART II

Protestant England

CHAPTER V

England after the Reformation

While in France, in the development of the Catholic community and the thinking of Catholic writers, it was possible to trace long-term trends from generation to generation, there is little sequential unfolding in England. As early as Thomas More we see the typical pattern of the English Catholic: one man alone, struggling against a hostile government and isolated scarcely less from his fellow Catholics than from his Protestant fellow countrymen. The historical position of the English Catholic from the time of Henry VIII's quarrel with Rome is that of the lonely dissenter. A French Catholic author writes to and about the French Catholic community, but an English Catholic author has little or no sense of belonging to an English Catholic community.[1]

Despite the hostility of the governments of Henry and Elizabeth, Catholics in England probably remained a large but silent and scattered minority until the death of the generation of 1535. After that they dwindled rapidly. Under Charles I they probably constituted about ten percent of the population.[2] During the Restoration in the second part of the seventeenth century, their numbers increased slightly, particularly in the brief three-year

79

reign of the Catholic monarch, James II, but at the accession of George I in 1714 they had shrunk to half their Restoration strength and were probably no more than five percent.[3] Many of the old noble families, stubbornly Catholic for generations, fell away during the eighteenth century, and their chapels, so long centers of clandestine worship for neighbors and tenants, were closed. By the end of the century the long attack by the government against Catholics under the penal laws seemed to have succeeded so well that such laws had become unnecessary and, in view of the philosophy of liberty of conscience generally accepted after Locke, the persecution of such a small minority— now shrinking toward three percent—began to seem to many unbecoming to an enlightened modern nation.

It is customary now to forget the severity of the old English penal laws. Englishmen often were ashamed of them and reluctant to see them used against neighbors and friends, and mention of them never occupies a conspicuous place in any English history. The fact is, however, that they did exist and were both stringent and effective. Under Elizabeth all power over the Church in England was taken by the crown. All clergy, judges, officials, university graduates, and even private schoolmasters had to swear to accept the queen as "Supreme Governor" in "all spiritual and ecclesiastical things as well as temporal." Any person found guilty of defending the spiritual authority of the pope was to forfeit all his property to the crown on the first offense, to be imprisoned for life on the second, and put to death on the third. Attempts of Catholics to free themselves by deposing Elizabeth and placing Mary Queen of Scots on the throne, Pope Pius V's bull releasing Englishmen from their allegiance to Elizabeth at a time when he mistakenly believed the majority of English were in rebellion against her, and the attempted invasion by the Spanish armada gave Catholicism a flavor of treason from the time of 1588. It was not long before there developed around Catholics in England a public pathology of

hatred. The attempt of a few isolated Catholics to blow up Parliament by laying a train of powder from a house next door, a
scheme that horrified those of their fellow Catholics who found
out about it, was marked forever in England by Guy Fawkes
Day. In 1677 a monument in London proclaimed that the great
fire of the previous decade had been set by the Catholics. The
perjured testimony of Titus Oates as to the so-called "Popish
Plot" in 1678 introduced a period of fanaticism marked by execution of Catholics on trumped-up charges of conspiring
against their country. In early novels figures of cruelty or
treachery were apt to be represented as Catholic, Dr. Mack-
shane, the brutal ship's surgeon in *Roderick Random* in 1748,[4]
the callous captain in the same book, and Dr. Slip-Slop, the
incompetent "male midwife" in *Tristram Shandy* in 1760.[5] And
an endless procession of conscienceless and conspiring Jesuits
haunts English fiction as well into the nineteenth century.[6] Alex-
ander Pope used to say that he longed for some occasion to
prove how different he was from what a Catholic was popularly
supposed to be.[7]

A Catholic who was also a loyal Englishman not unnaturally
developed a painful duality in his loyalties. That he believed
deeply in his religion goes without saying, for otherwise he
could not have held to it in such an environment, but he was
often also profoundly attached to all that was good in the Protestant community and eager to make his compatriots understand
what they most doubted about him, his solidarity with his fellow
citizens of good will. This duality can be seen from the earliest
days. Edmund Campion, though he refused under torture to
deny his faith, went to the scaffold asking the crowd to pray for
Elizabeth, "your Queen and mine."[8]

Campion was a convert. It is a curious fact that in the group
of Catholic writers we are to consider all but one, Hilaire
Belloc, were converts. In England, even when the waves of conversions that followed the Oxford Movement in 1833 and the

First and Second World Wars were over, there were 12,000 adult conversions in a typical recent year.[9] English converts seem to be a special breed, stubborn, independent, single-minded, often unusually gifted. When news came to Lord Burghley, Elizabeth's chancellor, that Edmund Campion, the famous young scholar and one of Oxford's most notable leaders, had fled the country in 1569 to become a Catholic, Burghley declared it was a great loss because Campion was one of "the diamonds of England."[10] When Campion returned as a Jesuit to make converts in his turn, as so many men of his type were to do, and was inevitably captured by Burghley's agents, he was offered a full pardon and a brilliant career in the English Church if he would apostasize. There was always among English Catholics a leaven of such converts, people of extraordinary character, with a sense of allegiance to both the non-Catholic world they had left and the Catholic world they entered. Margaret Clitheroe, who also died for her Catholic convictions, left behind a husband and children not of her faith. In prison, while steadfast in her loyalty to Catholicism, she showed no bitterness against her Protestant judges, and, like Campion, she prayed for the queen at the end, when by a mode of execution common at the time, she was pressed slowly to death under heavy weights.[11]

What may be termed the English "convert's view" seems to fall into one of two kinds of vision. With such people as Campion and Margaret Clitheroe, understanding of both Catholics and non-Catholics may result in such broadness of perception that even executioners are forgiven. Or, on the contrary, Protestant views may be utterly rejected. It must be realized that in a country where a vast and increasing majority was non-Catholic, conversion to Catholicism could easily spring from reaction against the whole life of the Protestant nation. There is probably a period in English history when this type of conversion becomes more prevalent.

There was always political anti-Catholic hysteria in England. The Catholic sympathies of Charles II at the time of the Restoration in 1660 were continually exaggerated, with many sinister forebodings of consequent dangers to English liberties. Charles was reconciled to the Church only on his deathbed, but the known conversion of his heir, his brother James, so alarmed Protestants by the prospect of a Catholic monarch that in 1672 a Test Act was passed, obliging all officeholders to deny transubstantiation and receive Communion according to the rites of the Church of England. And in 1678 an act barred Catholics from both Houses of Parliament. But the penal laws most onerous for Catholics in their daily life were those imposed after 1688, when the Catholic James II had been exiled and the loyalties of English Catholics were apt to include loyalty to the deposed Stuarts. After this time a Catholic could not keep arms or ammunition, could not own a horse worth more than five pounds, could not vote in any parliamentary election, could not be a barrister or solicitor, could not inherit land or purchase land, and was required to pay the land tax at double the usual rate. Although many of these provisions were not strictly enforced, the laws did secure their aim. Catholics were kept from any effective share in the economic or political development of the nation. It followed that any convert, besides testifying to his belief in a creed which ninety percent of Englishmen either found unimportant or with which they disagreed, also dropped out of English civilization as a whole. Increasingly, as the eighteenth century gave way to the nineteenth, those who were repelled by a rationalist, relativist, empirical and utilitarian philosophy, or who formed a distaste for industrial society, were apt to be attracted to Catholicism, which repudiated all these things. There was a tendency in England for prominent Catholic converts to link their conversion with social and political dissent. Cardinal Manning took a leading part in working for social justice for the striking dock workers in 1889.[12] William George Ward engaged in vigorous debate with the utilitarian, John Stuart Mill.[13] In the years before the First World War G. K. Chesterton[14] and Hilaire Belloc sponsored the distributists, who planned to replace England's steadily enlarging corporations with small independent businesses and farms.[15] Eric Gill attempted at Ditchling to demonstrate that a society based on handcrafts could exist and prosper.[16] And after the war Evelyn Waugh produced his satires, which rejected not only the entire life of modern England but the whole industrial, empirical, and utilitarian society of the Western world. English Catholics, and particularly English converts, held with particular vigor the idea shared by most Catholics everywhere after the industrial revolution: that commercial society with its orientation toward material profit was an enemy of the spirit. In Péguy's Utopia of the "harmonious city" the profit motive no longer existed, but use was made of the machine to free citizens for leisure in which to cultivate spiritual and aesthetic sensitivities. But Péguy's acceptance of the machine was unique among Catholics of the past. As was so frequently true of Péguy, one must look to the Catholics of later generations to see his ideas understood.

Opposition to commercial society and to the middle class in France came with the antipathy felt by perceptive Catholics for the pharisaical pseudo-Catholicism adopted after 1830 by the bourgeoisie in the interests of avoiding reform and maintaining the economic *status quo*. The same opposition developed for quite other reasons in England. When the penal laws were in force, English Catholics could almost never become members of the merchant or professional classes. Wealth was almost impossible for them to accumulate because of the system of fines; in the professions few posts except that of physician were open to them. Apart from the great nobles, who were able to maintain their Catholicism by influence or personal friendship with the reigning monarch and so gain exemption from the penal laws,

most Catholics were humble folk, artisans or farmers, who wor-
shiped in secret at the chapel of one of the Catholic lords, or at
the Masses celebrated by one of the wandering and hunted
Jesuits. The conversions that followed the Oxford Movement in
1833 were chiefly from the ranks of intellectuals, many of them
ordained in the Church of England. But, just as the educated
nobility of penal times were vastly outnumbered by farmers and
artisans, so in the nineteenth century intellectuals were outnumbered by the flood of poor Catholics from Ireland, who after the
potato famines in mid-century came in as cheap labor. Thus,
both before and after repeal of the penal laws, Catholics in England belonged generally to the top or bottom of society. The
middle class, increasingly dominant in English life, had been
shaped by the age of Cromwell and by the Puritan-Protestant
ethic. Catholics, even those few who were converts from the middle class itself, found middle-class culture alien to Catholicism,
and the industrial revolution with its emphasis on the Puritan
ethic intensified the Catholic reaction against all that was part
of the commercial and utilitarian orientation.

The romantic medievalism that characterized much of nineteenth-century Catholicism was marked in France as early as
1801 by Chateaubriand's *Génie du Christianisme*, a reaction
against the Revolution of 1789. A similar reaction appeared
later in England against the industrial revolution. When in 1829
most of the penal laws against Catholics were abrogated, and
Catholics could vote, sit in Parliament, and enjoy the normal
privileges of Englishmen, except attendance at the universities
(where graduates were required to subscribe to the Thirty-Nine
Articles of the Church of England), English Catholicism had its
own separate and distinct cultural flowering. Its flavor was
partly Italian and partly medieval, but always anti-industrial.
For some time the Protestant world of fashion had formed the
habit of occasionally attending for artistic pleasure Catholic services at the foreign embassy chapels, where the singers, usually

Italians, had long been admired. By the Relief Act of 1791 Mass became legal in any registered chapel whose priest took an oath of loyalty to the crown, and after this, and still more after the Act of 1829, the outward nature of English Catholicism began to change. For obvious reasons an English Catholic custom during the time of the penal laws had been inconspicuousness in dress of the clergy, in liturgy, and even in devotion, characterized by the gentle spirit of Bishop Challoner's *Garden of the Soul*, published in 1751. By the nineteenth century, however, inconspicuousness was no longer necessary. The isolation and secretiveness of the Catholic community had ended in 1829, and, as in France at the same period, there was increased awareness of the secular world, much criticism of it, and a desire to express as emphatically as possible that Catholics were "different." This "differentness" appeared first in the Catholic espousal of a Gothic and medieval spirit, marked in literature by the popularity in the 1820s of the convert Kenelm Digby's *Broad Stone of Honour*. Medievalism began to manifest itself also in the Gothic churches of the convert architect Pugin and the liturgical scholarship of Dr. Rock, chaplain to the Earl of Shrewsbury, who financed Pugin's work. The medieval ritualists and the ritualists who modeled their practice on current Roman custom entered into rivalry, but what is to be remembered is that both were manifesting the desire to assert Catholic identity in contrast to the dominant commercial and Protestant culture. At the same time it must also be remembered that, in their view, they themselves were not "separated" from the true English spirit, but English society since the sixteenth century had "separated" from its real heritage and from all of historic Christendom. Dr. Rock's book in praise of pre-Reformation English ritual was called *The Church of Our Fathers*. The attitude of Rock, Shrewsbury, and their group was that only rejection of current society could be an expression of the "true" English heritage.

This attitude had no parallel in France. Whatever the bitterness between those who followed the example of 1789 and parted from the Church and those who clung to Catholicism or returned to it, there was never in France at any period a feeling that the people who chose to follow 1789 were somehow un-French, insane, or inhuman. But in England, where for nearly three centuries less than ten percent of the population had been Catholic, it was felt during the Catholic revival that followed 1829 that ninety percent of Englishmen had not only strayed from theological truth but had also betrayed the nation and the entire Christian world in a way that could scarcely be accounted for. English Catholics developed a sense of mingled astonishment and outrage that French Catholics never experienced, and this gives the early separatist Catholic writers in England a characteristic vigor—which appears sometimes as exuberance, sometimes as violence. An example of exuberance is G. K. Chesterton's humorous story, *The Ball and the Cross*, where the non-Catholic world, which regards the Catholic one as lunatic, is shown to be itself the realm of the really mad. An example of violence is Evelyn Waugh's astringent satire, which regards the entire Protestantized world as degenerate. Somewhere between the buoyance of Chesterton and the bitterness of Waugh is the satiric sense of Ronald Knox, whose forays into modernist criticism develop the delightful dilemma of whether there was actually one Dr. Watson or two, and note that to modernists the only reasonable conclusion about Tennyson's *In Memoriam* must be to decide that the real author was Queen Victoria.[17] Satire became a natural vehicle for Catholics who rejected the non-Catholic world.

As early as 1870 the division between those English Catholics who rejected the surrounding Protestant environment and those who sympathized with many of its aspects caused a serious split. The most conspicuous adherents of complete rejection were Cardinal Manning, who even when Catholics were finally allowed to attend the universities in 1854, refused to the end of his long life to let them do so without special permission, and William George Ward, whose vivid quarrel with Mill has been noted. With rejection of the Protestant world went adherence to ultramontanism. Separation from the non-Catholic environment in England was to be marked by particularly fervent adherence to the center of world Catholicism, Rome. Ward in his pre-conversion days was a follower of Thomas Arnold in hoping that broad spiritual renewal could combat the moral degeneration he believed had been brought by commercialism. Later he became an enthusiastic supporter of the Oxford Movement, which he saw as seeking spiritual renewal by asserting the independence of the Church of England from the modern and corrupted English secular state, so that the English Church could be regarded as descended from the apostles rather than dating from the Reformation. But Ward's rejection of the secularism of his time found neither of these positions adequate. He was among the first who gave up the Oxford Movement's view of the "apostolic" English Church to declare that the true apostolic Church was the Church of Rome, which he entered in September of 1845, preceding Newman by a month. Ward was a leader among those whose rejection of the Protestant environment was signaled by devotion to Roman centralism, and he became one of the most effective English adherents of the party which long before the Vatican Council of 1870 hoped that papal infallibility would become a dogma.

Newman was a convert of the opposite type. The figure of Newman recalls the earlier spirit of Campion and Margaret Clitheroe, who brought with them into Catholicism a tenderness for the Protestant world they had left and an ability to see good outside the Catholic fold. Newman longed to bring into Catholicism the best attributes of the Protestant and secular environment. Newman's party, however, did not in his time prevail. Ward and Manning carried the day, and Newman's hope of a

Catholic university modeled on the best practices of Oxford and
Cambridge was to prove unfulfillable.[18] His article on "consult-
ing the laity in matters of doctrine" only resulted in complaints
to Rome and his enforced resignation as editor of Capes' and
Acton's liberal Catholic periodical, the *Rambler*.[19]

But Newman, like Lamennais, de Coux, and Lacordaire in
France, although he was defeated in his own period carried the
seed of time to come. A Church in which the laity shared leadership with the clergy, and which was receptive to good wherever it was to be found, was the Church of the future, and
his ideas on "development" were to play no small part in the
adoption by thinking Catholics of a flexibility which by mid-
twentieth century made possible the nature of the Second Vatican Council. At the time of the First Council Newman believed
that the declaration of papal infallibility was "inopportune."[20]
Indeed Newman believed that centralism, so strong among Catholics in England in his day and whose aftereffects were to place
most of the English delegates to the Second Council among the
relatively conservative,[21] was actually alien to the whole earlier
spirit of Catholics in England.

There was ample ground for Newman's belief that in England the Church had historically been characterized by decentralization. Even in medieval times there had never been any
Canossa for an English king. England's geographic isolation
gave her relative independence in centuries of the strongest papal domination, and this pattern persisted. At the time of the
French Revolution, the possibility of an Irish rebellion began
to make English statesmen want to draw the Catholic Irish into
the national life of Protestant England. A commission was
formed by English Catholics to determine what sort of oath of
allegiance to the English crown would be acceptable under
canon law, and the commission was not headed by any of the
vicars apostolic, who had represented the papacy in England
since 1685, but by the most prominent English Catholic noble-

man, Lord Petre. The nobility and their chaplains, not the underground bishops and clergy, were the most powerful members of the old English Catholic community. Lord Petre gave Pitt to understand that English Catholics were different from other Catholics, that the pope had always had less claim on their consciences, that the allegiance of English Catholics to the papacy was minimal, and that the old bogey of direction of Englishmen by any pope could be dismissed so far as the fear of interference in national affairs was concerned.

Lord Petre had a point, but the ecclesiastical outcry was intense, and long after the formal reestablishment by Rome of the English hierarchy in 1850, he was remembered as an illustration of the dangers of letting power slip into the hands of laymen. The problem between the bishops and Lord Petre was based on a misunderstanding. No English bishop would have held that a pope could or would interfere in English national affairs, and even Lord Petre would not have claimed that the pope did not have general direction in matters of conscience, although since his lordship was grand master of the English Freemasons, whom he regarded (with some justice) also as different from continental Freemasons, he was perhaps less dutiful in submission to the letter of papal rulings than he might have been. Even without the problem of Lord Petre's opinions, the distinction between matters of conscience and matters of national concern was and had always been hard to define, and also the question of papal infallibility was even then in the air, beginning to cause agitated discussion. The essential fact is that men like Lord Petre, or like Lord Acton, and, later, Baron von Hügel and his friend the modernist priest George Tyrrell, represented the opposite point of view from Manning's and Ward's. To Ward and Manning and the majority of English Catholics, allegiance to Rome was probably an emotional surrogate for their nation's rejection of its Catholic subjects. There is something that reminds one of the search for a lost father in William

George Ward's remark in the 1860s that he wished he could have an infallible papal bull every morning with his breakfast.[22] There is a strain of romanticism in Ward's extreme ultramontanism. On the other hand, men like Petre, Newman, Acton, and von Hügel are open to Protestant and secular influences and see goodness in all men and in many ways of life. With them it seems as if banished children were seeking to prove to their family, England, the unfairness of their banishment.

CHAPTER VI

The Precursors and
Minor Writers

The attitude of William George Ward, which emphasized Catholic exclusiveness and Catholic separatism, and the contrasting attitude represented by the long line of English Catholics from Campion to Newman, who were open to the outer world, are the antipodal centers of English Catholic development and reappear in the creative processes of English Catholic writers. The early writers, Belloc, Chesterton, and Waugh during the time of his first satires, were like the French early writers in defining their position as opposition to the non-Catholic environment. Frederick Rolfe, as we shall see, is an exception and directs his criticism at the Catholic community, particularly at the aloofness of the papacy from the modern world. But not until the time of Graham Greene does introspective criticism of basic Catholic thinking and the Catholic community find its way into the Catholic novel in England with the same passionate intensity as in France with the work of Mauriac and Bernanos. Graham Greene is open to the non-Catholic environment. He belongs to the line of Campion and Newman, just as Mauriac and Bernanos belonged to the line of Lamennais and de Coux. And it is Greene's work which equals and sometimes surpasses that

of his two great French contemporaries, while the books of the
English Catholic writers who base their attitude on separatism
usually compare in literary quality to the novels in France of
Huysmans and Bloy.

As a forerunner of Graham Greene in making the Catholic
community the subject of his criticism, Frederick Rolfe is a fascinating and prophetic figure. Rolfe, whose *Hadrian VII* was
published in 1904, was one of those people of great gifts who
have such keen perceptions and strong longings that they are
never able to strike a balance. Rolfe was a convert. He studied
for the priesthood but later left the seminary. He roamed
through Italy, where he formed an obscure relationship with an
older woman who gave him—so he said—the property of
"Corvo," after which incident he took the title of Baron Corvo.
Rolfe was also a homosexual. For most of his career he was
clearly an unscrupulous charlatan, but it seems that at no time
was he insincere in his belief in Catholicism. From the contra-
dictions in his life, it appears more than probable he was often
a little mad. But in any case, whatever the usual condition of his
mind, there were periods in which he had extraordinary insights, and *Hadrian VII* is an astonishing book. As one of those
converts who saw Catholicism from the point of view of the
Protestant environment from which he had come, Rolfe felt that
papal wealth and ceremoniousness were a violation of Christ's
teachings, he rejected completely the current Catholic spirit of
apartness, and he believed that many Catholic practices could
be changed, even when they had been built into the Church by
centuries of habit. His oddly chosen English Pope Hadrian VII
orders the opening of a blocked Vatican window, bricked up
since 1870. There he appears publicly, "despite the objections
of the cardinals," to give "the Apostolic benediction to the City
and the world."[1] Pope Hadrian leaves the isolation of the Vatican and walks in public procession to his coronation. In an
Epistle to All Christians and a bull on the text, "My kingdom is

not of this world," Hadrian renounces the papal claim to temporal sovereignty over the former papal states. He also sells the Vatican's treasures and gives the money to the poor.

In spite of Rolfe's liberal ideas, *Hadrian VII* is marked by the conservative ultramontanist belief of most English converts in the power of Rome, the single center. It is an exaggeration to see Hadrian as an early type of John XXIII, for Rolfe gives no portrayal of a tide of change surrounding Hadrian and following him. Hadrian does not stir Catholic thinkers of all nations and the Catholic people of all communities as John did. It is natural that Rolfe's book should make compelling reading today when the spirit of so many of Hadrian's reforms has been fulfilled, but the recent play, *Hadrian VII*, distorts the novel more than a little when it regards Rolfe's tormented dream as an analogy to present circumstances in the Church. *Hadrian VII* is not fiction of the highest quality. Its importance lies in its forecast of future Catholic thought.

For some years before Rolfe's *Hadrian VII*, writing a novel seemed to be a natural reflex for Catholics of the English renaissance. In 1848 Newman published *Loss and Gain,* the story of a likable upper-class young Englishman who is gradually brought to see the flaws of the Church of England and separates himself from it—but with so much tolerance, gentleness, and regret that the fiction is robbed of dramatic power. Cardinal Wiseman, the first cardinal of the reestablished hierarchy, wrote *Fabiola* in 1854, a romantic novel about the Church of the catacombs—so romantic that the favorite English theme of setting forth the unique courage of holding Christian convictions in a hostile world becomes, alas, a bore. Robert Hugh Benson, the son of the Church of England's Archbishop of Canterbury, a convert and a Catholic priest, wrote *Lord of the World* in 1907, a story of the final days of the Church, in which the last pope, an impoverished refugee hiding in Palestine, holds the loyalty of a few solitary and scattered Catholics through the days of persecution that precede Armageddon. The theme is the typically English one of a persecuted and concealed minority; the technique is that of a popular "adventure" story and reminds one a little of an earlier and more sedate Sabatini. Benson was a favorite author of Ronald Knox during his Anglican boyhood.[2] Benson influenced Knox's conversion, and no doubt the conversions of other less well-known people in the wave of enthusiasm for Catholicism among English intellectuals at the time of the First World War. It is to be noted that in all these early novels except Rolfe's, the emphasis even of Newman's mild story focuses on the "goodness" of Catholics and the "badness" of their opponents, the same black and white division that prevailed among the early Catholic novelists in France.

Among early English Catholic writers, Chesterton and Belloc are usually thought of together because of their joint political espousal of distributism, which brought them the name of the Chesterbelloc. In their fiction, too, they must be regarded together, although the fact is not as apparent. Both were separatists, but Chesterton was a joyous romantic, whose view of the general insanity of the non-Christian world moved him to as much mirth as bitterness, while what he saw as the sane clarity of faith filled him with sheer delight. Influenced by the revival of medievalism that from the 1820s marked the Catholic renaissance in England, he loved the time of Alfred, the early bards and poets, and the vitality of the Catholic past reflected in Chaucer:

> The giant laughter of Christian men
> That roars through a thousand tales.[3]

Chesterton had a cheerfully relaxed view of life and history that accords with the fact that, although he wrote Catholic novels from the early years of the twentieth century, novels dependent for their meaning upon Catholic separatism and the ideals of the English renaissance, nevertheless he did not feel it necessary formally to become a convert until his wife was ready to join him in taking the step in 1922.

Belloc shared Chesterton's view of the necessary tension between Catholic Christianity and modern secular culture, but he lacked Chesterton's easy joyousness, and in his writing was a realist where Chesterton was a romantic. Belloc produced a satire, *Emmanuel Burden*, in 1904, just three years before the appearance of Chesterton's engaging spoof, *The Man Who Was Thursday*. There is nothing light or engaging about Belloc's *Emmanuel Burden*. It is written in the guise of an admiring biography of a typical English bourgeois, a London merchant. As an exporter of cheap iron finger rings to Africa, where he exchanges them for valuable ivory, Burden is regarded by his biographer as not only turning a clever and blameless profit but also as carrying civilization to the dark areas of the world. Belloc's device of telling the story through an imaginary biographer who admires Burden is an example of deft satiric use of an unreliable narrator. Everything the biographer says must be taken as exactly the reverse of the meaning given, though his meaning is invariably that accepted by all "reasonable" people —to whom he frequently appeals. If Burden is beneficial in Africa, he is even more so in England, where his biographer sees the Burden family history as exemplifying the English ideal of utilitarian progress. A hard-working man, whose moral base is his heritage of the Puritan ethic of diligence and thrift, he and his family have long since sensibly discarded the religious aspect of their original orientation to become "modern," but they do remember with pride that Burden ancestors fought for Cromwell; and Emmanuel (whose name, "God-with-us," symbolizes his self-righteousness) has a strong sense of his personal contribution as a far-reaching man of affairs in the British empire.

Since the seventeenth century each Burden generation increased the Burden fortune which the Burdens "naturally ascribed to their considerable capacity, but which was perhaps also due to the evolution of modern industry."[4] Here, as sometimes happens, Belloc's mask as Burden's admiring biographer slips and he speaks in his own person. Belloc's indignation at the English Protestant middle class occasionally tricks him out of the detachment necessary for good satire. The latest representative of the Burden clan, Emmanuel's son, is portrayed with quite visible loathing. The young man's name, Cosmo, suggests that the Burden species is now not only English but worldwide. In Cosmo, Burden righteousness has eroded. While at the university Cosmo has indulged in an affair with an innkeeper's daughter, and when he is forced to buy back his letters, he falls into the grip of a Jewish moneylender, who quite easily persuades him to act the role of confidence man with his own father. Cosmo draws the older Burden into promoting a scheme to mine gold in an African territory called the M'Korio. There is of course no gold actually in the M'Korio, but with the name of Emmanuel Burden on their board, the swindlers are able to sell the stock profitably and get out of the speculation before the market collapses and ruins the remaining investors.

But Belloc's real story does not concern the successful swindle. Emmanuel Burden in his mediocrity and naïvete resembles Charles Bovary, and it may be that Belloc, who was half French and spent much of his youth in France, was influenced by Flaubert. But Belloc adds to Burden's biography a dimension alien to Flaubert's type of realism, a dimension perhaps also owed to Belloc's youth in France, where of the early Catholic precursors we examined in the first chapter he would certainly have read Bourget and possibly Huysmans as well. Belloc writes with emphasis on "interiority," on the soul in its relation to eternity, which we saw was central to the formation of the whole school of nineteenth- and twentieth-century French Catholic creativity, and which became the keynote of the aesthetic developed by Claudel and Maritain.

In Belloc's portrait of Emmanuel Burden, the London wool merchant and his son are creatures who, however repellent, have an immortal destiny. Their real drama is not Emmanuel's realization that he has been tricked, or Cosmo's founding of his career on his father's destruction, but the development of the Burden spirit. Belloc, like Chesterton, and like the other English Catholic novelists who follow, is orthodox in his view of free will. For all their stupidity, the members of the Burden family are the architects of the Burden soul. The Burdens' decisions, each growing out of the ones before it, are made from moment to moment as life flows on, and they shape the Burden nature ever more distinctly into the thing it finally becomes. Even though the process is a long one and bridges the generations, one cannot say that it is "determined" or that it makes freedom impossible for Emmanuel and Cosmo. The Burdens are carried by the momentum of their own ongoing choices, a momentum that stretches back no doubt to the first Burden and probably, as Belloc sees it, if not to Adam, at least to the end of the Middle Ages. The Burdens are victims of wounded human nature in a fallen universe and of a particularly Burden form of original sin, but they are shown assenting freely to their heritage and going on to shape themselves. This view, more complex and less melodramatic than Jansenism, nevertheless lends itself to effective scenes, especially when Belloc writes of death, and a particular Burden soul is fixed in the shape it has taken and faces eternity alone. Belloc describes the heart attack of the elder Burden, "loneliness caught him suddenly, overwhelming him; wave upon wave of increasing vastness, the boundaries leaping, more and more remote; immeasurably outwards with every slackening pulse at the temples. Then it was dark; and the Infinite wherein he sank was filled with that primeval Fear which has no name among men, for the moment of his passage had come."[5]

In Belloc's novel there is more than the question of personal immortality, however. To Belloc, the world through its Emmanuel and Cosmo Burdens receives its cultural and political as well as its spiritual shape, all of which Belloc condemns utterly. Here Belloc goes beyond his French predecessors, for he sees souls as creating an inheritable orientation, one with effects not only individual but historical. To Belloc, the Burden soul, degenerating from generation to generation, is truly a "burden," for it stamps an entire civilization by sheer weight of numbers. This theme of world degeneracy caused by spiritual impoverishment reminds one of Evelyn Waugh. But there is no reason to suppose that Belloc influenced Waugh. Their work is too unlike. One must rather believe that Waugh, like his predecessor, was relying upon observation of the English environment.

Emmanuel Burden is marred by farce, sentimentality, and lack of the detachment necessary for satire, but it is significant among early Catholic novels because it regards spiritual development as having an influence on history, on the condition of the nation and the world. But, as we will see in the next chapter when we come to the major writers, while Waugh takes up this theme, Greene does not. Greene's novels follow Mauriac's. Greene's characters are "persons" in Maritain's sense. In Greene's books history is a backdrop, a provider of ordeals on each soul's passage to eternity. But in America J. F. Powers, an admirer of Waugh, continued the trend that is first seen in Belloc. In Powers' satiric fiction the spiritually ill infect others who follow them or are near them, and Powers lends this process a note of historical ominousness that gives timeliness to his stories. Waugh and Powers, however, tend to be less powerful writers than the Catholic novelists who follow the tradition that began in France with the definition of "interiority" and the distinction between "persons" with souls to save or lose and "individuals" who are social and political units.

Emmanuel Burden now is seldom read. Its satire of a distinct period that gave it much of its effect when it was published in 1904 made it seem dull to later generations. Today, when most members of society in the West have given up colonialism and a majority no longer regards affluence as the key to all good things, it is hard to appreciate the outrage that Belloc's theme once represented. Most secularists and nearly all Catholics would now take the greater part of Belloc's insights for granted. Even Evelyn Waugh's almost perfect early satires have today lost much of their bite. As with Belloc, people have become accustomed to too many of Waugh's observations, and his power to outrage, which is the strength of this kind of writing, has dissolved. Regrettably, prophets cease to be prophets when their era of fulfillment has come.

Evelyn Waugh

It is a sad fact that timeliness, which may have been the strength of a satire when it was published, later usually makes it seem dated. No matter how brilliant the satirist, the period immediately after his death is almost invariably a bad moment to encounter him. The circumstances he mocked are far enough past to be stale but not yet far enough past to be interesting. Nevertheless, as Juvenal gives a searing picture of first-century Rome, so someday Evelyn Waugh may give our descendants a picture of the era just over. The perceptive critic, Frank Kermode, calls Waugh's *A Handful of Dust* "one of the most distinguished novels of this century."[1]

The excellence of a satirist's art depends upon skill, temperament, and circumstance. Waugh was ideally endowed with all three. The way he uses his skill reminds one of Dryden's description that satire should never be a "bare hanging" of its victims; the trick is to make the malefactors "die sweetly," after the manner of history's most refined executioner, Jack Ketsch.[2] A neighbor of Waugh's describes Waugh's way of using his favorite phrase to designate a human being: "poor beast." Waugh spoke the phrase not with "savage inflection" but with what was far more cutting, a "mixture of ridicule and pity with which he normally regarded humanity."[3] "Pity" in a satirist may of

101

course be strong. Indeed, however he may conceal it, it may be too strong and unconsciously blunt his edge. But this is never the case with Waugh. Pity is a trait he has just enough of—and "just enough" is all he has. Some of his books, notably *Decline and Fall* and *A Handful of Dust* stop barely short of depicting human folly and suffering so painfully that the reader is moved close to that state of revulsion which, according to Aristotle, would make even tragedy unbearable.

Waugh is a Catholic novelist who, like Chesterton and Belloc, focuses on criticism of the secular environment. *Decline and Fall*, written in 1928, expresses Waugh's view of English society in the years after the First World War. Its theme is that the moral fabric of the nation is rotting, eroded by aging commercialism, postwar licentiousness, and long-standing aspirituality. The central figure is Margot Beste-Chetwynde, a distinguished leader of the "smart set" who is received in the most exclusive circles. Margot is beautiful, charming, and wealthy, and is connected by marriage with the oldest families in England. Margot herself, however, is descended from three generations of recently enriched white slavers, a lucrative trade which she carries on with pleasure and natural aptitude. The cruelty of great wealth and its disreputable sources were never given a sharper or more absurd analogy. To illustrate what Margot's type is doing to civilization, Waugh makes her the purchaser of King's Thursday, a historic gem of perfect Tudor, which Margot remodels into "a creation of ferro concrete and aluminum."[4] To illustrate what she is doing to humanity Waugh gives her as victim the absurdly inept Paul Pennyfeather, a divinity student. Margot makes young Pennyfeather her lover, promises to marry him, and then leaves him to the police when they descend on her white-slaving enterprise, of whose real nature the chronically innocent Pennyfeather is of course entirely unaware. The later Waugh would not have hesitated to leave Pennyfeather in prison for life, but at this time he was not as misanthropic as he later became. By a series of comic improbabilities Pennyfeather is returned to his studies in divinity, and the story leaves him just as he is about to be ordained.

J. F. Powers regards *Decline and Fall* as Waugh's best book.[5] Powers, who owes more to Waugh than to any other writer and thus confirms the international character of the later Catholic novel, is naturally appreciative of Waugh's art, but his opinion of *Decline and Fall* does not overestimate the book's excellence. *Decline and Fall* is beautifully constructed: its three parts are as symmetrical as Margot Beste-Chetwynde's undertaking in modern architecture. The replacement of the Tudor seat of an ancient family, the Pastmasters, by Margot's atrocity in concrete and aluminum, the "newborn monster to whose birth ageless and forgotten cultures had been in travail,"[6] is symbolic of the whole course of the story. The extinction of the main line of Pastmasters followed by the substitution of their distant relation, Margot Beste-Chetwynde, has for its background the slow death from gangrene of Little Lord Tangent, accidentally shot in the foot by an incompetent referee at his school games. Little Lord Tangent (the three words used together suggest Little Lord Fauntleroy and all that the title expresses of Victorian security) and his accident on the playing field (one remembers that England's battles have been won on the playing fields of Eton) is reported at intervals throughout the book to be slowly dying. He represents England, humanity, youth, the future—one or all of these—but, in any case, his survival is impossible. The atmosphere of decay, the competence of all the mad and wicked, the lethargic helplessness of the innocent have the effect of some remarkable obscenity carefully preserved under glass.

Vile Bodies takes up the same theme, but less effectively. The "vile bodies" are the crowds at the hysterical postwar parties in the twenties of England's "bright young people." A bit of dialogue near the end may be worth quoting. Ginger, a repellent youth who seems to have spent much of his boyhood pulling the wings off flies, is eloping with the heroine. She is a woman of considerable natural discrimination and she is in love with someone else, but unhappily her beloved has no money. So she and Ginger, whom she despises, are on a plane beginning their honeymoon. Ginger leans over her to shout above the roar of the engines:

> "I say, Nina, . . . did you ever have to learn a thing out of a poetry book about 'This scepter'd isle, this earth of majesty, this something or other England'? D'you know what I mean? 'this happy breed of men, this little world, this precious stone set in the silver sea . . . this teeming womb of royal kings. . . .' "
>
> Nina looked down and saw inclined at an odd angle a horizon of straggling suburbs; arterial roads dotted with little cars; factories, some of them working, others empty and decaying. . . .
>
> "I think I'm going to be sick," said Nina.[7]

Vile Bodies was published in 1930. Waugh became a Catholic that same year. His own account of his conversion shows that underneath his misanthropy the background of his thinking much resembled that of typical English converts before him. Where men like Newman and Ward had reviewed in detail the whole history of confrontations between Rome and the ancient schisms, to decide that history had shown Rome to have been right and the schismatics wrong, Waugh voices the same conviction in layman's language, drawn not from research but from his travels as a wandering journalist.

> Foreign travel anywhere (in Europe) reveals the local and temporary character of the heresies and schisms and the universal, eternal character of the Church. It was self-evident to me that no heresy or schism could be right and the Church wrong. It was possible that all were wrong, and that the whole Christian revelation was an imposture or a misconception. But if Christian revelation were true, then the Church was the society founded by Christ and all other bodies were good only so far as they had salvaged something from the wrecks of the Great Schism and the Reformation. This proposition seemed so plain to me that it admitted of no discussion.[8]

This leap of faith, which accepts Catholicism as true partly because it is both old and widespread in the same single form, while Protestantisms are later and have different accretions that change from one locale to another, is very English. Where a Frenchman turns to logic and the proofs of Saint Thomas or of some more recent theologian, an Englishman is apt to look to history and circumstance.

The adoption of Catholicism gave Waugh firm ground on which to stand for his criticism of the secular world. It made him harsher; at the same time he retained enough youthful zest to keep a certain lightness—which later he lost. The comparison between early and late Waugh invariably reminds one of a rapier which by the continual addition of weight has turned into a sledgehammer. But in 1934, when Waugh wrote his third book, *A Handful of Dust*, this transformation had not begun. The circumstances that produce perfect satire were in exact balance: rejection joined to a firm underlying moral affirmation, deftness joined to a fury of brutality just within bearable limits.

In *A Handful of Dust* Tony Last is the only surviving adult descendant of an old and noble English family. He lives at Hetton, a countryseat rebuilt in 1867 in imitation Gothic. The rooms are named for the legendary personages of King Arthur's court. "Galahad" is for guests, quite untenable since the bed is so uncomfortable for the modern figure that no one can sleep in it. Here as a weekend visitor comes John Beaver, the only son of a widowed interior decorator and anchor man on the London hostesses' list of available dinner partners. John is about as deep as a teacup, but Tony Last's wife, Brenda, is so bored by life at Hetton that she takes John as her lover, thus living up to the name of her own suite in the tawdry castle, "Guinevere." Waugh spares no pains to show that Brenda as much as John Beaver is rotten to the core. On one occasion Brenda at a party is told that "John" is dead. She thinks that her lover is meant and nearly faints. But when she discovers that it is only John, her young son, she revives at once. The scene is the more effective because Brenda has been shown to have more rather than less humanity than the other people in her "set." Edmund Wilson has noted, as the secret of the peculiar chill with which *A Handful of Dust* strikes the heart, a sense of "terror."[9] These characters are its source: they are evil in the sense that they are utterly empty. Eliot's hollow men live before our eyes, and the world of *A Handful of Dust* is a depiction of an earthly hell—a most orthodox Catholic concept of it. Waugh's hell is the supreme negation, where every vestige of beauty and nobility, love and truth must die, yet without its inhabitants ever quite losing the knowledge that actual beauty, nobility, truth, and love do somewhere exist.

This unattainable vision is reflected in Tony Last, weakly reflected as in any true hell such reflections must always be weak, but as obsessive as it is unattainable. Tony is haunted by unnameable glories and untraceable strengths—whose source he cannot imagine but which he places somewhere dimly in the past and sees as transfiguring the bogus nineteenth-century Gothic of his "family seat." Tony is scarcely less self-centered and ruthless than Brenda and John. When Brenda's suit for divorce threatens so to impoverish Tony that he must give up the vision represented by his moldering castle, he refuses to cooperate in the suit and flees on a trip of exploration in the jungles of South America with a "Doctor Messinger," whose "message" is to beguile Tony with talk of a "lost city." Tony has a clear picture of it in his mind. "It was Gothic in character, all vanes and pinnacles and tracery, pavillions and terraces, a transfigured Hetton, pennons and banners floating in the sweet breeze, everything luminous and translucent. . . ."[10] Messinger and Tony do not find the city. Messinger is killed, and Tony falls into the hands of a madman who lives in the jungle. The madman makes Tony his prisoner and compels him to spend the remaining years of his life reading aloud over and over the volumes of a tattered set of Dickens.

Stephen Spender finds in *A Handful of Dust* "incipient tragedy." Although tragedy does not really exist in this work because it is impossible to feel sufficient empathy with its characters—even with Tony, or perhaps especially with Tony, for the less shallow man is less easily forgiven for his shallowness —it is true that *A Handful of Dust* does seem always on the edge of something deeper than satire. Spender describes it well when he says that "where people act ruthlessly and selfishly, tragedy, as it were, may be distributed over their lives, though each may be incapable of feeling its intensity."[11] But a more fitting description of the book seems to me to be "apologue."[12] In apologue the emotions aroused in the reader come not from sympathy for the characters but from assent to the statement made by the action. Apologue is a form that in England dates back to Samuel Johnson's *Rasselas*. Johnson's story is moving not because of the realism of the characters, who are not real at all, but because of the statement they illustrate—that perfect happiness cannot be achieved on earth. Waugh has taken up this old English form and used it to express his own modern convictions, and under Waugh's influence the form will again be taken up by J. F. Powers. The conviction expressed in *A Handful of Dust* is that our present world has been given over to emptiness. Its people are hollow. All good, even all significance, has been drained away.

If, as we have seen, Waugh's stories combine the loveless, the cruel, the empty, the grotesque, and the disgusting, it is obvious that these can be experienced only if the writer has in mind some standard that makes them what they are—if, in other words, he implicitly holds the opposite concepts: love, compassion, reason, beauty, and decorum. As a man, Waugh's longing for these was deep and real, but he somehow lacked the gift of being able to grasp them. His love of decorum in a disgusting world, of order in a chaotic one, betrayed him into an attraction to fascism. Other writers who in these years for similar reasons took positions on the far right included G. K. Chesterton, Hilaire Belloc, George Bernard Shaw, D. H. Lawrence, William Butler Yeats, T. S. Eliot, Ezra Pound, Wyndham Lewis, and Roy Campbell. Later, when it became clear what the fascist vision was turning into, Waugh, like Belloc and most of the rest except Pound, rejected the fascist cause, but the initial attraction had been there. Perhaps for people able to draw the chaotic and degenerate environment that appears in such work as Waugh's, the virtue of hope became so attenuated that, as with Tony Last's Hetton, no positive vision could come into actuality except as a monster.

Certainly there is something monstrous about the book in which after the war Waugh tried to set forth the positive side of his beliefs, although *Brideshead Revisited* published in 1945, is not a political monster but a monster of artificial religiosity. For anyone who knows the true depth of Waugh's religious convictions, *Brideshead Revisited* is painful to contemplate. Its hero, Charles Ryder, is the kind of idealist Waugh had previously mocked. He is a seriously depicted Tony Last, with the dream of glory and good really located somehow in "old families" or in "the past." We know that Waugh himself often vaguely held forth on similar lines to his friends, and it is not hard to guess that much of the most biting satire in *A Handful of Dust* came from Waugh's strength in his own newly found faith as he turned his focus on the secular world he found so completely wanting in decency, courage, humanity, and love.

The story of *Brideshead* is the story of the Flytes, a symbolically named English family. This book is Waugh's one attempt to scrutinize the Catholic community, and it was written late in the process of convergence, in the days following the Second World War. Nevertheless, to find orientations comparable to

Waugh's in *Brideshead Revisited*, one must go all the way back to Chesterton, Huysmans, and Barbey d'Aurevilly in the period of most acute Catholic separatism. Waugh's "good Catholics" are represented by the sincere Lady Marchmain, and by Julia and Sebastian Flyte and Charles Ryder when they reform and are converted at the end of the book. Invariably, the converted and the "good Catholics" are also "good people." On the other hand, Catholics who offend against the rules of their religion, Julia and Sebastian in their youth, and the secularists Charles Ryder and Rex Mottram, are in varying degrees "bad." It is too simplistic a morality to make compelling fiction. The most Waugh can achieve is melodrama and sentimentality.

The theme of *Brideshead Revisited* is symbolized by the Marchmain family name, Flyte. The most basic flight is from the good: from truth and serious effort, obligation and love as these must be lived from day to day by sincere Catholic people. These flights take different forms in the different characters. Lady Marchmain, daughter of an ancient Catholic family, married the heir of a Protestant noble house, who to please her became a convert. Marchmain's bride is a saintly woman, and, finding her goodness unbearable, Marchmain flees into an affair with a coarse and reassuringly normal widow. All the Flytes are similarly refugees. Sebastian Flyte, Ryder's Oxford friend who is unable to take life or anything else seriously, flees into alcoholism. Julia Flyte, who despises the conventional dullness of her Marchmain background, flees into marriage with Rex Mottram, a newly rich colonial, making his way by marriage and money into the power he craves. But at the end all "flights" fail. The Hound of Heaven is on their trail and brings each to bay, Lord Marchmain in a deathbed conversion, Sebastian in a life of humility as a lay brother in a North African monastery, and Julia in a heroic renunciation of Charles, whom she has learned to love, but as a divorcee cannot legitimately marry. He, too, is divorced, so the situation is compounded. "I've always been bad," Julia says. "Probably I shall be bad again. But the worse I am, the more I need God. I can't shut myself out from His mercy. That is what it would mean, starting a life with you, without Him."[13] The closing pages show Charles on his knees in the Marchmain family chapel during his wartime "revisit" to their ancestral home of Brideshead. "I said a prayer, an ancient, newly learned form of words and left. . . ."[14] He is either a convert or on his way.

If *Brideshead Revisited* proves nothing else, it demonstrates that sentimentality and the religious dimension cannot mix in a modern novel without destroying its impact and its art. Filtered through sentimentality, what is intended as power becomes melodrama and what is introduced to touch the emotions descends to bathos. Hollywood was eager to film a story so in accord with its own standards. Waugh went to California, but when he discovered how the producers saw *Brideshead* he turned down the fee and refused to assign the rights. Later he rewrote portions of the novel, eliminating some of the Sebastian passages, but Charles Ryder as narrator was irremovable. One must pity Waugh for the fate of finding that, when in *Brideshead* he attempted to write a nonsatiric story about values for which he cared, he could not achieve the excellence he attempted. He must have felt that in his maturity his talent had failed him. But if in the mature Waugh there had been sufficient compassion and humanity to make a Charles Ryder genuinely a hero, probably the young Waugh could never have given us a Tony Last or a Paul Pennyfeather. The books which assure Waugh his place in literature are his satires. Their vitality is such that when one reads them the "lost generation" and all the tragic emptiness that beset England after the First World War live again in startling immediacy. When that period is a little more veiled by the passage of time, Evelyn Waugh will come into his own again as the great writer he was, the keenest satirist his era produced.

CHAPTER VIII

Graham Greene

Evelyn Waugh believed that compelling serious drama could be created within the framework of the English Catholic novel, and he attempted a scrutiny of the Catholic community. He himself failed, but another Englishman, whom Waugh could never like or understand, was to succeed. This was of course Graham Greene.

Greene is such a complex artist that before one can even hope to know what he was attempting to do one must look at his origins. James, Conrad, and Mauriac were the chief writers who influenced him. Most obvious is his connection with Mauriac and through him with the whole carefully developed, highly self-aware French critical Catholic tradition we discussed in Chapter I. Like J. F. Powers, who is under the influence of Waugh, Greene, with his debt to the French, affirms the international character of the later Catholic novelists. In Greene's essay on Mauriac he says that the salient trait of Mauriac's characters is that they have "the solidity and importance of men with souls to save or lose"[1]—Maritain's "essentialism," Claudel's "permanence," as worked out by Mauriac as he developed his fiction, and studied by Greene as he read and admired the Bordeaux novels. The fate of souls which will be saved or lost is the strongest source of drama in Greene's stories. Though his handling of it derives from the French tradition, nevertheless, as with all debts Greene owes, he changes the gift he receives and develops it in his own way—as we shall see.

From Conrad, particularly from such characters as Jim in *Lord Jim*, Kurtz in *Heart of Darkness*, Singleton in *The Nigger of the Narcissus*, and Heyst in *Victory*, Greene derives much of his knowledge of the drama that can be generated by examining the nature of man's responsibility to his fellowmen. He adds, however, a purely Catholic development, Péguy's theme that a human being may long to give for others not only his life but his soul. Until the time of Péguy, Catholics took it for granted—as was and is catechistically taught—that the first duty to God, to all good, was one's own salvation. Greene's compassionate police commissioner, the Catholic Scobie, says, "I know the [official] answers as well as he [the priest] does. One should look after one's own soul at whatever cost to another, and that's what I can't do. . . ."[2] Much of the self-centeredness, limitation, and lack of human solidarity modern Protestants believed they saw in certain Catholics came from this teaching, which Scobie rejects. Greene understood the accumulated encrustations of popular misconceptions among Catholics about Catholic orthodoxy. He worked to eliminate them, and in Newman's sense "develop" the fullest possible true meaning. Greene believes the biblical teaching, greater love hath no man than that he lay down his life for his friend, but he also believes that there should be added as a logical corollary the principle that man must be ready to lay down not only his temporal but his eternal life. As the priest says in recalling Péguy in *Brighton Rock*, "greater love hath no man than this, that he lay down his soul for his friend."[3] Curiously, among all other Catholic novelists, the one who shares with Greene the most urgency in pressing this theme is Bernanos, whom Greene never admired because he found Bernanos' work coarse and clumsy, but whose Abbé Donissan in Péguy's pattern offers his salvation for others, while in Mauriac's work the theme does not appear. Greene, however, makes it specially his own and develops his own variation. Like all his dramatic themes, its central element is the search for the highest measure of love, a search that leads into a paradox, yet again the drama is one whose power depends on evoking and enlarging for modern times a timeless teaching. Whoever shall seek to lose his soul in Greene's superbly generous way shall save it, as Rose does in *Brighton Rock.*

The search to determine the highest measure of love, the effort to ascertain the nature of the obligation men owe their fellowmen have of course been Catholic concerns all through history, but they are not narrowly or exclusively Catholic. Protestants and many secularists have been engrossed by these same problems. Thus Greene again must be said to resemble Bernanos, particularly the Bernanos of *The New Story of Mouchette,* which, as we saw, depends on Catholic values but opens out to universality. Greene's characters are often Catholics, his themes almost always are, and thus he is a "Catholic novelist," but one does not find in Greene the exclusively Catholic doctrines that Mauriac uses so often as a mainspring of dramatic action. One cannot find in Greene, for example, any character whose central function is like that of Mauriac's Marie in *Vipers' Tangle,* who earns grace for her father by her prayers.

We must say a word about Greene's backgrounds. Greene has the isolation and individualism that marked English Catholics from the time of the Reformation. Unlike Mauriac, Greene has no sense of his own national Catholic community as the subject of his scrutiny or as an audience to be converted to his ethical and religious views. Greene writes as naturally about Catholics in Mexico as about Catholics in England, and his books are addressed to Catholics wherever they may be, and beyond them to all readers everywhere. Yet this fact does not mean that Greene is not an "English Catholic writer." Paradoxically, the chief characteristic of the English Catholic community was the obliviousness of most of its members to the fact that there was such a community.

Also, before going on to look closely at the novels, one must make at least a few preliminary observations about Greene's technique. Volumes could be written about his achievements in developing the novel. There is room here for only the briefest description. Undoubtedly Greene takes from James the use of personality reflectors. In James' *The Ambassadors,* for instance, Lambert Strether is one sort of person with his friend Waymarsh, another sort of person with Maria Gostrey, and develops still a third (and ultimately dominant) side of his character with Madame de Vionnet. In *Brighton Rock,* to take only one book of Greene's, Pinkie is a swaggering leader with his gang, a hate-filled inferior with the "big gangster," Colleoni, and an obsessed hater of women with Rose. As in James, all the component personalities combine to create the whole personality as it finally develops. But compared to Greene, James seems to write in slow motion. Greene shifts from one person to another, one place to the next, one action to consequent action with a rapidity that can only be called cinematographic. The effect is as if Greene were swinging the boom of a huge camera. The changes come the more swiftly because for plots Greene uses the patterns of the modern thriller, with intrigue, betrayal, mystery, suspense, surprise, and particularly the chase as main elements. Countless critics comment on the affinity between Greene's novels and the cinema and note not only the number of Greene's novels and entertainments that have made successful movies, but that Greene himself was a movie critic, serving in that capacity from 1935 to 1939 on the *Spectator* and *Night and Day.*[4] However, as far as I know, only George Steiner, an enthusiastic admirer of Greene, has observed that Greene's photographs are almost entirely deprived of color. His is nearly a black and white world, bleakly emptied of all but the most subdued hues.[5] Mauriac felt the link between this cinema world and the contrast

Greene makes us experience as he moves us about in the seedy, run-down, ugly, shabby surroundings of fallen man, like a muffled environment underwater, and then suddenly irradiates it with grace. It is the contrast that gives the vitality, in Mauriac's word: "Une transposition cinématographique de la vie qui me toucherait peu si elle n'était en prise directe avec l'éternite."[6]

This effect requires of course almost constant change in depth of focus. At this Greene is adept. Usually the eyes through which one visualizes a scene are the character's, the center of consciousness is also his, as in James; but Greene is not an author who effaces himself from his work, a cameraman who fails to use the lens to its widest angle. When in *The Power and the Glory* the whiskey priest and the Indian woman with her dead child come upon the enormous crosses in the wasteland, a far more sensitive awareness than either the priest's or the woman's begins directly communicating with the reader. The same is true of Pinkie's drive in the rain and of Scobie's storm in the last pages. Greene, in writing of Mauriac, from whose work Greene developed this part of his technique, gives this description:

> In such passages one is aware, as in Shakespeare's plays, of a sudden tensing, a hush seems to fall on the spirit—this is something more important than the King, Lear, or the General, Othello, something that is unconfined and unconditioned by the plot. "I" has ceased to speak: I is speaking.[7]

Such direct contact between author and reader might threaten to make the reader become too conscious of the presence of a "storyteller." Occasionally this does happen in Mauriac, but never, I believe, does it happen in Greene, in spite of the fact that his use of the "thriller" plot mechanisms might seem to threaten realism. The "thriller," however, is for us unfortunate moderns not merely a pattern of fiction but a pattern of life. Greene is careful to give it to us as directly—one might say, as violently—as possible. As Morton Dauwen Zabel points out, Greene's stories come from life: *Brighton Rock* from the Brighton race gang murders, *The Power and the Glory* from Canabal's persecution of religion in Tabasco, *The Heart of the Matter* from the wartime Gold Coast, where Greene himself served.[8]

In *Orient Express*, published in 1932, the first book that shows Greene's power to captivate a reader by a tale superbly told, there first also appears the theme of universal love on whose development the force of Greene's later dramas depends. The form this theme takes in *Orient Express* is one that Greene later uses again and again. Greene, as we have said, is obsessed by the responsibility a human being may be made to feel for his fellowmen; and in this book Dr. Czinner, the doomed and movingly portrayed Communist revolutionary, embodies this sense of responsibility. Dr. Czinner, for all of his revolutionary convictions and the topical orientation of this novel of the thirties, when so many European states were under the shadow of fascism, is very recognizably the English Catholic writer's typical lone figure of faith and fidelity in a cynical and treacherous world. By Greene's favorite device of repeating his central theme for emphasis, the same lonely virtue of fidelity and responsibility is also central in the character of Mydans, the Jew, and of Coral Musker, the young chorus girl, who is the earliest member in Greene's long procession of touchingly responsible child-women.

England Made Me in 1935, Greene's most brilliant ensuing book until *Brighton Rock* in 1938, is another story in which Greene again examines his favorite theme, this time in its negative aspect as irresponsibility. The central figure this time is the international financier, Krogh (modeled on Ivar Kreuger). Krogh's utterly faithless irresponsibility is reflected in lesser and engaging irresponsibility of feckless young Anthony Farrant. In Krogh we are shown that irresponsibility, if total, is the passport to success in the amoral world of modern industry (an invalid contention, if one considers the ultimate fate of Ivar Kreuger, but Krogh's end has no part in the book; we are led to believe that he goes on successfully). In Anthony Farrant we are shown that if a man's irresponsibility is fettered by any remnant of decency, he not only will not get on in the modern world but the modern world will destroy him. The sympathy we feel for the characters raises the story above the level of a moral allegory directed at a Europe writhing in the grip of worldwide depression, but its dramatic framework is once more of the simplest sort: the good suffer, the evil prosper, much as in *Orient Express*; and both books, compelling though they are to read, are far below the level of Greene's later achievements.

Orient Express is listed among Greene's works as an "entertainment," while *England Made Me* appears as a "novel." It is well to keep in mind Greene's distinction between the two because it sheds light on his goals as a writer. In a radio broadcast in 1955 he said, "In one's entertainments one is primarily interested in having an exciting story as in a physical action, with just enough character to give interest in the action, because you can't be interested in the action of a mere dummy. In the novels I hope one is primarily interested in the character and the action takes a minor part."[9]

Brighton Rock started out as an entertainment and was later listed as a novel. One can see why. The characters do not exist for the sake of the plot in *Brighton Rock* as we read the finished book (whatever may have been their role when Greene began to write this sequel to an earlier entertainment), but the plot exists to display the characters. To develop these characters and the relationships between them, Greene has to put the plot through so many twists and turns that it is only because, as George Steiner says, Greene is one of the great storytellers of our time that he avoids startling his reader by repeated improbabilities. As it is, the pace carries the reader on, and only the third or fourth perusal will give rise to difficulties.

Brighton Rock is Greene's first venture into using a Catholic setting. His central character, Pinkie, the young gangster who lives by making racecourse bookmakers pay him for protection, was born into the poorest working-class environment. His Catholic parents were as ignorant and brutalized as any in Bernanos' dead parishes. Pinkie nevertheless from his schooling absorbed a certain amount of Catholic belief, which he distorts to fit his idea of how best to cope with his life. Pinkie makes the Catholic popular idea of hell as a place of eternal flames and endless pain the focus of his "religion." He sees his own environment as a reflection of this hell, and his aim is simple: he intends in his earthly hell always to be one of those who inflict pain instead of one who receives it.

This much Pinkie takes from his early life. But, contrary to the claims of some of Greene's critics, particularly conservative Catholics among them, Pinkie does not illustrate a Jansenist or Calvinist or even Darwinian infringement of free will.[10] It is rather that Pinkie partakes of the quality of those heroes of the classical world whose fate looms on a horizon shaped by their past. Thus far there is a strong neopagan element in Greene. But it is combined with the Christian doctrine of sufficient grace. The reason the plot of *Brighton Rock* has to wind through so many convolutions is that Pinkie must be given so many obvious opportunities to revise his views and escape the eternal hell he dreads, opportunities he often nearly takes and which he rejects as his clear and conscious choice. Early in the book, when he is with Rose, a sixteen-year-old waitress who comes from a background almost exactly duplicating his own, Pinkie quotes the saying, "Between the stirrup and the ground, he something lost and something found." Rose, who never let her brutal environment distort her faith but rather clung to faith the more devotedly as a source of light and hope, supplies the word that Pinkie's unconscious has wiped out: "Mercy."[11] Pinkie's broodings on hell are reinforced when one day at the racecourse he has a direct experience with pain and is slashed by razors, instead of being as usual himself the slasher. In agony and fear

he thinks of what eternal pain might really be and begins to
brood on mercy.

Greene has put Pinkie into a situation which over and over
again illustrates the orthodox Catholic belief that people are the
architects of their own souls, determine their own characters,
and have sufficient grace to save themselves whatever their background. Rose, the little waitress, is in love with Pinkie, but her
innocence and particularly her "softness" fill Pinkie with contempt, which is reinforced by his fear and hatred of everything
to do with sex. Pinkie cannot escape Rose, however, because she
has stumbled upon evidence that can convict him of murder. He
is determined to silence her—and yet he puts off doing so,
touched by Rose in spite of himself and moved by his fear of
hell. But Pinkie has as completely perverted his Catholic faith
as Rose has kept hers inviolate. Even if he kills Rose, he thinks
there will be no obstacle to his ultimate escape from hell. "He
could deal with Rose; and then when he was thoroughly secure,
he could begin to think of making peace, of going home, and his
heart weakened with a faint nostalgia for the tiny dark confessional box, the priest's voice. . . ."[12]

Pinkie realizes that he and Rose are a natural pair. Greene
has doubled the traditional English figure of faith: Pinkie feels
that he and Rose are linked because, while the pagan world
knows only right and wrong, he and Rose have been trained to
understand good and evil. Pinkie also feels that he and Rose
complement each other: he is "evil"; she is "good": "What was
most evil in him needed her; it couldn't get along without goodness."[13] Pinkie's corruption of Rose, making her a knowing accomplice of murder, marrying her in a civil ceremony to ensure
that she cannot give legal evidence against him, mark his progress on his chosen course. Before he undertakes to marry Rose,
he thinks, "He had graduated in pain: first the school dividers
. . . next the razor. He had a sense now that the murders of Hale
and Spicer were trivial acts, a boy's game, and he had put away

childish things. Murder had only led to this—this corruption. He was filled with awe at his own powers."[14] Sex is to Pinkie the symbol of sin, and sex is what he makes Rose share with him —as he sees it, the ultimate degradation of them both. He finally decides to murder her by feigning to make a suicide pact and persuading her to kill herself. But, right to the end, possibilities of repentance haunt Pinkie. Always he cannot bear music. It opens to him visions of release so beautiful that he cannot endure them. Even as he advances in evil, so does the temptation to good advance within him. Sitting in a movie with Rose, he listens to music. It "went on—it was like a vision of release to an imprisoned man. . . . It was as if he were dead and were remembering the effect of a good confession. . . . He said at last, 'Let's go.' "[15] Even when he has fully formed his plan to bring about Rose's death, the hope of his ultimate escape does not leave him. "He thought: there'll be time enough in the years ahead—sixty years—to repent of this. Go to a priest, Say, 'Father, I've committed murder twice. And there was a girl— she killed herself.' "[16] Pinkie's ongoing choices are shaping him. Repentance is always more difficult, and farther away. In the end, Pinkie, blinded by the very vitriol he once bought to throw in Rose's face, plunges over a cliff; and his death overtakes him while his redemption still remains embryonically within him, forever unrealized. *Brighton Rock* is a fearful study in the Catholic's belief in human freedom.

The book would fail if Pinkie were not a convincing character. Rose is equally convincing, and she must have been far harder to draw. She is another of Greene's child-women who live by responsibility for others. She knows Pinkie is a murderer, she sees him reflected in a similar but lesser degree of evil in each member of his gang, and she realizes on their last ride together that his plan is to bring about her death. "It didn't matter; she loved him; she had her responsibility."[17] Even in the end, if Pinkie is to be damned, she is determined not to leave him but to be damned with him: "she felt responsibility move in her breasts; she wouldn't let him go into that darkness alone."[18] As Pinkie has grown in evil, so Rose has grown in compassion, loyalty, and selfless love.

The emotion aroused by *Brighton Rock* is more complex than anything attempted earlier by Greene. It depends of course on consent to Christian orthodoxy, either by genuine conviction or by willingness to suspend disbelief until one closes the book. But whether one is a convinced believer or simply a reader who accepts the "mythology" of Pinkie's "hell" until the story is over, one will not be troubled by sentimentalism, for Greene's stylistic approach to his drama is astringent in the extreme. There is the portrayal of Pinkie, who, haunted by the visions of escape, still chooses hell but who, even in his plans for Rose's death, can think of ultimate forgiveness—surely one of the most telling expositions of the Narcissism of a completely self-circumscribed identity in all of literature. There is the portrayal of Rose, which evokes the moving experience of watching the character of this sixteen-year-old child rise to match her fate. For Pinkie she will give up her hope of eternal life, a particularly moving version of the Péguy theme, for in a devout young girl of Rose's type, for whom there has never been any hope but the hope of heaven, this is a measure of love that cannot be excelled. Finally, there is the closing measure of love— in which the priest makes it clear to Rose that God accepts this kind of sacrifice only within his own love; that Péguy, when he also wished to make it, probably died a saint. But neither Greene nor the priest give any conclusive verdict in this book as to Pinkie's ultimate fate. Because of Rose there is hope even for Pinkie. The priest says, "You can't conceive, my child, nor can I or anyone—the appalling . . . strangeness of the mercy of God."[19] "Mercy" is the key word in this story.

There is a curious figure in *Brighton Rock*: Ida Arnold, buxom, promiscuous, good-natured and hearty, a woman who loves life and lives by the "difference between right and wrong," thus providing a secular and pagan background for the Catholics, Pinkie and Rose, who live by the difference between "good and evil." Clearly Ida, with her ouija board and hunches, her bonhomie and her idea that right is simply helping people to live and enjoy life, is not as moving a character as Rose or Pinkie. Compared to them she has no depth; she is a hedonist who lives entirely on the surfaces of existence. Yet Ida in her way has "mercy" as Rose has on her much deeper level, and Ida is kind to her friend, Fred Hale. And it is Ida who, outraged at Pinkie's gang's murder of Fred, pursues Pinkie to his doom. To Ida, taking away mortal life is the worst thing anyone can do. But the attitude into which we are led concerning Ida is not hostile or even contemptuous, it is merely ambivalent. After all, without Ida, Rose would die and Pinkie go free. So it would seem that, in creating Ida, Greene approached at least halfway toward peace with a kind of creature Catholic writers had always most despised, the worldling who lives only by the values of the world. Ida is a latter-day pillar of the bourgeoisie, a modern female version of a type not far from a poorer and more virtuous Cosmo Burden. If a Catholic writer in 1938 could be even slightly favorable toward this type, he had traveled far along the road of extending his hand to all people of good will. In Ida, I believe, we see a bitter old intransigence, common to Catholic writers in both France and England, beginning to fade.

The Power and the Glory, published in 1940, marks a tremendous advance in Greene's ability to generate more complex emotions from his handling of Catholic themes. In *Brighton Rock* he opposed evil to good, evoked the power of evil's triumph in Pinkie, and then the power of seeing a good person, Rose, develop the magnitude of character to match an evil fate. In *The Power and the Glory* he does something far more difficult: he opposes good to good—and does justice to the dramatic force of each side's opposition to the other.

The story is a simple one. A lone priest, the familiar figure of a solitary man of faith hunted by his enemies, has for years held out in Garrido Canabal's Tabasco, where all religion is banned as treason to the Mexican revolutionary state. The natural thing to do with this pattern is to make the hunted man good, his hunters evil—as Catholic Englishmen had seen this situation since the time of Campion. But Greene's priest is an alcoholic, driven to drink by his years of fear. Furthermore, cut off from the Church and from all support of ecclesiastical discipline, the priest, one lonely drunken night in a remote village of the parish he attempts to serve, has fathered a child. As he himself says, he is a "bad priest." Yet by a paradox with which Greene deals expertly, he is also a very good one. Again and again he turns back to tend the dying or to give the sacraments just as he is on the brink of escape. Greene finally does let him escape over the border—for without this interlude the endless pursuit would exhaust its drama—but he goes back a last time into what he knows is a trap that will mean his capture and death. An American fugitive gangster is dying and has sent a message that may mean a wish to make a final confession. The gangster has been hunted at the same time as the priest but with far less eagerness on the part of the state. In the juxtaposition of the priest and the gangster there are reflections of Christ and Barabbas, for the police would far rather catch the priest. There are also reflections of Christ and the good thief, for although the priest elicits no formal expression of contrition from the gangster, the man dies warning him to "beat it, Father," and tries to give him his own most precious possessions, his gun and his knife—actions of love and concern for a fellow being which make a "good death" so far as this man is capable of it. With Greene's usual astringent irony, which prevents weakening a strong story with sentiment, the priest does not see this "goodness." As he goes to his own capture by the police waiting outside, he believes that in his final effort to help a dying man accept grace, he has merely failed again.

If the priest could not see the "goodness" of the gangster, many of Greene's readers were equally blind to the "goodness" of the priest. *The Power and the Glory* brought a torrent of complaints, and finally Greene received an official letter from Rome: the Holy Office condemned the book because it was "paradoxical" and "dealt with extraordinary circumstances." Considering the uproar that Greene's saintly "bad priest" had caused in conservative Catholic circles since the book's publication, the official letter was a mild rebuke. As Greene observed,[20] the matter remained private; there was "no public condemnation" of his refusal to revise his story of a modern martyr, based on an actual case of a "whiskey priest" told him during his research visit to Mexico. The story, with its focus on men's hearts rather than their actions, was a probing of intentional ethics that made use of a much more sophisticated application of Catholic orthodoxy than any previously displayed in a Catholic novel. Greene was very deliberate in demonstrating exactly what he was doing. He went to elaborate lengths to contrast the realism of his story with the usual pious "saint's life" by presenting at intervals throughout the book a group of Catholic children whose mother is reading to them from a conventional hagiography of the kind Bernanos so despised, a story of the "rosy saints" of Catholic popular myth. The children are bored at so much unreality, the perceptive little boy Luis is even hostile; but at the end the execution of the real "whiskey priest," a martyrdom whose human anguish can be felt even by the child, turns Luis against his former hero, a Communist lieutenant of the security police, the whiskey priest's pursuer and victorious enemy. The final page shows Luis opening the door to a stranger, and at the man's frightened announcement that he, too, is a hunted priest, Luis stoops quickly to kiss his hand.

If Greene's portrayal of a "bad priest" who was at the same time a saint aroused anger and bewilderment among Catholics in the 1940s, his portrayal of the Communist lieutenant as a typical "enemy of the Church" seemed to many even more outrageous. For, as the priest says, his pursuer is a "good man."[21] The lieutenant has the innocence of imagination that characterized Marxists in the 1930s, and he believes that all the poverty, ignorance, and backwardness of Mexico can be instantly dissolved simply by getting rid of the Church, confiscating its wealth, destroying its role in education, and freeing the populace from superstition. As the priest is a "responsible" man whom responsibility summons back into danger again and again, so the lieutenant is a "responsible" man—responsible above all to boys like Luis, to whom he shows his gun in his character as a people's soldier, and to whom he tries to explain his dream of a free, educated nation. Greene repeatedly uses children to focus the bearing of his story. The lieutenant's and the priest's sense of responsibility is reflected not only in Luis' assumption of responsibility for the new fugitive priest at the end of the book, but early in the story in the responsible little girl, Coral, who shelters the whiskey priest, successfully misleads the police, and has as a foil her irresponsible father. A symbol of the Republic's hopeless wooing of children like Luis is the always deserted playground, which occupies the former site of the cathedral.[22] Finally, the crux of the whiskey priest's martyrdom is that he offers his salvation for the ransoming of the soul of his own corrupt child, who represents the future to him, as Luis represents it to the lieutenant.

The lieutenant, ascetic, proud, and for all his sincerity too puritanical to arouse real sympathy (Greene has loaded the dice skillfully in favor of the humble, fallible priest) is nevertheless a variation of one of Greene's favorite types, the humanist radical, whom he first portrayed in Dr. Czinner.[23] In the confrontations between the priest and his enemy, it is clear that one

good man faces another, and that only their opposite dedica-
tions keep them apart. This sort of thing has been the blood and
bone of the more serious kinds of drama at least since the time
Aeschylus set Apollo against the Erinyes, and Greene's use
of the form marks a significant advance in craftsmanship, but
there were many readers who found Greene's "good" Communist as scandalous as his "bad" priest. Not unnaturally, their
most eloquent spokesman became the conservative Evelyn
Waugh, to whom Greene's explorations of the ethics of intention
and the anatomy of the heart were, and forever remained, a
shocking enigma. But non-Catholics were often equally bewildered. In 1949 George Orwell said, "in outlook he is just a mild
Left with faint C. P. leanings."[24] Of course Greene was nothing
of the kind. He was simply the first modern Catholic writer to
apply without flinching the ancient dogma that God judges man's
heart not his acts.

As far back as *Orient Express* Greene had been working
in this same direction. Dr. Czinner is a revolutionary and a
"bad man" in the eyes of many conventional and reasonable
people of the time, but no one who reads the book can doubt that
within the framework of Greene's Catholic orthodoxy Czinner's
devotion to the best that he knows makes him a man close to
God. Czinner dies at the hands of the enemies of the people he
is trying to help. His fate thus foreshadows that of the whiskey
priest, who is a "bad priest" but is nevertheless a martyr and a
saint. In *The Power and the Glory* Greene develops the theme
at several levels. Even the gangster, dying with thoughts of
further murder on his mind, at the same time makes a "good
death" because he is concerned not for himself in his last mo-
ments but for the hunted priest by his side. Greene is able to
make us see these people as a just and merciful God would see
them. In so doing Greene also makes us see God as he wants us
to see Him. The world's ideas of good and bad, Greene points

out, have nothing to do with how a man is judged by an all-seeing and merciful Creator.

Greene's books were a symptom of Catholic thinking that was increasing in depth, but inevitably his work collided with the pious rigidity inherited from the nineteenth century. Nevertheless his widely read fiction exerted a strong influence. The "open Church" of the 1960s, with its acceptance of all "men of good will" had in its background the puzzled, slowly comprehending, worldwide Catholic audience on which Greene's themes were working in the 1940s and 1950s. These were the decades when the separatism that had dominated the nineteenth century was surrendering to the older recognition that had begun with such men as Campion and continued with such men as Newman: that there was good in all people. Greene's work was a sign of the accelerated convergence between the Catholic and the non-Catholic worlds.

The Heart of the Matter (1948) was another step forward in Greene's handling of Catholic themes and characters. In the compassionate English West African police commissioner, Scobie, Greene probes his old concept of the "responsible" protagonist to the greatest depth he reaches in his fiction. Basically the novel is another version of a conflict between two loyalties, each valid on its own level. This time the conflict is internalized in the heart of a single responsible man, who cannot abandon his loyalty to his wife or his loyalty to his mistress, although the two loyalties are incompatible and their conflict leads him into offense against his greatest responsibility of all, his loyalty to God. Compassion was a primary trait in the Communist Dr. Czinner as the complement to his sense of political responsibility; it was even more primary in the Catholic Rose, whose focus was on eternity; and with the whiskey priest compassion motivates most of his actions. In Scobie, the police officer whose Catholicism has been central to his life of service in protecting his fellowmen, pity becomes an obsession. Scobie pities his wife, Louise, and pity for her leads him into his first trap, borrowing money from the Syrian diamond smuggler, Yusef, in order to send her to South Africa for a vacation. While Louise is gone, it is pity that leads Scobie to love the defenseless shipwrecked young widow, Helen Rolt, who becomes his mistress. When Louise returns, it is pity for her and fear that she will be hurt by hearing of his affair with Helen that causes Scobie to let the suspicious Louise trap him into going to Communion. Louise, we should note parenthetically, is very recognizably a variation of Mauriac's favorite figure of the "eternal Tartuffe," a pious Catholic hypocrite, who deceives herself as much as she deceives the people around her. Scobie is unable to obtain absolution for his affair with Helen because his pity for her will not let him leave her. He is also unable to stay away from Communion because his pity for Louise will not let him confirm her suspicions. At last Scobie falls into a depth of self-disgust that makes him feel that men who make such sacrilegious Communions as his strike Christ across the face, and he pities even God. An earlier thought of Scobie's was that pity must be endless in the universe. "If one knew, he wondered, the facts, would one have to feel pity even for the planets? if one reached what they called the heart of the matter?"[25]

Scobie's corruption by pity is not ended but only confirmed by his sacrilegious Communion. His pity for Louise, his terrible sense of responsibility for her, and his fear that she will be so shattered by hearing of his love for Helen that all her fragile security and her very personality may be destroyed lead him to complain to Yusef about the native "boy," Ali, who has been Scobie's faithful servant for years but through whom knowledge may by circular routes now reach Louise. What Yusef means by his promise to make Ali safe Scobie does not consciously realize, but when the endangered Yusef, who has forced Scobie to be his accomplice in a smuggling venture about which Ali also

knows, has Ali killed, Scobie understands he has been the insti-
gator of the murder of the man who was probably his one devoted friend.

In Scobie, Greene engaged in a piercing reassessment of
what had been his most fruitful theme. His previous books had
exalted the responsible man. But in Scobie, Greene showed that
the sense of responsibility for others could actually come from
lack of trust. It is lack of trust that drives Scobie to make himself responsible for what Ali might do or say. Scobie himself
realizes this. After Ali's death he thinks, "You served me and
I did this to you. You were faithful to me, and I wouldn't trust
you."[26] Scobie's relationship to his God is similar. He imagines
God urging him to resolve his dilemma by either leaving his
wife and joining his mistress, or giving up his mistress to go
back to his wife: "One of them will suffer, but can't you trust me
to see that the suffering isn't too great? . . . his own voice replied
hopelessly: No. I don't trust you. I love you, but I've never
trusted you. If you made me, you made this feeling of responsibility that I've always carried about like a sack of bricks."[27]

Greene has arrived at an extremely subtle study of evil, an
evil that is able to "camouflage"[28] itself behind good, in this
case responsibility. Greene shows the world in the grip of "an
enemy who works in terms of friendship, trust, and pity."[29] The
dramatic theme that formed Scobie is deeper than any Greene
brought to the creation of earlier protagonists, deeper than any
he would ever achieve again. Scobie's virtue itself is his flaw.
This is of course again a kind of drama that is very old. It was
familiar to the Greeks; Sophocles in Antigone shows that the
courage and leadership of Creon were themselves the source of
the hubris that blinded him. Once more we see a neopagan
element in Greene. But again it is combined with Christian orthodoxy and Christian love and mercy. Scobie, who kills himself
to avoid doing any more harm, offers to God his very lack of
trust in God, his terrible "responsibility" that he has carried

"like a sack of bricks" and which he believes now will by his suicide damn him. Scobie offers his damnation itself for the salvation and happiness of those he loves. It is the Péguy motif once again, in a powerful and complex variation.

Many of Greene's readers found *The Heart of the Matter* scarcely less a scandal than *The Power and the Glory*. Was not Scobie a good man and a good Catholic? Yet was he not shown taking his own life? Was not Scobie damned? The argument raged, with many coming to the conclusion that Scobie was indeed damned. Among those who took this side in the dispute were of course many secular or Protestant readers who were simply accepting what they regarded as Catholic mythology and had erroneous notions; but also among them were many Catholics, who should have known better—and who from reading Greene's books probably indeed were painfully beginning to understand distinctions they had never seen before.

At the end of *Brighton Rock* Greene evoked a direct shadowing of the supernatural. He did it very skillfully as Pinkie in his cherished automobile is driving Rose to what he intends to be her death:

> An enormous emotion beat on him; it was like something trying to get in, the pressure of gigantic wings against the glass. *Dona nobis pacem.* He withstood it, with all the bitter force of the school bench, the cement playground, the Saint Pancras waiting room, Dallow's and Judy's secret lust, and the cold unhappy moment on the pier. If the glass broke, if the beast—whatever it was—got in, God knows what it would do. He had a sense of huge havoc—the confessional, the penance, and the sacrament—an awful distraction, and he drove blind into the rain.[30]

In Scobie's death agony, after he has taken the pills that will simulate his fatal heart attack, there is the same sense of a force attempting to enter. As in *Brighton Rock* it is skillfully kept from definition. One is aware only that it lies somewhere between the pressure of grace and the presence of God. Pinkie had thrust it away. Scobie, on the contrary, does his best to respond, even in his moment of death:

> It seemed to him as though someone outside the room were seeking him, calling him, and he made a last effort to indicate that he was here. He got on his feet and heard the hammer of his heart beating out a reply. He had a message to convey, but the darkness and the storm drove it back within the case of his breast, and all the time outside the house, outside the world that drummed like hammer blows within his ear, someone wandered, seeking to get in, someone appealing for help, someone in need of him. And automatically at the call of need, at the cry of a victim, Scobie strung himself to act. He dredged his consciousness up from an infinite distance in order to make some reply. He said aloud, "Dear God, I love . . ." but the effort was too great and he did not feel his body when it struck the floor. . . .[31]

When one bears in mind Greene's lifelong development of the theme of God's mercy, and when one looks back on his fiction with today's larger view of Catholic orthodoxy that does away with such mistaken encrustations as the notion of some sort of automatic damnation for suicides, one remembers Pinkie's verse about the stirrup and the ground, and one feels sure that what Scobie found was indeed mercy, a compassion and responsibility infinitely greater than his own. As in all Greene's novels, the measure of the protagonist before God is his love. And the measure of God is the same, except that God's love in its illimitable vastness is immeasurable. Here again we see that Greene's best work goes back to forms that are very old, and far more complex than dramas in which the good suffer and the evil prosper, as in the early *Orient Express* and *England Made Me.* If Scobie's destruction by his own best trait recalls Sophocles, the ending of Scobie's life, like the ending of *Brighton Rock,* recalls the Aeschylean mode of religious wonder and awe. With this book the "metaphysical dimension" Mauriac felt was the most essential element in Catholic fiction, and which Maritain and Claudel had defined as the highest aim of all Catholic art, reached its most satisfying fulfillment. Of all the Catholic novels treated in this essay, *The Heart of the Matter* comes closest to being perfect of its kind. Unfortunately, for our purposes, Greene's plots are so complex that our brief interpretations here cannot do any of them justice. One can only urge readers to seek the books out for themselves. They are worth the effort.

There is one aspect of Greene's plots and his casts of characters which we have not discussed, but to which he owes much of the impression of variety one feels in the novels. Though Greene, as we have seen, often tempers his criticism of the secular world and gives a sympathetic portrayal of such figures as Ida Arnold or the whiskey priest's enemy, the Communist lieutenant, nevertheless criticism of the non-Catholic environment survives strongly in his work. Much of it is as savage as any we saw in earlier novelists such as Huysmans or Belloc, whose chief subject was their attack on the secular world. The secular figures whom Greene draws savagely are minor characters and his attack always exists as a minor antiphony for his major themes, but his secular villains are nonetheless despicable, with no more redeeming qualities than Belloc's Cosmo Burden or Waugh's Margot Beste-Chetwynde. One encounters them with a shudder of distaste or a spasm of anger that widens the range of feelings Greene is able to evoke. Such characters are the gross Italian gangster, Colleoni, in *Brighton Rock*, who reminds one of Belloc's Jewish moneylender, or Wilson, the spiteful, shallow, would-be poet who is the suitor of Scobie's wife Louise in *The Heart of the Matter* and belongs to the same species as the repulsively inane "English gentlemen" who appear in Evelyn Waugh's early satires. Thus, though Greene's central orientation is criticism of the Catholic community rather than any attack on the secular world, the attack survives as a minor element and enriches his work just as a similar survival enriches the work of Mauriac and Bernanos with the portrayal of Raymond Courrèges or the Malorthys. With the European Catholic novel-

ists, bitterness toward the secular environment remained a factor long after they turned their attention to the Catholic milieu.
In America this bitterness was less compelling—as we shall see.

After Greene produced his finest novel, *The Heart of the
Matter*, his strength seemed somehow impaired. A study of the
works that followed gives one the impression that whatever he
experienced while developing the character of Scobie must have
exhausted him. From the time of his first novels Greene's theme
had been responsibility. In 1932, in his earliest widely read
entertainment, *Orient Express*, the antifascist Dr. Czinner was
a protagonist who dedicated his life to the political liberation of
his fellowmen. In 1935, in the depths of the financial crisis that
shook the world, Greene examined the theme on its economic
side and portrayed the amoral financier, Krogh, a type of creature who, Greene felt, had by his irresponsibility brought about
the sufferings of the countless millions of starving and unemployed. Later Greene examined figures of heroic responsibility,
and created the child-woman, Rose, in *Brighton Rock* and the
whiskey priest in *The Power and the Glory*.

But after *The Power and the Glory* in 1940, Greene apparently began to reassess his major theme. The reassessment must
have been painful, for responsibility had been not only Greene's
answer to life as he saw it in the 1930s but it was the answer of
the whole intellectual world of that era. The feeling was that irresponsibility had brought on all of the world's crises from depression to impending war. It was believed that if France had
prevented the remilitarization of the Rhineland, if England and
France together had prevented the Austrian anschluss, if a firm
stand had been taken to protect the innocent people of Abyssinia
from Mussolini's brutal seizure, if the people of Manchuria had
been given aid against militaristic Japan, a world being driven
toward self-destruction by Hitler, Mussolini, and the Japanese
aggressors might have taken another course. Liberals in particular looked back in anguish to lost opportunities and came to

the conclusion that the selfishness of self-centered people and self-centered nations had doomed humanity to the bloody struggle then so clearly impending. The assumption that irresponsibility was to blame for the situation of the prewar world and could have saved it was so central to the credo of most thinking people that no one questioned it.

The Power and the Glory had been particularly moving in its treatment of the theme of responsibility because the protagonist was a priest and the book traced the theme to its deepest roots, which lay in the Christian origins of Western civilization and Christ's commandment of love from man to man. *The Power and the Glory* is written by an artist who is carried by surging self-confidence in the rightness of his evolved beliefs, and who feels his command of his talent reaching a peak. When one puts down *The Power and the Glory*, however, and picks up *The Heart of the Matter*, one is immediately aware of a change in spirit. *The Heart of the Matter* moves deliberately—painfully. It is one of those works in which one can almost sense the sweat on the author's pen. The brilliant cinematographic flashing from scene to scene is gone, the plot unfolds with terrible slowness, a crescendo of inexorability.

Scobie, the policeman, the protector of society, pities everyone; he wants to shelter everyone. And Greene, reluctantly and certainly with great suffering, finds against his hero. To "police" the world is morally wrong. Later, in 1955, when Greene entered his relatively quiescent period and began reworking ideas from the major fiction, he would similarly find "wrong" the actions of a nation that was currently out to "police" the world, and the outcry in the United States at the criticism of its actions in Asia in *The Quiet American* would be righteous, astonished, and intense.

Where did Scobie go "wrong"; what was the nature of Greene's painful and astounding reassessment of the theme that had lain at the heart of his own beliefs and of the Western world's convictions since the 1930s? Greene's Scobie is shown as "corrupted" by the force of his pity. He is in the grip of the world's "enemy," who uses pity, decency, kindliness, and concern as a disguise. Only at the end of the book does Greene point to the cause of "corruption" by pity. Scobie is a man chronically unable to trust in the ultimate goodness of the universe, the final "responsibility" of a loving Creator. When Scobie imagines God urging him to solve his dilemma by either leaving his wife and joining his mistress or giving up his mistress to return to his wife, Greene gives us that significant passage quoted earlier: "One of them will suffer, but can't you trust me to see that the suffering isn't too great? . . . his own voice replied hopelessly: No. I don't trust you. I love you, but I've never trusted you."

Thus in his portrait of Scobie Greene reversed his great theme. Love of man for his fellow beings is the second commandment; the first and greatest is love for God "with all thy heart, with all thy soul, with all thy mind." An ineradicable part of this love of God must be trust, and Scobie does not trust. Greene's theme now is that a man should indeed help and serve his fellow beings, but there are limits beyond which he cannot go, and times when trust in God must replace his own efforts. Scobie's lack of trust is self-destructive, and his ultimate suicide is inevitable.

In *Brighton Rock*, *The Power and the Glory*, and *The Heart of the Matter* Greene had been like an embodied spirit of compassion, contemplating more and more deeply in each book the nature of man's fate in a fallen world. It would seem that the ordeal of writing *The Heart of the Matter* may have driven him spiritually into dryness, and, intellectually, he may have said, if not all, at least the utmost he had to say. The later Greene is like his own Querry in *A Burnt-Out Case*. Only one book, *The End of the Affair*, whose craftsmanship was such that it evoked the warm sponsorship in America of William Faulkner, can even remotely be compared to the major novels; and the theme of *The End of the Affair* is significant: it is love and loyalty to God over love and loyalty to man; it is trust in God's own "responsibility" and a placing of final trust in the goodness of creation when one reaches the place beyond which one's own efforts cannot prevail.

Looking back after fifteen years, one realizes that the steady deepening of Greene's achievements ended in mid-century, at the time of the reassessment of his great theme. Afterwards he turned increasingly to the mode of fiction that had always enabled Catholic writers to express their vision and yet maintain the detachment that is the artist's protection against pain. Satire is prominent in the skillful entertainment, *The Third Man* in 1950; it provides the framework of *The Quiet American* in 1955; and it is almost the entire substance of *The Comedians* ten years later. Thus Greene finished on somewhat the same note as Waugh had started. Satire, though weaker in its impact than serious drama, can force almost unbearable insights. Swift was most notably expert at this sort of thing, drawing the utmost in emotion from his readers in spite of comic distance. Waugh does not have quite that deep an effect, nor does Greene, who in satire must bow to Waugh as his master. The best work by any Catholic novelist using strong satiric elements was to begin about the time Greene's finest work was tapering off.[32] It developed in quite another location and from an entirely different sort of talent, from a young American woman named Flannery O'Connor. Catholicism in America and the American Catholic novel are the subjects of the section to follow.

PART III

Pragmatic America

CHAPTER IX

Catholicism in
the United States

The traditional characteristics of American Catholicism are generally traced back to 1634, when George Calvert, the first Lord Baltimore, sent the ships, *Ark* and *Dove*, to found his plantation in Maryland. It was not the first attempt by an English Catholic noble to develop a haven of religious freedom in the new world. In 1607 Lord Arundell of Wardour and the Earl of Southampton had tried to establish a colony in what is now Maine. But this settlement failed, while the Maryland settlement took root and grew; and it is to the history of his particular foundation that we owe some of the most important traits that have distinguished Catholics in America from Catholics in other parts of the world.

For example, although the "twenty gentlemen" of Lord Baltimore's contingent were Catholic, a number of their servants and followers belonged to the Church of England. Furthermore, in subsequent years Protestant settlers kept coming in. Toleration and cooperation between the opposing religions, therefore, became a habit in Maryland; and it was never quite to be overthrown. Although in 1649 Bennett and Claiborne, the commissioners in Virginia, hearing of Charles I's execution, invaded

Maryland, summoned an Assembly from which all Catholics were excluded, and repealed the Act of Toleration, Cecil Calvert made friends with the Protector and convinced him the welfare of the colony required that toleration be reestablished. Later, when after 1688 the Catholic Calverts were deposed, first William and Mary and then Queen Anne, interested in the prosperity of the new world, interfered to mitigate the harshness of the English penal laws as they might otherwise have been applied by some of Maryland's Protestant governors, causing Catholics to leave. Although by that time there was a large Protestant population, most of the wealth was held by the old Catholic families. Restraint was therefore in the interest of both sides.

We see the roots of another tradition of equal importance in the attitude in 1776 of prominent Maryland Catholics as typified by one of their leaders, Charles Carroll. The head of the colony's wealthiest family, he was accused by a Tory opponent of favoring American independence because his Catholicism made him an enemy of England's Protestant king. He replied by distinguishing between his religious and political convictions: they were, he said, entirely separate. His political convictions were in themselves sufficient to motivate his stand on independence: he was "interested in the prosperity of his country"; he was "a friend to liberty" and "a settled enemy to lawless prerogative."[1] This separation of politics from religion was seconded by Charles Carroll's cousin, John Carroll, a priest. Although John Carroll after much persuasion accompanied the delegation of the Continental Congress in its fruitless expedition to attempt to persuade Canada to join the rebellion, he was reluctant to undertake the mission, and his deliberate inconspicuousness while in Canada illustrated his often expressed belief that the clergy should remain aloof from civil affairs.[2]

In 1806, more than two decades later, when John Carroll had been for fourteen years the American Prefect Apostolic and had stamped his apolitical stand upon the early American

Church, he characteristically took pains to avoid an occasion of possible political offense by asking the secretary of state, James Madison, how the administration would view Carroll's alternative courses in the new territory of Louisiana. Madison's attitude was in keeping with Carroll's own. He replied that although the character of Sedella, the opportunist and amoral Spanish friar leading Louisiana's dissidents, was well known, the government must remain aloof in accord with the provisions of the Constitution against interference in religious matters.[3] Thus, both from the side of the Church as represented by its hierarchy in its elemental beginnings, and from the side of the government as represented by its most fundamental document the Constitution, the declared separation of Church and state became established in practice—at a time when such separation was still generally regarded as impossible.

This is not to say that Catholics in the new world had always had smooth sailing. Except for Maryland, and for Pennsylvania where toleration was a Quaker principle, the "religious freedom" sought by most colonial settlers had been entirely for those of their own persuasion, and in pre-Revolutionary days prejudice against Catholics was even harsher than in England. John Cotton, the Congregationalist leader who died in 1652, expresses the general spirit of his community:

> The Holy Ghost puts no difference between Popish Pagancie and Heathenish Pagancie. . . . Popery is but Pagancie refined; and the estate of Popish people dying in Popery is more dangerous than the estate of Pagans dying in their Ignorance.[4]

In 1688 there was still a death penalty for priests in New York and Massachusetts, and it was 1806 before the last of the ancient English penal laws gave way and the election of a Catholic, Francis Cooper, to the New York legislature occasioned repeal of the statute requiring all elected officeholders to take an oath forswearing allegiance to any foreign ecclesiastical power.

Thus, there were from the beginning two contrasting currents in America. One was the prejudice that stemmed from colonial Puritanism; the other was the spirit of cooperation that sprang from the Maryland foundation, which became the central diocese of Baltimore. And for a long time in the new nation it was toleration rather than its opposite that prevailed. As late as the 1860s, when the future Cardinal Gibbons was a young missionary bishop in North Carolina, it was his custom when touring his diocese to ask a Protestant pastor for the loan of a church if, as was frequently the case, there was no Catholic church or suitable Catholic private house available. Then in the borrowed church the traveling bishop would celebrate Mass for scattered local Catholics and give curious Protestants an opportunity to observe the Catholic liturgy. Or, if there were no Catholics, Gibbons would gather those Protestants who cared to come and would explain the points of the Catholic faith. On a typical tour in 1869 Gibbons reached New Bern, where he confirmed twelve people, half of whom were converts, and preached at a Sunday Mass to a large congregation "the great majority of whom," he noted in his diary, "were Protestants."[5] In Fayetteville he preached in a packed church with Presbyterian and Methodist ministers in attendance, and in Goldsboro he preached in the town hall to an audience of eighty.[6] Whatever the frictions that rose later between Catholics and Protestants in America, there remained this time-honored tradition of mutual tolerance and curiosity that was so much part of the American spirit among both Protestants and Catholics that it was always ready to be restored.

One reason tolerance persisted so long was that for many years the number of Catholics was relatively small, and the scattered congregations were not usually recognized by the rest of the population as having any conspicuous unity. Carroll in his first report to Rome in 1785 estimated the number of Catholics at 25,000. The total population at that time was around four million, making Catholics a minuscule minority. But after the first quarter of the century, and particularly after the years of heaviest immigration, this picture began to change. In the decade from 1830 to 1840 there were 600,000 immigrants. From 1840 to 1850 the number nearly trebled, to 1,700,000. In the decade following it made another leap, to 2,600,000.[7] Catholics, particularly Irish Catholics, were the most cohesive group.

Although the hostility of American non-Catholics toward the Catholic immigrants, especially the Irish, soon became extreme and for many years quite obscured the earlier spirit of toleration, the feelings of the immigrants toward their new surroundings never grew to match this hostility. What happened to the feelings of the immigrants was that they became deeply ambivalent. A love-hate relationship developed in the fullest sense of the term, and for this there was good reason. Whatever the bitterness felt by these newcomers as resentment against them mounted and signs began to appear in places of employment, "No Catholics need apply"; nevertheless, conditions in America represented an enormous improvement over the near starvation from which they had come. America was, at least comparatively, a land of freedom and opportunity. On the other hand, to the native population, particularly to its poorer classes, the immigrants represented the threat of cheap labor. Hatred was single-minded and sincere.

This hatred was fertile soil for fantasies. By many Americans the tide of immigration was seen as a national disaster, and sometimes even as an anti-American conspiracy. The famous Presbyterian preacher, Lyman Beecher, horrified his audiences with accounts of a papal plot to take over the Mississippi Valley. In 1834, after one of his sermons in Boston, the Ursuline convent was burned to the ground. In New York Bishop Hughes protected his convents by arming bands of sturdy Irishmen with clubs and billies. Samuel F. B. Morse in 1834 published a book, *The Foreign Conspiracy Against the Liberties of the United States*, and two years later he ran for mayor of New York on the Nativist ticket. Morse's hat had been knocked off in Rome when he didn't remove it as a procession of the Blessed Sacrament passed by, and no form of personal assault could have assumed more sinister intimations of superstition, anti-Protestantism, and idolatry than did this episode as Morse related it to his followers.

The Nativists flourished in the thirties but went into eclipse in the middle forties. They were quickly succeeded, however, by the Know-Nothings, so called because when asked about their purposes or meetings their reply was, "I know nothing." Believing that they were fighting a hydra-headed, foreign, and frighteningly silent Catholic conspiracy against the United States, the Know-Nothings tried to become silent conspirators in their turn. After some early political successes, their organization faded away around the time of the Civil War. But they were forerunners of similar groups—the American Protective Association founded in 1887; the Ku Klux Klan, most active against Catholics in the years preceding and following the First World War; the Protestants and Other Americans United for the Separation of Church and State. This last is still flourishing at the present writing. It was founded in 1947.

Catholics in America were too busy to react with much overtness to hostilities. The armed Irish bands of Bishop Hughes were exceptions, not the rule. Catholics in general had only two aims: the first was to preserve their Catholic identity and traditions; the second was somehow to persuade their adopted country to accept them nevertheless as free and equal citizens.

Maintaining Catholic identity was achieved by collecting into parishes with a strong sense of community and by establishing Catholic schools. The efforts of New York's Bishop Hughes to secure special schools within the tax-supported state system added materially to Nativist antagonism. In 1842 the

Irish Catholic Democratic vote in New York ensured the passage
of the Maclay Act, which by legislating that educational policy
was to be decided by separate districts enabled Hughes to keep
out the Protestant Bible and Protestant prayers district by district, a measure that made Protestants more than ever certain
that the invading Catholics were immoral heathen whose priests
did not dare let them read the Bible for fear they would find
out what was in it.

It was not easy for Catholics to channel their school taxes
into their own schools. Usually they carried a double burden
and were taxed for the secular and strongly Protestant schools
while building their separate Catholic systems. But, meanwhile,
everything was done that a burning sense of dedication and anger against the injustice of the double tax could do to secure
some of the tax money for Catholic areas. Occasionally, as in
1870 in Savannah, a bishop would arrange with a local school
board to take over and maintain the parochial schools, in which
the board paid the teachers and even selected the textbooks, except for history, geography, and literature. In 1873 the Church
at Poughkeepsie for a dollar a year leased its schools to the public system, which then repaired and supported the schools. Under Bishop Ireland in the 1820s a new plan was developed at
Faribault in Minnesota. Parochial schools were rented to local
school boards during the day, and classes in religion took place
before and after school hours. Any pretense of nondenomina-
tional instruction was hollow, however, for the teachers at Faribault were Dominican nuns. Efforts of this kind continued in
many parts of the country and in different forms. The scheme of
shared time is a modern example of continuing Catholic attempts to obtain a portion of return on school taxes. Lately,
when Catholic schools have had drastically reduced support as a
result of the diminution of Catholic separatism since the war
and specially since the Second Vatican Council, less is made of

the once burning issue of distinctly Catholic schooling. Whether the result will be to weaken Catholicism in America remains still to be seen.

In the nineteenth century many of the new parochial schools seemed "foreign" to most Americans, a feeling that increased hostility against them. Pan-Germanism was strong in those days, and about a quarter of the immigrants were German.[8] While the Irish had no language barrier, Germans, Poles, Italians, and other groups often lived in special language sectors and frequently not only intended to maintain their Catholic identity within the American community but their national identity within the Catholic community. Immigrants of this type usually wanted their children taught in the language of their country of origin. They fought vigorously for bishops of their own nationality, and, led by the well-organized Germans, agitated in Rome against the "American Irish Church."

But national separatism was doomed to defeat. The majority of Catholic immigrants were Irish, the church hierarchy was largely Irish, and the Irish were determined that, while religiously they were and would remain Catholic, and nostalgically they would retain their Irishness, nationally they had and would continue increasingly to have all the traditional rights of Americans. When in 1877 Gibbons came to Baltimore as archbishop of the oldest Catholic diocese, he inherited the attitude that stemmed from the time of Charles Carroll's declaration in 1776 that while in religion he was a Catholic, in politics he was a "citizen."[9] To understand why this attitude was retained and grew, one must remember that in England and Ireland until 1829 there had been the harshest kind of government repression; in France and Germany after 1876 there was keen and increasingly crippling public and official hostility marked by suppressions and exiles; and in Italy after 1870 the new national government fought Catholic influence wherever it was found and confiscated the territories that had belonged to the papacy since the eighth century. Against this background, the situation in America looked bright.

Occasional efforts by hostile Americans to hamper Catholicism by legislation were usually futile. In New York, where Bishop Hughes not only got the Maclay Act passed but at one time backed a Catholic Party ticket to try to elect an Irish Catholic named O'Connor mayor of New York City, anti-Catholicism struck back by strengthening the state statutes empowering elected bodies to manage religious properties. This was a vulnerable area for the Church in America. "Trusteeism," as it was called, had been a problem ever since the Revolution. Because the law vested control of church property in the people of whatever church was concerned, Catholics in some areas, usually led by a dissident priest, had on occasion insisted both on controlling church property and on "calling" in Protestant fashion a priest of their own choosing rather than accepting the bishop's control and the bishop's appointee. Several priests had defied their bishops and led their parishes into schism over this issue.

But New York's Bishop Hughes was made of sterner stuff. From the beginning he treated the law concerning religious property as a dead letter. He relentlessly acquired deeds to diocesan churches and used ecclesiastical powers, including the threat of excommunication, to subdue recalcitrant trustees. And gradually this pattern prevailed throughout the country. The Catholic tradition of direction from above—from which most Catholics in any case found it unthinkable to depart—overcame the issue known as "trusteeism." One should note, however, that latent democratic tendencies always existed in the Church in America, despite the authoritarianism of most bishops during the post-Civil War nineteenth century. The able John England, Irish bishop of Charleston who died in 1842, in those early days set up a Convocation of the Clergy and a House of Representatives for laymen. When after the Second Vatican Council certain American priests and laymen adopted new patterns of

increased church democracy and found some bishops supporting them, they were picking up an old American tradition.

Legislative efforts by enemies of the immigrants to curb the
strength of Catholicism did not end with trying to stir up trusteeism. In 1875 President Grant in a message to Congress pro-
posed a constitutional amendment forbidding the teaching of
"sectarian" matters in any school supported wholly or in part
by public funds and exclusion from school taxes of any school
conducted by a religious denomination. The amendment made
no headway, and for years compromises like those at Faribault
and Poughkeepsie continued to function. Grant also recom-
mended taxing church property, a proposal that fared no better.

Meanwhile, Catholics, particularly after James Gibbons was
made cardinal in 1886, continued to behave as much as possible
like ordinary Americans. Gibbons disliked the kind of separa-
tive hostility that in an earlier day had been made customary
by Hughes. To Gibbons and those in the hierarchy who followed
his lead, the goal of American Catholics should be to express
their gratitude to their adopted country and persuade it to accept them on an equal footing by demonstrating that they were
as patriotic as anyone else. In 1879 Gibbons ordered public
prayers on Thanksgiving Day: "We should not let Protestants
surpass us in our expression of loyalty and devotion to our country," he said.[10] Nor was Gibbons separatist even in religious
matters. In 1887, like the ministers of the various Protestant de-
nominations, he offered prayers at the Centennial of the Federal
Constitution in Philadelphia.[11]

As early as his trip to Europe as a young monsignor of
thirty-six accompanying Baltimore's Archbishop Spalding to the
First Vatican Council in 1870, Gibbons had become convinced
that American democracy was the best possible soil for Catholicism. When in passing through France young Monsignor Gibbons noted the beauty of French church properties and thought
of the American struggle to establish churches and schools for

its hordes of poor, a French bishop had replied ruefully, "Monsignor Gibbons, I cannot even build a sacristy without government approval."[12] Gibbons made use of the incident in his first book, written five years later, an essay designed to explain Catholicism to Americans. Published in 1876 as *The Faith of Our Fathers*, it was reprinted thirteen times and sold 65,000 copies,[13] an immense distribution for that day, which had to come from both Catholic and Protestant readership.

The type of practices defiantly inaugurated by Hughes represented what came to be called the "conservative" attitude. It was separatist, oriented toward European customs, and belligerent. Gibbons represented what came to be called the "liberal" attitude. It was integrative, patriotically American, and conciliatory. Generally conservatism prevailed in the East, liberalism in the South and West, with most victories going to liberalism. In the worldwide issue of ultramontanism that was causing so much division abroad, most Americans were on middle ground. Spalding arrived at the Vatican Council agreeing with those who felt that, although papal infallibility was a truth, proclamation of it was "inopportune." Then, however, repelled by what he felt to be the extremism of French and German inopportunists, he voted with the majority. This little slice of history showing Americans selecting theological alternatives from European leadership without either pronounced opinions or theological initiative of their own is typical of American Catholicism. And when we come to look at the American Catholic novel, we will see that theological innovation, such as that which animates *The New Story of Mouchette* or *The Power and the Glory*, is not a dramatic force in the works created by our Catholic writers.

There is no better way to measure the successful efforts of the Catholic liberals to integrate Catholics into American society than to observe the contrast between the reception given the first papal representative, Pius IX's Bedini in 1853, and what occurred forty years later when another attempt to send a representative was made by Leo XIII. Bedini was to carry a letter to President Franklin Pierce and then to tour the country. The hope of Pius IX was to make a tentative step toward some sort of official representation in Washington.[14] But the antipapal feelings of Italian Carbonari who had immigrated, the general American sympathy for Italian Republican aspirations, the Nativist tide of anti-Catholicism, and the rise of Know-Nothingism combined with false rumors that Bedini had been implicated in the execution of Italian Republicans to cause riots wherever the unfortunate legate attracted attention, and in Cincinnati he was nearly lynched. Wisely Rome withdrew him. Partly because of this earlier prudence and the long period of quiet that followed, partly because of changed circumstances, when Rome sent Archbishop Francis Satolli in 1892 to take a display of historic maps to the Chicago World's Fair, the reception was entirely different. By then the conservative Pius IX was dead, the liberal Leo XIII was pope, Italy had been a constitutional monarchy for two decades, the question of ever restoring the papal states was dying everywhere and among American Catholics was a vanished issue, and the blending of Catholicism and democratic patriotism was progressing rapidly under Gibbons. Convergence, not separatism, was the aim of Gibbons; and the leadership of the Church in America was in the hands of men who shared Gibbons' views. We hear echoes of Gibbons' typically patriotic language in Satolli's address in 1893 to the American Catholic Congress in Chicago: "Go forward, in one hand bearing the book of Christian truth and in the other the Constitution of the United States."[15] The phrasing is so typical of Gibbons that it is hard to believe he did not write it out for Satolli to speak. Though Satolli became a delegate in the American manner and had no official post *vis-à-vis* the government, he had considerable power over the Church, and his time was spent settling disputes between priests and their bishops, disputes which previously had to go to Rome, causing delay and confusion.

In 1892 Leo XIII was pleased and encouraged by the liberal Catholicism that had developed in America. When Satolli arrived in the United States, the nature of the American Church had been set for a century by its history in the new world. It was a Church completely cut off from the American civil government and glad of it. It was grateful for the opportunities provided by the United States for its hordes of immigrants and regarded patriotism as a religious duty. Above all, it was a busy and hard-working practical organization. The American Catholic cleric was from the beginning, typically, a man of action. He was a missionary in frontier territories, an educator of previously uneducated immigrant masses, and a builder of schools and churches, who battled for his parishioners against exploiters of the immigrant poor.

Protection of the working class had long been characteristic of the Church in the world of the immigrants. It was a largely Catholic organization, the Knights of Labor, which, under the leadership of the Catholic, Terence Powderly, in 1886 compelled capital in the person of Jay Gould to meet labor on equal terms for the first time. The American ritualistic societies, which were endemic in those years and of which the Knights were one of the largest and most powerful, were on occasion condemned by Rome as tending to become heretical semireligions in the pattern of European Masonry. There was also agitation against the Knights by Eastern conservatives in the hierarchy, who were in areas where some Catholics even at that early date were beginning to become middle class, and who were not nearly as prolabor as the Southerners and Westerners. But Gibbons and his fellow liberals, who were deeply moved by the hardships of the poor and the abuse of great wealth,[16] at this time had the ear of Rome; they fought for toleration of the Knights and won.[17] Meanwhile in the parishes ordinary priests were almost always wholeheartedly friends of the workers and often of the Knights, since the great majority of congregations still belonged to the laboring class. Later, Cardinal Gibbons, like Cardinal Manning in England, was instrumental in furthering the arguments that moved Leo XIII to publish the labor encyclical *Rerum Novarum* in 1891, just a year before the establishment of Satolli brought about the closer ties with Rome.

The alliance between the Church and labor in America reached back before the period of immigration. It can be traced to the early writings of the journalist and former Unitarian member of Brook Farm, Orestes Brownson, who was influenced by Lacordaire and by English Chartism, but whose views on exploitation went far beyond either. Brownson illustrates the persistent anti-industrial, antiexploitative stand taken by so many people in the nineteenth century who were to become converts to Catholicism. The Catholic ethic of brotherhood and cooperation both intrinsic in Christian doctrine and inherited from the guild spirit of the Middle Ages was in natural collision with the Puritan Protestant ethic of self-sufficiency and competition. People who rejected the Puritan Protestant ethic found Catholicism congenial. Even without influences from across the Atlantic, Brownson's conversion was both natural and in accord with nineteenth-century conversions elsewhere in the Western industrialized world. Brownson published his book, *The Laboring Classes* in 1840 and became a Catholic four years later. He considered wage slavery so much worse than any other evil that he believed the lives of Southern plantation slaves were secure and easy in comparison. Probably for this reason he agreed with the Catholic Chief Justice Taney on the Dred Scott decision in 1856, although condemnation of the slave trade by the papacy was centuries old, dating back to Pius II in 1462; and Gregory XVI had renewed the Church's stand in 1833.

Just as the alliance between American Catholics and the cause of the workingman reached back fifty years before Satolli's coming, so it stretched forward into the future, and achieved a culmination in the work of Minnesota-born Monsignor John A. Ryan, professor of labor relations and of moral theology at Catholic University.[18] Ryan was a typical Western Catholic liberal in the tradition of Minnesota's Archbishop Ireland. In 1919 Ryan drew up for the National Catholic War Council—later the National Catholic Welfare Conference—a document of central importance in American labor history. Entitled *Social Reconstruction,* its suggested reforms rallied not only liberals among American Catholics but were characteristic of most liberal programs. It is interesting to note how many of Ryan's proposals passed into American law or custom. Among his recommendations were minimum wages, public housing, health and old age insurance, legal enforcement of the right to organize, control of monopolies, an age limit for child labor, progressive taxes on income, inheritance, and excess profits, establishment of cooperatives, participation of labor in management, and worker ownership of stock in corporations. The president of the National Association of Manufacturers voiced the shock of the contemporary conservative community when he called Ryan's program "socialistic propaganda under the official insignia of the Roman Catholic Church in America."[19] In Ryan's work not only the traditional, antiexploitative orientation of the Church played a part but the sufferings of the immigrants. They had loyally adopted the country which had given them opportunity, but the long history of prejudice and injustice had caused deep wounds. An unhealthy manifestation of the inevitable resentment would have been anti-Americanism, hatred of the secular environment, or separation from the modern world in any of its forms. Luckily there was little of this because the energies that might have gone into feeding it were sublimated into the drive for reform. Nevertheless, as we shall see in the stories of J. F. Powers, sympathy for the workers, a drive for social justice, and hostility to the rich remained a hallmark of American Catholics, and the tradition was particularly strong in the Middle West, the West, and the South.

Even more important than Catholic liberalism, however, was a certain American orientation of the Catholic temperament, which began in the earliest times and continues today. As we have seen from our brief survey, activism, concern with practical, concrete affairs, from the beginning filled the lives of Catholic priests and of most Catholic laymen. What such priests and their lay companions were actually doing was giving a Catholic slant to particularly American characteristics, the feeling for liberty and justice, the desire for swift pragmatic action with visible results, the respect for hard work and material accomplishment. In addition, the fact that the American Church was cut off from interference by the American government, and until 1892 also was more cut off than the Church in other countries from the Catholic center in Rome, combined with the high value Americans set on energy and initiative to give most American Catholics a sense of independence and of the merits of individuals who get results. Portions of the Puritan ethic began to be absorbed by American Catholics and in subtle ways to transform the spirit of American Catholicism.

Although the nature of the transformation caused no official disquiet until 1895, circumstances that were finally to result in attracting Leo XIII's attention began much earlier. One of the most active and effective Catholic missionaries in the turbulent years of expansion following the Civil War was a young priest named Isaac Hecker. The son of German Protestants of the artisan class, Hecker had begun life as a baker[20] and learned at an early age to know the life of the American workman from the inside. After corresponding with Orestes Brownson, he was introduced to the Transcendentalist group and became a member of Brook Farm and of Fruitlands. Transcendentalism did not always go down well with the practical young ex-baker. Alcott, Emerson, and Thoreau seemed to him both to lack logic in doctrine and the necessary practical gifts required for living in community.[21] Converted with Brownson in 1844, Hecker joined the Redemptorists. Expelled for disagreement with a superior, largely over the question of whether the Redemptorists should commit themselves to German parish work or to work for the conversion of American non-Catholics, he founded the Paulists with the approval of Pius IX on behalf of the latter aim.[22] As a lecturer he attracted large audiences. He undertook to persuade Americans that the Church was not the enemy of patriotism, as Nativists had so long claimed, but that religion was patriotism's greatest ally—the message Gibbons was to take up.[23] In 1865 Hecker founded the periodical, the *Catholic World*, and a year later organized the Catholic Publication Society to distribute inexpensive pamphlets on a national scale. Hecker was sensitive to certain American ideas, which he wanted to draw into Catholicism and which, in the words of Father Walter Ong, were "liberty, the ideal of hard work, expansiveness, 'optimism,' and resourcefulness,"[24] an attitude that was to become typical of many American priests.

Hecker died in 1888. In 1890 a Midwestern Paulist, Father Walter Elliott, published *The Life of Father Hecker*. First signs of the coming storm were obscure. Monsignor Preston of New York, the diocese of Archbishop Corrigan, a conservative who had often disagreed with Gibbons, took issue with several of the various views publicly discussed after the book's publication— views widely prevalent in the Church in America. The beliefs Monsignor Preston thought he saw prevailing among enthusiasts for Elliott's book were these: that the government and atmosphere of the United States was the best possible and most suited to Catholicism; that all religions were conducive to salvation and Catholicism was only better and more complete; that the separation of Church and state was an unmitigated good in all circumstances; and that the papal states and temporal power of the pope were unnecessary.[25]

In 1897 the French Abbé Klein translated *The Life of Father Hecker*, and the beleaguered French Catholic Republicans hailed it as a charter for their hope of a free Church in a free state. But by this time the favorable view that a few years earlier Leo XIII had taken of French Republican Catholicism and the American system of separation of Church and state was beginning to fade, though the fading was not yet acknowledged in America, where the pope's approval had had a long and conspicuous history. Ten years before, in 1887, at the time of the celebration of the centennial of the American Constitution, Leo had written officially to Gibbons to say, "We desire that you should assure the President of Our admiration for the Constitution of the United States . . . because under its protection your Catholic countrymen have enjoyed a liberty which so confessedly has promoted the astonishing growth of their religion."[26] The previous year, when Gibbons had been made cardinal, he had said in his official sermon at his titular Roman church that while "despotism" harmed the Church, in the "genial atmosphere of liberty" it flourished, points Gibbons could make at that time with sure expectation of papal agreement, for the hostilities of European governments against the Church were painful, recent, and continuing. In 1892 Gibbons' good friend, Minnesota's Archbishop Ireland lectured in France at the request of the pope, and Ireland's exposition of the freedom of the Church from government interference in the United States was enthusiastically received.

This year, 1892, was the height of the pope's attempted *ralliement* of Catholics to the French Republic. It was also the height of papal approval for what was called the "American system." But then, as the *ralliement* began obviously to fail, a cloud appeared in the relations between Rome and Baltimore. Leo in a letter to the American hierarchy, *Longinqua Oceani* in 1895, observed that the Church in America might have been even more fruitful if it had enjoyed official status with the government. Three years later, after the publication in France of Abbé Klein's translation of *The Life of Father Hecker*, Abbé

Charles Maignen wrote the articles that resulted in his book
Études sur L'Américanism: le Père Hecker est-il un saint?
Maignen claimed that Hecker was "Protestantized," replacing
obedience to ecclesiastical direction with private initiative,
which he "covered" by calling it the inspiration of the Holy
Spirit, and also that Hecker impoverished Catholicism spiritually by watering doctrines for the sake of making converts.[27]

Leo XIII apparently felt that all the arguments of Maignen
and those who agreed with him contained a germ of truth, but it
was the accusation that America slighted the virtues of the spirit
to which he paid most attention in the condemnation of "Americanism" that shocked the liberal leaders of the American
Church in 1899 when the pope issued the encyclical *Testem
Benevolentiae.* Leo distinguished several errors. The Church
must not modify doctrines to suit modern civilization. It is in-
correct to assume that external spiritual direction is no longer
necessary. The natural virtues must not be extolled over the supernatural nor the active over the passive. It must not be thought
that the vows of religious orders are not compatible with Christian liberty. The irony of the condemnation was that Hecker was
a mystic and an expert spiritual director, he had been praised as
such by Elliott,[28] and far from being a despiritualized priest
who substituted action for prayer, he made prayer and contem-
plation the root of action from his earliest days.[29] But there existed in America tendencies that were indeed fair targets for the
criticisms that brought about *Testem Benevolentiae.* The priests
and missionaries in the new world had been so busy building
churches, working for social justice, overcoming poverty, establishing schools, and preaching missions that many of them now
behaved as if every good were to be achieved by active effort
with pragmatic results. Furthermore, in their reaction against
Nativism,[30] they often seemed to regard the act of fitting
smoothly into American life as the first duty of American Catholics, and to equate patriotism with religion to such a degree

that men like Ireland could not imagine any conflict between religion and patriotism. Ireland said, "I neither put Church before Country nor Country before Church. Church and Country work together in different spheres."[31] If the life of the spirit was not in actual retreat among American Catholics, it had certainly begun to suffer considerable confusion.

The intensity of the shock of the American liberal hierarchy at the publication of *Testem Benevolentiae* measures the degree to which liberals had been blind to criticism. The encyclical was only a culmination of a series of actions that had followed Leo's changed views after the failure of the *ralliement* led him to stop depending on some version of the American system for Catholic freedom in France, and after Archbishop Satolli had begun to come under the influence of American conservatives and express to Rome observations made by opponents of Ireland and Gibbons. In 1896 Dennis O'Connell, Gibbons' friend, personal delegate, and liberal rector of the American College in Rome, was forced to resign. The following year the liberal Bishop Keane was suddenly relieved by the pope of his office as rector of Catholic University. There were other repercussions, and men like Gibbons and Ireland were first stunned and bewildered, then inclined to attribute the whole issue to a misunderstanding.

Gibbons dutifully expressed American submission to *Testem Benevolentiae* but there is no sign that he afterwards made allowance for dangers from excess pragmatism or believed that American Catholics were riding perilously near spiritual shallows. His typical association of religion with patriotism never underwent any change. In the very process of installing Conaty, who was named by the Holy See as the new rector of Catholic University, he said, "The Constitution is adapted to the growth of the Catholic religion and the Catholic religion is suited to the Constitution. They fit together like two links of the same chain."[32] If Gibbons had been told that his statement was perhaps indeed true, but that it and possibly the entire attitude represented by some liberal Catholics was lacking in depth, he would have thought his critic had gone mad. Supporting the nation, furthering freedom and equality, educating the illiterate, working for social justice, of what could these be accused?

If the cult of activism and the effort to fit into American life had continued to flourish only as patriotism or the quest for social reform, their later development would have been less serious, but the spiritual impoverishment that early critics had felt in it made headway in predictable directions. The laboring population of the old immigration became, by the second or third generation, middle class—first, as we have noted, in the East, and then in the rest of the country. Middle-class desires, middle-class morality, and middle-class diversions gradually replaced the old needs, the old causes. By the 1930s if a young curate from a poor family was to be found taking a liberal point of view on labor questions or spading up the earth with the over-worked parish gardener or loaning his overshoes to a marcher on a depression picket line, as is the case in one of J. F. Powers' stories,[33] his pastor on the other hand owned an expensive car, was a friend of wealthy parishioners, and accepted funds from corporation heads, receiving them with gratitude whether or not company policies dovetailed with *Rerum Novarum* or *Quadragesimo Anno*. The views of the American middle class, with its heritage from the Puritan Protestant ethic, were now changing American Catholicism still further. It is this change Powers is opposing. He is at the same time opposing the distortions of "Americanism." The pastor in Powers' story, in spite of his illiberal, antilabor views, was a descendant of Gibbons and Hecker, an heir of the nineteenth century. He was a seeker of welfare for his parish and prestige for Catholicism by trying to fit into American life as *he* saw it in his own new time. The aims of "Americanism" were still his, though oddly turned around, for such a pastor would regard with suspicion the social action that had been the mainstay of earlier Americanists. The monsignor of Powers' story found his young curate "reading *The Catholic Worker* one day and had not trusted him since."[34] By 1930 to most pastors, fitting into the American scene meant fitting into the middle class, which was the material support of the Church. Spiritually impoverished by a long heritage of Americanist belief in the importance of getting results, such a pastor as the one portrayed by Powers was blind to the spiritual implications of his position. Indeed he was blind to most spiritual implications of any sort, including those of his own unspirituality. Until Powers came along and made the American unspiritual priest the subject of satire, he was—to himself, to most American Catholics, and to most Americans—so much part of a customary picture that no one gave him any particular attention.

There was, however, in the United States a trait in the development of Catholic thought which made it certain that in the long run the flaws of despiritualized Catholicism would be seen. This trait was Catholic Puritanism, whose central ideas are similar to those we encountered in France as Jansenism. The elements of American Catholic Puritanism are encountered more as an atmosphere than as a heresy, and they are more difficult to pin down than the French Jansenist heritage which stemmed from the specific errors of Port Royal. Nevertheless, one can say that there is a distinctly American Catholic spirit which has two sources, an earlier one in the Jansenism imported into the United States from France, and a later one that came after the Irish immigration with the Irish religious reform. Certain attitudes are found separately or in combination. Human nature may be regarded as so depraved that it is believed man's first natural impulse is to do evil. Sex may be regarded as the most serious of sins, if not synonymous with sin. Beneficent human actions may be seen as not resulting even partly from man's choice but entirely from supernatural grace. And, finally, in consequence of these views of almost total natural depravity, man's free will in choosing his own fate may be regarded as minimal, while God's election is an irresistible force. There is a strong resemblance to French Jansenism, but Jansenism's traits have been exaggerated and reinforced.

It would seem that French Jansenism was established very early in the new world. Its greatest object of attack was always Jesuitism. In Louisiana, before the papal bull ordering the suppression of the Jesuits had been issued, Louisiana did not wait for the action of the French government—which also anticipated the bull—but forcibly expelled its Jesuits as soon as news reached the colony that suppression had been decided.[35] Wherever there were French priests in any number there were apt to be some who had Jansenist tendencies, and not only was the first American seminary, Saint Mary's in Baltimore, founded in 1790, staffed by French priests, but also for years French seminaries trained American priests or sent over French priests to minister to Americans. Bishop Loras, born in Lyons in 1792, was brought to this country in 1829 by Bishop Ortier of Mobile, and became the first bishop of Dubuque in 1837, having brought two more French priests and two seminarians to work with him.[36] Bishop Fitzpatrick, who instructed Hecker in 1844 before his conversion, had been trained in France, and Archbishop Hughes of New York suggested that Hecker go to France to prepare for ordination.[37] Archbishop Hughes' predecessor in his diocese had been French. Archbishop Ireland of Minnesota had been trained in France. French ideas and background were widespread.

American Jansenism with roots in French influence met a current that undoubtedly strengthened it during the Irish immigration. Maynooth, the first Irish seminary, was founded in 1795 and had two French priests on its staff. French refugees and French priests were present in Ireland from 1793. More important, however, was the Puritan spirit of the Irish religious reform of the nineteenth century. Irish morals had fallen to a low ebb during the disorders of earlier years. A letter of the bishop of Elphin in 1826 reported, "attendance at Mass on Sundays, not to talk of festivals, was disregarded and innumerable couples had lived as man and wife who had never been married and many others in flagrant and notorious adultery." "Hundreds of persons had not been at Confession for 20 years. . . ."[38] One of the great difficulties in Ireland had been the large population, too large for the country to feed, and, as far as the Church was concerned, too large to be reached by the limited number of priests. By 1840, however, famine and emigration reduced the Irish in Ireland by twenty percent,[39] and was to reduce them still further until by mid-century that stricken and tragic country for the first time had a population of relatively manageable size. A series of energetic bishops, priests, and missionaries inaugurated a religious reform that became a major civilizing influence. Because of the conditions it had to combat, the reform from the beginning was Puritanical in spirit, dwelling most heavily on moral and sexual sins.

Irish priests coming to America during and after the migrations carried this spirit with them, particularly in later years as the Irish Reform Movement became more powerful. Great numbers of the immigrant Irish had been forced by famine and destitution into an almost animal level of existence long before they left Ireland in the typhus-ridden "coffin ships"; and, as the survivors collected in American ghettos, conditions there became much the same as those described by the bishop of Elphin. In the task of humanizing this people reduced to barbarism, their priests adopted the Irish reformist focus on chastity and the dangers stemming from original sin. The strain of Jansenism already present in the United States fitted in well with the teachings of the reformers, and there resulted a blend of ideas that stressed man's natural sinfulness, the dangers of sex, the weakness and infirmity of man's flawed will, and the need for God's grace, which one found still being preached in typical missions and parishes around the country well into the years after the Second World War. These doctrines had been all the more easily absorbed because the Catholic immigration had established itself in a Protestant world where a Calvinist heritage with similar teachings was as old as colonial times.

Thus American Catholic Puritanism took vigorous root, and it is no accident that Flannery O'Connor makes her symbolic heroes members of American fundamentalist sects. Catholic Puritanism's shortcomings, its inclination to minimize freedom of the will and God's granting of choice to all men, its habit of seeing the powers of darkness as stronger than the powers of light in life on earth, tend toward theological error. There is no denying, however, that, in its very gloom, American Catholic Puritanism had a keenness of vision typical of any people who scrutinize themselves and others expecting the worst. This trait, which makes it a deadly foe of all errors other than its own, is a substantial asset in giving a writer ideas of his environment that lend themselves to drama, particularly of the darker variety.

In the United States the Catholic Puritan spirit was perhaps also aided by the fact that immigrant communities developed a sense of inferiority. They tended to feel that their own cultures were lower than those of the surrounding or secular environments. Critical self-appraisal and lowered self-esteem are typical reactions of underprivileged minority groups in America. Where Mauriac, Bernanos, and Greene attacked only false religion, J. F. Powers and Flannery O'Connor often seem to attack all religion. The Catholic novelists we considered in other countries pointed out decadence in the secular world and the false religiosity of corrupted Catholicism, while they saw a contrasting world of genuinely religious people. Even though the genuinely religious were often as fallible as Graham Greene's whiskey priest, nevertheless they were closer to the good than were their opponents. J. F. Powers and Flannery O'Connor, however, seem to regard the world of religion as at least as dark as the world of secularism, and, if good exists in their characters at all, it is simply as the result of God's grace. In the American Catholic novels there is no Curé d'Ambricourt or Abbé Donissan or any figure corresponding to Rose, the tenderly portrayed heroine of *Brighton Rock*.

The determinist tendencies of the Irish Catholic Puritan reformers may have been particularly hard to resist because of the low state of theological studies in Ireland. Original sin and reliance on grace are simple doctrines, while the doctrine of balance between man's free will and God's foreknowledge is complex. In Ireland under the English oppression the land of the saints and scholars had become a land of intellectual as well as physical starvation. For centuries the only university was Anglican. If Catholic Reform Puritanism came to the United States with the Irish, so did many of the stigmata of Irish intellectual poverty, which accorded readily with the tendencies of nineteenth-century American Catholics to value pragmatic mission work and church building over any possible contribution toward exploring theological complexities. When the board of trustees of the newly founded Catholic University approved a request to have the hierarchy circularized in order to increase its meager student body, Gibbons complied with a letter urging every bishop to send at least one candidate, but it is significant that Gibbons himself was reproached indirectly for poor attendance from his own diocese.[40] The shortage of priests and the demands of practical parish work made higher studies almost impossible. An attitude spread throughout the American Catholic community that, while it was necessary to overcome the illiteracy of the immigrants, further learning was of little importance compared to maintaining and spreading the faith. The need for intellectual training in the very enterprise of maintaining the faith was for years—indeed until recently—very largely overlooked.

Those who could most readily understand the dangers of American Catholic Puritanism with its lack of emphasis on education, its view of natural depravity, and its slighting of human choice were most notably Jansenism's ancient European enemies, the Jesuits, with their emphasis on freedom of the will and its necessary training. After the order was reestablished in America in 1806 through a papally tolerated link with the never-suppressed portion of the Society that had survived in Russia because of Catherine the Great's esteem for Jesuit scholarship, American Jesuits became the educators of the upper class of Catholics but not of the American Catholic people. In the same pattern as in Europe after the restoration of 1814, it was years before Jesuit views and Jesuit schools were able to reach the populace. The attitude of American Protestants, to whom the word "Jesuit" had long represented all that was supposedly most dishonest and amoral about Catholicism, no doubt was instrumental in inhibiting spread of the order's influence.[41]

That Catholic novels begin so late in America is probably due to the low regard in which American Catholics for so long held the life of the intellect. Most American Catholics did not become sufficiently self-aware intellectually to produce or even read significant Catholic literature until the decade before the Second World War, when Mauriac, Bernanos, and Greene enjoyed their first wide audience. Before that period, there were in the nineteenth and early twentieth centuries American writers who were Catholics—the poets Joyce and Aline Kilmer, the essayist Agnes Repplier, for example—but none of them were "Catholic writers." Willa Cather did not write "Catholic novels" in the sense we have used in this essay. Her books are typical of the best of American regional fiction and represent the spirit of a developing country. *Death Comes for the Archbishop* does show Archbishop Latour and Father Vaillant as followers of their master, Christ, but the novel's theology is universally

Christian rather than Roman Catholic and cannot be said to come within the terms of our definition: that Catholic novels to be so called must depend for their mainsprings of dramatic action upon Roman Catholic theology, or upon the thinking of one of the world's large Roman Catholic communities, or upon development of Roman Catholic ideas in Newman's sense. The popularity of *Death Comes for the Archbishop* when it was published in 1927 may show, however, a diminution of the anti-Catholic prejudice toward Catholic culture in the United States, although the political prejudice was still strong, as was to be virulently illustrated when Alfred E. Smith ran for president the following year.

With J. F. Powers and Flannery O'Connor, novels which depended directly upon the history of thought within the American Catholic community began to be written, and a new American art was born. Although "development" of ideas seldom could provide themes because of the low state of American theological studies, the typical orientations of American Catholic traditions often did. Forty-four million Catholics, nearly a quarter of the population, were living in a country where, as in France and England earlier, the separation of the Catholic community was breaking down and curiosity about the lives and beliefs of Catholics was rising. It was helped by the revival of the particularly American spirit of toleration which was as old as the nation, and which finally by the time of John F. Kennedy was to do away with even most political prejudice. At the same time self-understanding surged to higher levels among American Catholics, who became ready for the sort of self-scrutiny that in Europe had produced the best Catholic novels. J. F. Powers and Flannery O'Connor then appeared and found their audience waiting for them.

J. F. Powers

J. F. Powers published his first book of short stories, *Prince of Darkness*, in 1948. Most of his best achievements in the short story are, I believe, in this early collection. It is well to begin by categorizing them briefly because they indicate how he developed a variety of skills which later, in his novel *Morte d'Urban*, came together.

For instance, the short story, "The Old Bird," is a sensitive, furious portrayal of the sufferings of an unemployed man too old to get any job except as a clerk in a wrapping room; "The Trouble" is the story of anti-Negro whites rioting through a Negro ghetto in the South and beating a Negro mother to death; and "The Eye" is about a Negro who saves a white woman from drowning and then is lynched for having supposedly raped her. All three are apologues: that is, as we saw earlier in the work of Evelyn Waugh, the strongest emotions come not from our sympathy for the characters but from empathetic anger at the statements made by the action. With Powers these are statements not about the decadence of the secular world—which was Waugh's theme—but about social injustice in the United States, an American Catholic preoccupation more than a century old, and a central spur to action since the time of Ryan. Powers was born in southern Illinois, and it will be remembered that Cathol-

icism in the West and South was historically the most liberal.
Conservatives were in the earlier days generally found in the
East. Even Powers' first fiction, however, is not limited to themes
of social justice and criticism of the non-Catholic environment.
The very early "Lions, Harts, Leaping Does" is based on the
teachings of John of the Cross and is a gentle but profound
appraisal of the spiritual limitations of a dying American Fran-
ciscan, a character study of a man who has had a dry and extremely narrow spiritual life, but who endures his dark night
of the soul with steadfast simplicity and goes to meet his God
like a bird let out of a cage. But there is no gentleness in the title
story, "Prince of Darkness," and very little in the other story
about priests, "The Wrong Forks." Like all the Catholic writers
we have examined, Powers finds the world corrupted in spirit,
and he is in angry and uncompromising opposition. "The Wrong
Forks" almost as much as "Prince of Darkness" is a savage satire, a depiction of the unspiritual American priest as he
emerged into the twentieth century. Before we proceed to examine Powers' priests, however—the portraits for which he is
best known—we should note that in his first collected volume he
shows mastery of three quite different but often overlapping
forms: he can express his opposition by satire, by penetration of
character, or by the use of statement we have called apologue.
His satiric plots are bitter, as in "Prince of Darkness," yet he
never carries them into the viciousness that would make the
reader put down the book. His character portrayals are compassionate, as in "Lions, Harts, Leaping Does," yet the tenderness
does not overflow into bathos. And in his use of apologue he
makes his points with the conviction of sheer rage, but even in
"The Eye" his characters are too real and the reader is too convinced by them ever to dismiss the work as propaganda.

Powers' novel, *Morte d'Urban*, which was published in 1962
and won the National Book Award, is like "Prince of Darkness"

and "The Wrong Forks" concerned with criticism of the American Catholic community and is a study of an American priest. A good way to approach the novel, therefore, is to see first how Powers handled these two earlier short studies. "The Wrong Forks" is the story referred to in the last chapter in which a conservative pastor, loyal to the upper-class interests of the parishioners who financially support the Church, duels with his liberal young curate, who comes from a working-class background and doesn't know how to use his forks properly. The crisis comes when the pastor receives a check as a personal gift, an annual offering from the "Rival Corporation," which is "plagued by strikes and justly so."[1] Young Father Eudex (a name suggesting "judex" or judge) also receives a check from Rival. First, as he tells his outraged pastor, he considers endorsing it, a hundred dollars, to the strikers' relief fund. " 'So,' Monsignor said calmly—years in the confessional had prepared him for anything."[2] The tone of the satire throughout is of this muted variety. At first you hesitate before you are sure it is there; then it begins to snag your attention like barbed wire. Powers is merciless in applying it to the monsignor, gentler and more humorous in applying it to the young priest, but the latter is a flawed hero. He neither sends his check to the strikers' relief fund nor performs any other act of significance to his depression period. He ends by merely tearing his Rival check to shreds and flushing it down the toilet. He is thus exposed as a man of good intentions condemned to ineffectiveness, which Powers shows as a particularly painful condition, one carrying with it a sense of guilt and absurdity.

Although Powers tellingly satirizes both the old priest and the young one, it cannot be said that what he satirizes in either is lack of spiritual depth but rather a failure to get results. If we are to say that the two priests, each in his own way, is an activist in the American tradition, with respect focused on pragmatism, so at this time is Powers himself. There is no sign yet that he attributes ineffectiveness to failure of the spirit. That insight is yet to be expressed.

"Prince of Darkness" is a stronger satire than "The Wrong Forks." We have sympathy for Father Eudex, but we have no sympathy for Father Burner, who gets his title as "Prince of Darkness" from his hobby of developing photographs in his darkroom. Father Burner left the seminary as an activist of the most devoted kind. For an ordination gift he asked for a watch instead of the usual chalice—" 'time is money,' was his thought, 'sacred, like the host.' "[3] One is reminded that Cardinal Gibbons' first dated and extant sermon was on "The Good Use of Time."[4] American Catholic tradition was firm in regard to the most energetic possible use of man's mortal span, and Father Burner's further step was simply a natural one for his generation in the priesthood. He had joined the middle class and adopted the modern business sense: he equated time with financial gain.

Father Burner has all the habits of a priest of his type. He is an enthusiastic golfer, saying to himself that he is not "too proud to meet souls halfway wherever it might be, in the confessional or on the fairways."[5] He is not an aid to "souls" in either place. A devastating scene shows his failure in the confessional, and the uselessness of his endless games of golf is indicated by a fellow priest's joke, "Saint Ernest Burner, Help of Golfers, Pray for Us!"[6] Father Burner's activism is even more ineffective than that of Father Eudex, for while Eudex's activities in gardening or lending strikers his overshoes at least had some point, Father Burner's have no point at all. Burner takes flying lessons (action for its own sake, since he can hardly suppose he will meet souls on the airways) and in his fantasies he imagines himself a German war pilot. Until the First World War the family name had been Boerner, not Burner, and in his war hero role Father Burner affixes a "proud 'von.' "[7] Powers is

reflecting the old Irish Catholic hostility to the more national-
istic immigrant Germans. The scene also recalls the patriotism
of Irish Catholics, for clearly it is an additional mark of
Burner's general repulsiveness that he imagines himself a *German* war pilot.

It is refreshing that at least Powers does not show Father
Burner advancing rapidly in the Church. Burner is the oldest
man in his seminary class still without a parish. The climax of
the story comes when the archbishop, one evening after Father
Burner has been summoned to help with confessions at the Cathedral, gives him an envelope and tells him not to look at the
message until after his Mass in the morning. Father Burner of
course opens it in his car that night as soon as he is safely away
from the Cathedral. He supposes that it is the long-awaited ap-
pointment giving him his own parish. It is a transfer making
him once more an assistant in a new locality.

There are foils for Father Burner in the story, a young vicar
general, whom the archbishop has been promoting swiftly, and
the archbishop himself. But while there are details apparently
intended to indicate that these are spiritual men, the details are
slight. The archbishop has holes in the toes of his bedroom
slippers,[8] and seems to have what Powers, as a liberal intellectual in the American Catholic tradition, would consider a correct attitude toward the rich: " 'Yes, the rich have souls. . . .
But if Christ were really with them they would not be themselves
. . . that is to say, rich.' "[9] But the archbishop shows a cat and
mouse malice in handling Father Burner, and the portrait of
holiness—if any is intended—soon disintegrates. So with the
young vicar general: if, indeed, as is rumored among lesser
men "of the cloth" he is "troubled with sanctity,"[10] there is no
sign even of humanity, either in his brusque reminder to the
penitents kneeling in the Cathedral that they should get themselves into confessionals without further delay, or in his coolness
to Father Burner as he announces that the archbishop will see

him. One cannot accuse these stories of Catholic Puritanism in the sense that Powers' characters do not have free will. Free will is demonstrated in Father Eudex as he wrestles with various alternatives in deciding what to do with his check and in Father Burner when he opens the archbishop's message, but in Powers' total view there is certainly that element of Puritanism which views the influence of original sin in the flesh and on earth as stronger than the influence of light. The men of light—the archbishop and the vicar general—are, like Father Eudex, flawed figures. On the other hand, the "prince of darkness" is complete in his unspirituality. Powers' stories have a bleakness we have not seen since we looked at Mauriac, and, as we will see, this bleakness persists in his novel. Waugh at least presented us with an innocent victim, Paul Pennyfeather. In Powers, if innocence is present at all, it is never drawn fully enough so that we can be really sure it is there.

Powers' novel, *Morte d'Urban*, has for its hero an almost perfect specimen of the modern American activist priest. No doubt as a former seminarian Powers had more insight into Americanism in the priesthood than the average American Catholic. Certainly he understands it, and he dissects its modes of progress with a skill almost surgical in its merciless precision. Father Urban was recruited for the priesthood by Father Placidus. Father Placidus' "main concern after his religion was athletics" and "after God and Sport came Song. . . ." Father Placidus was usually "on the road," a traveling salesman for Catholicism, preaching for a minor order of missionaries and retreatants, the Clementines. Or he was off taking the Clementine Choristers or the Clementine athletic teams "on the road" in their turn.[11] Father Urban is the heir of Father Placidus. When Father Urban preaches missions, the parish churches clamoring for his presence will hardly hold the crowds because his sermons are ornamented with similes from spectator sports and please their audiences with an easy mixture of Rotary uplift and afterdinner comment. Like Father Placidus before him, Father Urban is such an activist that difficulties only spur him to added resourcefulness. When the unsympathetic head of the Clementines transfers the too successful Father Urban to a remote country branch of the Order, an old house in Minnesota willed to them by an eccentric Catholic, Father Urban gets a wealthy Catholic friend, Billy Cosgrove, to buy the surrounding land, and creates the area's most popular retreat house, one with a golf course. When Father Urban takes over a run-down local parish whose facilities are too small for the burgeoning Catholic suburb growing out of the real estate developments surrounding it, he energetically inaugurates a parish census and prepares for building a larger church. Whatever Father Urban's failings, lack of pragmatic success is not among them—and this is a reversal of the situation Powers portrayed with Father Eudex and Father Burner. Powers has developed. His target this time is failure of the spirit, not lack of success. Powers has looked at the American Catholic community and seen in it the fulfillment of the worst of the fears that almost half a century earlier had led to *Testem Benevolentiae*.

Morte d'Urban is prefaced by a quotation from Barrie, "The life of every man is a diary in which he means to write one story, and writes another. . . ." The diary Father Urban meant to write is quite clear. He intended to be a popular missionary (Powers has drawn a cruel parody of Hecker's descendants) ;[12] a great builder (all successful American priests had to be "brick and mortar men" from the time of the immigrants) ; and a friend of influential people who can assist the Church (this has precedent too: one recalls Cardinal Gibbons' friendships with United States presidents). Urban is likable, he has a quick intelligence, and he is skilled at manipulating people into what he wants them to do.

Nevertheless, everything goes wrong. For one thing, Urban, who himself shuns most of the seven deadly sins and is not proud, envious, lustful, lazy, gluttonous, or given to anger, is surrounded by people who do have these shortcomings. Billy Cosgrove, the BCL (Big Catholic Layman) who is his rich sponsor, is a fool and a brute and eventually deserts Urban in anger because on a hunting expedition the priest will not let him drown a swimming deer. The bishop, who might have turned over to Urban the area where he prepared so effectively to build, instead of giving the parish to the Clementines, appoints a new rector, and Urban is never able to bring forth the fruits of his labor. The bishop is suspected of having his eye on the mission-cum-golf course Urban has developed and of planning to appropriate it to the diocese as a seminary. In an accident the hostile bishop, while playing golf with Urban, hits him on the head with a powerfully driven golf ball. The bishop apparently is not unacquainted with compunction, and he afterwards leaves the Clementines their golf course, but the stricken Urban not only has to be hospitalized, but when he is elected as superior of the Clementines, his injury makes him so forgetful and confused that the benefit the Clementines hoped to get from his well-known energy never materializes, and the Order slips back into the habitual ineffectiveness that always characterized it outside the immediate sphere of its members like Urban or Placidus.

In his book on Powers, John Hagopian makes a good deal of the elements from Malory in *Morte d'Urban* and seems to believe these carry some hidden significance not yet quite clear. Though it is important to note this framework, I rather doubt that Malory is used as Mr. Hagopian seems to believe. It seems obvious that *Morte d'Urban* does not involve any detailed one-for-one correspondence with Malory, but that the evocations of Malory are a loosely infused mocking refrain designed to reinvoke at suitable intervals the wildly dissonant thematic unity of the serious with the insanely funny that give the work resonance. To cast the life of Father Urban, the supersalesman of the Church, as a parody of epic was a brilliant inspiration. The

story of Father Urban is as serious as it is comic. If we understand the consequence of the existence of priests like Father
Urban in the American Catholic community, our laughter at his
blunders is mingled with bitterness and outraged concern. Powers has put the mock heraldic shield of Urban on the title page.
On one side are the skyscrapers of the city; on the other, the
pines of the Clementines' country retreat. The shield is topped
by Urban's helmet, which ends in a stag's head. The motto, "Be
a Winner," is underneath. In the center is Urban's castle of
temptation, where he encountered Sally Thwaites, who attempted to seduce him.

It is Sally who gives us our deepest insight into Urban's
character. He is trying to persuade her to return to the Church,
and she says,

> "Do you enjoy my company?"
> "As a matter of fact, I do."
> "But that isn't why you're here, is it?"
> "No, not exactly. I don't feel it should be, do you?"
> Sally didn't reply to the question. "You say you're always dis-
> appointed by people who're trying to go it alone."
> "Not by the people themselves but by their reasons."
> "Has it occurred to you that people might be disappointed by
> you and your reasons, and even more by you?"
> "I'm not sure I know what you mean," said Father Urban.
> "I mean you're an operator—a trained operator. . . ."[13]

Sally's accusation that Urban is a "trained operator," a professional "operating" within his profession, and that as a man
of God he is spiritually barren, has by this time been sufficiently
demonstrated for the reader so that he has considerable sympathy with her. This does not minimize the shock, however, when
Sally then considers it appropriate to take off her clothes and
stand naked before Urban, for while Urban is not a saint neither
is he a sinner, but occupies some amorphous ground in between.
Failing to get a response, Sally furiously throws her shoes at

him and goes ashore, leaving him marooned. The scene is wildly funny, a masterpiece of the incongruous—yet it is entirely convincing, something that between a Sally Thwaites and a Father Urban might easily take place.

The scene occurs near the end of the book. It reveals the reason for Father Urban's failures—not any shortcomings of intelligence or will, but sheer emptiness. Where his spirit should be, Urban has a vacuum. He cannot draw to himself the spiritual allegiances of other people: he cannot win the bishop's respect, change the brutal Billy, or convert the unbelieving Sally. The effect that Bernanos' Donissan has on Mouchette, or d'Ambricourt has on the Countess, the effect that the martyrdom of Greene's whiskey priest has on the boy, Luis, is completely beyond the powers of a Father Urban, although he is far more practical and able than Donissan, d'Ambricourt, or even the persistent and resourceful whiskey priest.

A great deal of Powers' art is in his style. Here is his portrayal of a minor character, a young priest gone wrong, whom Urban straightens out and gets to spend less time praying and more on useful Christian activities, such as raising money.

> It became pretty clear to Father Urban that Johnny in his last two years in seminary, had fallen into the clutches of Manichees on the faculty. Unlike them, he had been bold. In fact, he had got so far out of line in his final year—giving up smoking and so on— that he'd come within an ace of not being ordained. For about three years, you might say, Johnny had been in a coma. Johnny had been all right before. In high school he had been voted all-state in hockey.[14]

This paragraph explains why there are never any d'Ambricourt-type priests in Powers' books. In Powers' view of American Catholicism, the d'Ambricourts would never make it through an American ordination.

Father Urban's change of character after the episode with the golf ball again raises the question of free will in Powers' fiction. We cannot say that Father Urban is like Father Eudex in weighing alternatives and choosing his way. Rather his way is chosen for him by the accident. Father Urban is not shown responding to grace, he is shown being overwhelmed by the bishop's blow. To the degree that Urban is helpless before circumstances, he at the end becomes a puppet, and Powers has swung away from his earlier orientation to enter more deeply into the spirit of the American Jansenist and Irish Puritan heritage. It is hard to stir much emotional response to the puppet-like Urban at the end. Whatever our sympathy for him before, we feel a reduction in dramatic power, and the astringent comedy of the "conversion by golf ball" does not leave us as moved as we would have been if Urban had been led to change his character by some process of self-criticism or growth of insight. But this is precisely the point. Father Urban was simply not capable of that much self-criticism or growth of insight. If his conversion had not come about by golf ball, it would not have come about at all.

The bitterness in this book is darker than any that appeared in Powers' earlier work, even in such cruel stories as "The Eye." In "The Eye" human beings were responsible for the events. In *Morte d'Urban* chance determines Urban's fate. Chance brings Urban Billy Cosgrove, the BCL who finances his projects and is responsible for so much of his spiritual inanity. Chance throws Sally Thwaites into Urban's path. Chance directs the bishop's golf ball. Many other events are equally strokes of ill fortune. It would appear not only from the story's conclusion but from the whole course of the action that the order of being itself is shown as malignant. The fragile acceptance of grace which Urban demonstrates by his humility in the closing pages is a thin radiance illuminating a darkened void. Again one recalls Mauriac, but one feels that Powers, the heir to American Catholic Puritanism, has an even more somber view than that taken by the descendant of the French Jansenists. For Mauriac, grace is all-powerful and we are often reminded of the life that Catholics believe follows death. Powers never turns our attention toward eternity, and his novel thus is cast further into shadow by lack of the dimension that had been important in Catholic aesthetics since Maritain and Claudel, and, if we except Powers' master, Waugh, had played a part in nearly all the European Catholic novels since Huysmans and Belloc. Powers is so astringent, indeed so flatly earthbound, that any mention of an afterlife, or even any intimation that it exists, would be dissonant—impossible to take seriously simply by the mode of his fiction. The same of course was true of *Decline and Fall* and *A Handful of Dust*, but Waugh was not writing about the Catholic community.

In Powers' design for *Morte d'Urban*, the chief source of its effect is in its statement, and the book functions as an apologue, the form we first saw when considering Evelyn Waugh. The statement Powers makes in *Morte d'Urban* is that America's priests are despiritualized and are at the heart of a despiritualized American Catholic religious life. When we considered the early growth of the Catholic novel in France, we saw that the major French Catholic authors avoided the moralizing form. Writing a novel to illustrate a thesis was not the mode of creative procedure adopted by either Bernanos or Mauriac. Waugh, however, wrote to illustrate his findings about his world, and Powers does the same. The problem with this kind of writing is its reliance on the central statement. Once Powers has made his statement that America's priests are despiritualized, he seems to have used up a large part of what he has to say. When the statement has been registered, the novel's impact exhausts itself— specially if one is familiar with Powers' short stories, many of which make the same statement. Powers, however, for some time has been in Ireland working on another book said to be about a priest and his curate, and the *New Yorker* has published stories which may indicate a new direction in which Powers is now moving. In the stories a middle-aged pastor is given a young assistant of the post-Vatican II type. The assistant's focus is on such matters as liturgical simplicity and social reform. His simplicity tends to come out as sappiness; his reformism seems to be largely a matter of poses. Apparently the unspiritual revolutionary is to be Powers' new target. Social reform as a Catholic aim has been primary with Powers since the beginning, but deleting all spiritual awareness in favor of social awareness is seen as the blasphemy it is. This constitutes a provocative insight in the best self-reflexive tradition of Catholic art. One may, therefore, expect Powers' work in progress to be an interesting and perhaps compelling element in the continuing dynamic of developing Catholicism.

Flannery O'Connor

Flannery O'Connor's achievement is very different from that of J. F. Powers'. Her stories do not lend themselves to extracting formulas. As with Mauriac, Bernanos, and Greene, to separate thesis from plot in a work of Flannery O'Connor's is impossible. The thesis *is* the plot and the plot *is* the thesis.

If we found it rewarding to get a preliminary view of Powers' technique by first glancing at his handling of the short story, such an introductory scrutiny is even more illuminating with Flannery O'Connor, whose work is more complex. One of her most easily understood stories, as well as one of her most enjoyable, is "The Artificial Nigger." Its chief characters are, as often in her fiction, an adult and a child—in this case an old man and his grandson. Mr. Head is an elderly Southern Cracker, an ignorant, shrewd, unschooled, poor country dweller. He is like many of Miss O'Connor's figures in whom we are intended to see ourselves: he is a smaller, simpler reproduction of everyman, distorted to such a degree that as we see ourselves more and more clearly, we are more and more outraged by a sense of the grotesque. We begin our encounter with Mr. Head by looking down on him—we who are educated people, or at any rate educated enough to read Flannery O'Connor and at least we think we understand her meanings, until deeper penetration teaches us how much we have been missing and makes us wonder unhappily how much we may be missing still. Mr. Head not only supposes he comprehends himself and the world, he fancies himself an example, for "only with years does a man enter into that calm understanding of life that makes him a suitable guide for the young."[1] Mr. Head's grandson, Nelson, represents the young whom Mr. Head intends to guide. Nelson is a ten-year-old who has youth's inborn conviction that he knows everything.

The action begins on the day Mr. Head takes Nelson on his first trip to the city. Hardly are they off the train before Mr. Head, that omniscient guide, gets thoroughly lost. Worse, he wanders into the Negro section, a mysterious, awesome, contemptible place inhabited entirely by black people. Where Mr. Head and Nelson live there are no "niggers," and Nelson has never seen one. The old man and the boy are badly shaken— black faces staring at them, not a white face anywhere. The duel between the old man who considers himself worthy and the child who considers himself complete is unresolved, however, for neither admits his state to the other. The pride of each refuses to fall, though inwardly it is tottering.

At last Mr. Head and Nelson find their way back to the white section, where they sit down in exhaustion and Nelson falls asleep. Mr. Head seizes his advantage.

> He justified what he was going to do on the grounds that it is sometimes necessary to teach a child a lesson he won't forget, particularly when the child is always reasserting his position with some new impudence.[2]

Mr. Head walks a few paces and sits on a garbage can around the corner. Nelson when he wakes will not see him.

The boy opens his eyes. Finding his grandfather gone, he gives a shout of terror and begins to flee through the streets. He hurtles into a woman with a bag of groceries. She falls, screams that the boy has broken her ankle, and shouts "Police!"[3] just as the pursuing Mr. Head catches up. The terrified boy clutches the old man.

> Mr. Head sensed the approach of the policeman from behind. He stared straight ahead at the women who were massed in their fury like a solid wall to block his escape. "This is not my boy," he said. "I never seen him before."

The women are horrified by so blatant a betrayal. Nelson obviously *is* Mr. Head's boy because the two look exactly alike. Silently they open a lane before the old man and he walks through it. Nelson follows twenty paces behind. There is no policeman. Mr. Head had imagined him.

After a while Mr. Head stops and offers to buy Nelson a coke. Nelson simply turns his back. Estranged, the two go to catch the train back to the country. But then by the road in front of someone's walled residence they meet an astonishing vision. Someone has created and someone else has installed in front of his dwelling a seated plaster statue—of a Negro holding a watermelon. For the old countryman and the boy amazement at so incredible a phenomenon is identical. "Mr. Head breathed, 'An artificial nigger!' . . . 'an artificial nigger!' Nelson repeated in Mr. Head's exact tones."[4] This "great mystery," symbolic of all the mysteries of the universe beyond the ken of either, acts upon them, "dissolving their differences like an action of mercy."

> Mr. Head had never known before what mercy felt like because he had been too good to deserve any, but he felt he knew now. He looked at Nelson and understood that he must say something to the child to show that he was still wise and in the look the boy returned he saw a hungry need for that assurance. Nelson's eyes seemed to implore him to explain once and for all the mystery of existence.
>
>   Mr. Head opened his lips to make a lofty statement and heard himself say, "They ain't got enough real ones here. They got to have artificial ones."[5]

Getting off the train at the junction where he lives with Nelson, Mr. Head, that would-be guide of youth who at the beginning of this day, "might have been Vergil summoned . . . to go to Dante, or better, Raphael, awakened by a blast of God's light to fly to the side of Tobias,"[6] takes a final step into the piercing illumination of self-knowledge.

> Mr. Head stood very still and felt the action of mercy touch him again but this time he knew that there were no words in the world that could name it. He understood that it grew out of agony, which is not denied to any man and which is given in strange ways to children. He understood that it was all a man could carry into death to give his Maker and he suddenly burned with shame that he had so little of it to take with him. He stood appalled, judging himself with the thoroughness of God, while the action of mercy covered his pride like a flame and consumed it. He had never thought himself a great sinner before but he saw now that his true depravity had been hidden from him lest it cause him despair. He realized he was forgiven for sins from the beginning of time, when he had conceived in his own heart the sin of Adam, until the present, when he had denied poor Nelson. He saw that no sin was too monstrous for him to claim as his own, and since God loved in proportion as He forgave, he felt ready at that instant to enter Paradise.[7]

This short story, surely one of the masterpieces of the form, shows how Flannery O'Connor works. Her symbolism and her use of grotesques to implement it remind many readers of Faulkner, but Faulkner does not have the metaphysical dimension of sins from the beginning of time. He does not write stories of souls, as Flannery O'Connor does, following in the tradition established by Maritain, Claudel, Bernanos, Mauriac, and Greene. The vision of "true depravity" with which she works is Jansenist, as Jansenism has filtered into and been reinforced by the American Catholic Puritan tradition, which is paralleled by the distortion of Calvinism surviving in the fundamentalist sects of the Southern countryside. The clarity of understanding that makes the reader see the absurdity of the human pretensions represented by both Mr. Head and Nelson is the commonsense American shrewdness that at their best marked people like Gibbons and Isaac Hecker and made them the effective, no-nonsense men of insight that they were. And the compassion, the mercy that irradiates the entire story and shows us how an all-wise Creator, as Flannery O'Connor wishes us to see Him, judges mankind in Mr. Head, is universal Catholicism at its most appealing, as is the luminousness of grace that moves Mr. Head at the end. No more than Powers does Flannery O'Connor direct our attention to life after death, but in her stories, as in the work of Bernanos, the eternal enfolds life on earth.

The symbolism of *Wise Blood*, Flannery O'Connor's first novel, will yield to no such ease of interpretation as "The Artificial Nigger." Begun in 1948, published in 1952, *Wise Blood* is very early O'Connor. She was still working out not only the methods of conveying her insights but those insights themselves. We can grasp the outlines of her meanings only as in a mist. My belief is that they were not clearly defined at the time even in her own mind. Nevertheless, *Wise Blood* is a powerful novel.

The hero is Haze Motes, a young Southern Cracker, whose grandfather was a country preacher, "with Jesus hidden in his head like a stinger,"[8] and who always felt with dread and rebellion that he was born to follow the same course. From earliest youth Haze is determined *not* to follow it, and he decides very early that the way to avoid Jesus is to avoid sin, or if he does sin, to pay for it, as he does one day when he is twelve and has sneaked into a carnival tent to view a naked woman. On his return home he fills his shoes with stones and walks a long and painful distance. "He thought, 'that ought to satisfy him.' "[9] To Haze, if you don't sin or if you keep the score even by penance, Jesus can't get at you to redeem you because there is nothing to redeem you from.

Drafted into the army, Haze carefully stays away from sin, which appears to him at once in its expected form of sex. Disdainfully he refuses invitations from his companions to accompany them to brothels. But the army makes a change nevertheless in the well-named "Haze." He decides with the same stubbornness of action and confusion of thought that always characterize him, that he has found an even better way to avoid Jesus: he will refuse to believe in Him or to acknowledge that there is such a thing as sin. That way he won't need redeeming and there can be no Redeemer. As soon as Haze is discharged from the army he buys a blue civilian suit and a flat-brimmed hat and starts spending his nights with Mrs. Leora Watts, whose address he finds in a lavatory, "the friendliest bed in town."[10] Since sex is the worst sin, by indulging in it freely Haze can prove he doesn't believe that sin exists and that, therefore, he has no need of the Jesus whose figure has haunted him since his childhood.

In his electric blue suit and black hat Haze looks exactly like a country preacher. This dismays him at first, and he emphatically informs Mrs. Watts that he is "no goddam preacher."[11] Then, however, after an encounter with a blind missionary, who is begging with his dwarfish daughter as they distribute leaflets entitled "Jesus Calls You,"[12] Haze is moved to begin some counterpreaching of his own. His preaching is a special sort: he preaches the "Church Without Christ."

Miss O'Connor has great fun with Haze Motes' Church Without Christ. Haze, who can see the mote in everyone else's eye, is quite blind to any beams in his own. His Church Without Christ is an ever-shifting parody of the more conspicuous ways man has invented to satisfy his religious sense and avoid religion while doing so. Haze begins his preaching with a grotesque version of Pelagianism.

> "I want to tell you people something. Maybe you think you're not clean because you don't believe. Well you are clean, let me tell you that. Every one of you people are clean and let me tell you why if you think it's because of Jesus Christ Crucified you're wrong. . . ."[13]

Swinging into his career, Haze buys an old Essex car for fifty dollars and standing on the nose of this symbol of the machine age ("Nobody with a good car needs to be justified")[14] he embarks on an exposition of secularism. Flannery O'Connor's depiction of it as an antireligion that is actually a pseudoreligion is delightful. Haze cries:

> "Listen, you people, I'm going to take the truth with me wherever I go. . . . I'm going to preach there was no Fall because there was nothing to fall from and no Redemption because there was no Fall and no Judgment because there wasn't the first two. Nothing matters but that Jesus was a liar."[15]

Deepening his theme, Haze goes on during subsequent evenings to secular humanism, again in the religious terms that reveal the pseudoreligion:

> "I believe in a new kind of jesus . . . one that can't waste his blood redeeming people with it, because he is all man and ain't got any God in him. My church is the Church Without Christ."[16]

He then embellishes his growing creed with relativism:

> "I preach there are all kinds of truth, your truth and somebody else's. . . ."[17]

To this he adds some facets from existentialism:

> "but behind all of them truths there's only one truth and that is that there's no truth. . . . No truth behind all truths is what I and this church preach! Where you come from is gone, where you thought you were going never was there and where you are is no good unless you can get away from it. Where is there a place for you to be? No place."[18]

Flannery O'Connor finally has him take a stab at positivism, in new and old variations:

> He said it was not right to believe anything you couldn't see or hold in your hands or touch with your teeth. He said he had only a few days ago believed in blasphemy as the way to salvation, but that you couldn't even believe in that because then you were believing in something to blaspheme.[19]

While Haze is given his different pseudoreligions to parody, he is at the same time surrounded by grotesquely symbolic figures from the secular world who are woven into the plot. There is Enoch Emery, as rasping in personal contact as the name suggests. Whining, begging, pleading for friends and friendliness, Enoch Emery is a pimply, lustful, treacherous rustic of eighteen with a genius for arousing revulsion wherever he goes. Enoch works in the center of the city, in a park whose "heart" is the city zoo, where the "heart" in turn is a templelike building mysteriously labeled "MVSEVM," and where the most exalted and mysterious exhibit is a small mummy under glass—a full-sized man once, so the legend says, but he has been "shrunk" over the course of his history to a doll-like effigy. Enoch, the urban countryman (the name is that of the oldest son of Cain, who gave his name to one of the cities Cain founded)[20] has heard Haze preach, and believes that both he and Haze have "wise blood," but that his blood is even wiser than Haze's. What Enoch's wise blood tells him to do is to steal the shrunken man from the MVSEVM and give to Haze as a "new jesus" for his Church Without Christ.

Wise Blood keeps the reader smiling. What more appropriate new jesus could one find for a modern humanist than this mummy advertised to have been once a man but now "shrunk"? Haze by this time has a more suitable mistress than Mrs. Watts. His new partner is the daughter of the blind missionary, who turns out to be neither blind nor to believe in God. The daughter, Sabbath Lily Hawks, promises to teach Haze to "like sin." Since for both sin is sex and Haze doesn't enjoy sex, she cannot succeed. But good use is made of Sabbath Lily. Sitting with Enoch Emery's stolen mummy in her arms, she is the center of a weird tableau—the madonna of unbelief with the new jesus of shrunken man. But Haze is a genuine truth seeker and the mummy is a fake that enrages him. Smashed by Haze, the new jesus proves to be not a man at all, shrunken or otherwise, but an empty skin partially stuffed with sawdust.

Enoch's role in the story does not conclude with his failure to induce Haze to accept the mummified "man" for his church. Enoch's dream as a successful city dweller is to have friends— crowds of respectful friends; and the creature Enoch most admires is a "gorilla man" who, dressed in a fur costume to make him look like a real gorilla, stands outside the city's movie houses whenever a gorilla movie is showing and shakes hands with the crowds. Enoch sneaks into the gorilla man's truck, clubs him, steals his suit, buries his own clothes in a forest, and goes out to make an impression. But the first people he meets, a pair of lovers, scream and flee instead of greeting him as Enoch has always seen the gorilla man greeted. If Haze represents the soul oriented to seeking out truth, god or no-god, and to probing the mysteries of the universe, Enoch represents the soul oriented to people, who passes from pleas for the admiration he longs for to a stance that is one of force and domination. Both are gifted with "wise blood," an intuition that leads them toward what counts in man's fallen life on earth, but the goals they seek are different. Enoch is a man of this world; Haze is a man of what lies beyond. We will see when we look at Flannery O'Connor's second novel that this idea of two contrasting and often opposing types, the rebellious God-haunted soul and the frustrated man-oriented soul, is one that she pursues and develops with ever greater clarity. It is of course a development of the two most basic tendencies we have seen as characteristic of the Catholic novelists: criticism of the secular world and criticism of the "religious" community. Flannery O'Connor balances one against the other and achieves in *Wise Blood*, and later in *The Violent Bear It Away* a wonderfully contrasting symmetry. The apostles of "religion" are opposed by the apostles of secularism. Souls on either side would be equally dark, except that the "religious" are in a position to be overwhelmed by grace, a force to which the secular characters of deepest dye are immune, Enoch Emery in *Wise Blood*, Rayber in *The Violent Bear It Away*. Rayber, as we shall see, has traces of vulnerability to God, but Enoch Emery's immunity is complete. There seems to be no free will in the matter. Enoch is as he is. God's grace simply does not shine on him. God, as Flannery O'Connor sees him, is not notably endowed with compassion, and this fact may trouble some readers, who feel a certain lack, a certain dryness, a certain harshness. One may feel a keen intellectual interest in seeing so Jansenist a view so vitally alive in modern times, but, if one is an orthodox Catholic who persists in looking beyond the cloak of Flannery O'Connor's delightful humor, one is apt to experience a bit of uneasiness.

Next to Enoch Emery in importance as a figure setting off Haze Motes is Hoover Shoats, an unbeliever but a professional promoter of religious enterprises. Robert Fitzgerald, whose garage apartment Flannery O'Connor was renting when she wrote *Wise Blood*, tells of the delight with which they celebrated the invention of this name:[21] "Hoover" with its suggestion of a vacuum cleaner (he is a chronic sucker-in of other people's ideas) and "Shoats," with its evocation of piggishness (while Shoats' auditors wallow in religious sentiment, he wallows in profit). Hoover Shoats hears Haze preach and decides that Haze provides a marvelous opportunity for partnership, since without Hoover's talents added to his own, Haze is financially helpless: "you innerleckchuls . . . don't never have nothing to show for what you're saying."[22] But Haze will not accept the classic alliance between the "innerleckchul" and the secular man of business. He rejects Hoover with considerable violence. So Hoover hires a man to imitate Haze, names him Solace Layfield, and has him go Haze one better. Instead of preaching the Church Without Christ and exhorting his hearers to seek truth, Solace Layfield invites the people to have their cake and eat it too: his church is the Church of Christ Without Christ, and what he invites those joining it to do is to believe whatever sentimentalism makes them comfortable.

Haze, misty-minded but a genuine truth seeker and also a man of action, cannot put up with this. Pursuing Solace Layfield one evening after Hoover Shoats has gone, Haze pushes Layfield's car off the road and runs over him, deliberately backing the Essex over the fallen man a second time, killing him. Layfield is not "true,"[23] and this Haze cannot abide.

Thus Haze becomes a murderer. At this point in her fable, I believe, Flannery O'Connor bogged down. She needed a conversion scene for Haze. As Fitzgerald says, she "didn't know how to finish him off." About then she read for the first time the Oedipus plays. In Fitzgerald's words, "she went on . . . to end her story with the self-blinding of Motes, and she had to rework the body of the novel to prepare for it."[24]

This preparation is expert. The missioner whom Haze met in the book's beginning is given a history that is the reverse of Haze's. Haze begins as a nonbeliever and ends as a believer. The missioner is revealed to have begun as a believer and to have ended by believing in nothing. On a day long ago, as a proof of the vitality of his faith, the missioner had advertised that he was going to blind himself with quicklime. He did splash lime on his face and he has worn dark glasses ever since, but actually his nerve failed him at the time of the supposed blinding and he did not let any lime get into his eyes. Since then his faith has been as false as his blindness.

After Haze runs over Solace Layfield, he decides to go to a new town. But on the road a policeman stops his ancient Essex and, discovering Haze has no license, pushes it off a cliff. If we remember that "no one with a good car needs to be justified," we will wonder what will become of Haze now that he is deprived of this symbol of the machine age. Haze sits on the edge of the cliff and stares:

His face seemed to reflect the entire distance across the clearing and on beyond, the entire distance that extended from his eyes to the blank gray sky that went on, depth after depth, into space.[25]

The conversion then takes place—"conversion" in the sense of the original Latin root "converto," to turn around. Haze becomes the opposite of everything he has been. Getting up from the edge of the cliff, he walks back to town. Buying quicklime, he blinds himself. He packs stones into his shoes. He wraps barbed wire around his chest. The austerities the saints performed to make their peace with God are paralleled by those of the converted Haze Motes, who eventually falls into a ditch and dies of suffering, illness, and exhaustion. Meanwhile, his landlady, Mrs. Flood, whose aim in being alive is to make the most of every worldly comfort in the manner of all people like her who "flood" the earth, feels that her lodger, who pays her well out of his army pension, is cheating her by somehow getting more out of life than she does; and also that the blind Haze, whose ruined eyes are mere pinpoints of light, can see something she with her normal vision cannot see. Mrs. Flood is very recognizably a figure of the Catholic writer's usual blinded worldling. She is a more repellent Ida Arnold, viewed with Flannery O'Connor's uncompromisingness instead of Greene's tolerant compassion.

Obviously this novel, particularly after Haze Motes' conversion following the loss of his car, is open to differing interpretations. What does Haze experience as he sits on the edge of the cliff? Does his stare into the horizon show, as I believe, an encounter with grace, which overwhelms him and makes him in spite of his lifelong battle against Christ, a man of God, a believer, and a follower of the Redeemer? If so, in what sense is he afterwards truly a man of God? When he tells Mrs. Flood, "I ain't treatin' with you,"[26] and so implies that his penitential way of life is a negotiation with Christ, what does Miss O'Connor intend to portray? I doubt if Haze Motes, the penitent, is supposed to represent achieved saintliness. Rather he is a man attempting a typical form of a very old, confused, and painful approach to God. He is doing just what he says: "treatin'," as penitents have tried to "treat," negotiate, pay since the time men first began to believe in God. The mode of Haze's "treatin'" is grotesque, as all of his story has been, but does not the reflection of a certain type of metaphysically haunted man emerge with considerable accuracy from this symbolic story? If one believes in free will, one must certainly quarrel with the sudden transformation of Haze as he sits on the edge of the cliff, but if one inherits Jansenist and Catholic Puritan ideas, as so many American Catholics do, may it not seem a true enough depiction of what freedom man has, as grace is accepted by the rebellious murderer, who was in spite of everything a seeker after truth?

Whatever the interpretation one brings to the story, no one will read it without being moved. Whether one's reaction is assent, disagreement, or suspended judgment, *Wise Blood* is superb symbolic writing. As we noticed before, some of the best Catholic novels in which man is depicted as pitting himself against the mysteries of the universe develop a quality one usually associates with the Greeks. This is particularly true of Flannery O'Connor. As she has drawn this story, Haze Motes, in setting his course against his destiny, tries to withstand a force that cannot be withstood. When he undergoes his reversal on the edge of the cliff, he who has had sight but could not see and so has been one of the dead-in-life, becomes a blind man who sees —and ultimately a dead man who lives. The enormity of his Oedipal self-blinding becomes a measure of the fathomless vision that develops within his soul as he seeks purification. As the Greek tragic heroes move us by their magnificence as they develop to meet their fate, so in this parable of dark paradoxes there is something that touches the quick of vital dramatic tension as the grotesque protagonist, giving himself over at last to

his destiny, plunges into the anguish of trying to undo his previous course and make himself "clean"[27] for his election. If one
accepts the necessary theological orientation and Flannery
O'Connor's view of a freedom that indeed exists and can create
resistance but is limited by God's plan for each soul, it could be
the story of any sinful God-pursued man, the story of mankind
itself. It is tempting to take this as the meaning which Miss
O'Connor was striving to convey.

Flannery O'Connor's second novel, *The Violent Bear It
Away*, is easy to interpret compared to *Wise Blood*, but even it
will reward the reader who has the patience to go through it several times. The entire fable may be seen in a new light—depending on the freshly realized significance of a corkscrew, the
suddenly understood new meaning of a hat. In Flannery O'Connor's material the most ordinary objects are transfigured; the
most humorous lines are full of provocative metaphysics. As she
herself wrote in 1962, in a note to *Wise Blood* a decade after its
publication, "all comic novels that are any good must be about
matters of life and death."[28]

The Violent Bear It Away was published in 1960, two years
before this note. It is a comic novel which, like *Wise Blood*,
sharpens satire into the grotesque and raises symbolic comedy
to the level of universal parable. Mason Tarwater (the first
name suggests a builder; the second, a sharp purge popular in
folk medicine) is an eighty-four-year-old moonshiner and dirt
farmer who, called by the Lord as baptizer and prophet, has re-
tired after a full life to Powderhead, his inherited clearing in
the Tennessee woods, to train his successor, young Francis
Marion Tarwater, his fourteen-year-old great-nephew. Young
Tarwater (his first names are those of the famous Revolutionary
general, the "Swamp Fox," known for the cleverness of his eva-
sive tactics) is a sharp-faced, nimble-witted boy who is interested in becoming a prophet if he can make the sun stand still
as Joshua did, but otherwise prefers freedom to being a servant

of the Lord. The crisis comes on the day of his great-uncle's death. Instead of burying the old man in a safely deep grave to await the Day of Resurrection, the boy gives up the unpleasant and exhausting task of digging in the Tennessee earth and goes to get drunk at the still. As soon as his great-uncle was dead, the voice of a "stranger" began to haunt young Tarwater, first pointing out the unfairness of having to labor to bury the bulky old man and then, as Tarwater gets drunk, speaking Tarwater's thoughts with more and more seductive cogency.

> It should be clear to you, his kind friend said, how all your life you been tricked by that old man. You could have been a city slicker for the last fourteen years. Instead, you been deprived of any company but his, you been living in a two-story barn in the middle of this earth's bald patch, following behind a mule and plow since you were seven. And how do you know the education he give you is true to the facts? Maybe he taught you a system of figures nobody else uses? How do you know that two added to two makes four? Four added to four makes eight? Maybe other people don't think so. How do you know if there was an Adam or if Jesus eased your situation any when He redeemed you? Or how do you know if He actually done it? Nothing but that old man's word and it ought to be obvious to you by now that he was crazy. And as for Judgment Day, the stranger said, every day is Judgment Day.[29]

By this time in the story we have been presented with a skillful succession of flashbacks, usually through Tarwater's memories of his thoughts on various occasions when the old man recounted the history of his life. Old Tarwater had a sister who married an insurance man named Rayber. City dwellers (and, in the old man's view, utterly corrupt) they engendered a son, young Rayber, whom old Tarwater kidnapped at the age of seven, brought to Powderhead, baptized, and instructed in the truths of his salvation before the father came out and forcibly took the boy home. Back in the city, however, the boy betrayed the old man's teachings. Instead of giving his life to seeking and spreading salvation, he embarked on a career that was the modern parallel of those pursuits: he became a schoolteacher, and worked up to being administrator of aptitude tests for his district. Baptized as an apostle of religion, he turns into an equally dedicated apostle of secularism. Old Tarwater did not for a long time believe that the seeds of Rayber's baptism were dead beyond recall, and at one time went to him in hopes of prophesying the truth back into him. But the old man left in outrage when he found that Rayber had written for a "schoolteacher magazine" an article on him as a neurotic type almost extinct in the present age.

Rayber's ideas are as decided as the old man's. He doesn't of course expect any Day of Resurrection, and, instead of the trouble of preserving a body by burial, he believes in the simplicity and neatness of cremation. The old man's greatest dread, which he expresses to young Tarwater, is that somehow after his death Rayber will get possession of his body and cremate it. He has "raised" Tarwater not only to succeed him as prophet but to bury him at his death.

Rayber had an only sister, whom in the interests of life-adjustment he persuaded to take a lover, a young divinity student. Pregnant, she died in an automobile accident, surviving just long enough to give illegitimate birth to Francis Marion Tarwater, whom old Tarwater promptly kidnapped in his turn, driving Rayber off with a shower of bullets when he and a "welfare woman" followed the old man and the infant to Powderhead. The divinity student, meanwhile, overcome by guilt, had taken himself out of the way by suicide. The reasons Rayber and the welfare woman, a Miss Bishop, did not make more attempts to reclaim young Tarwater were that the welfare woman took an invincible dislike to young Tarwater's face, which even in babyhood was about as mobile as granite, and also that they married and had a child of their own, Bishop. Old Tarwater sees the hand of God in the fact that Bishop turned out to be beyond the reach of Rayber's power to corrupt, for Bishop is feebleminded, mentally fixated forever at the age of five. His mother deserted him soon after this fact became obvious, leaving him behind while she pursued welfare work in the remote corners of the world, as far as possible from her son. For Flannery O'Connor, "welfare workers" are a kind of culmination of the apostleship of secularism represented by Rayber, and in the life of Bishop's mother who deserts her own son she shows what she thinks of the attachment to truly human values of those who devote themselves to so-called "welfare."

By the time young Tarwater gets drunk and passes out at the still with the "stranger's" voice whispering his own rebellious thoughts into his ear, Miss O'Connor has set up the dichotomy of her parable. On one hand is old Tarwater, the man of God, despised by the community of sensible people and in retreat at Powderhead to prepare his successor to explode upon the world. On the other hand is Rayber, the humanist and schoolteacher, who, as the old man reports contemptuously to young Tarwater is "free": " 'He's going to be his own savior. He's going to be free!' The old man turned his head to the side and spit. 'Free,' he said. 'He was full of such-like phrases.' "[30] If "freedom" is the burden of Rayber's efforts to convert the old man, a different kind of "freedom" is the burden of the old man's teaching of young Tarwater.

> "You were born into bondage and baptized into freedom, into the death of the Lord, into the death of the Lord Jesus Christ."
> Then the child would feel a sullenness creeping over him, a slow warm rising resentment that this freedom had to be connected with Jesus and that Jesus had to be the Lord.
> "Jesus is the bread of life," the old man said. . . .
> The boy sensed that this was the heart of his great-uncle's madness, this hunger, and what he was secretly afraid of was that it might be passed down, might be hidden in the blood and might strike some day in him and then he would be torn by hunger like the old man, the bottom split out of his stomach so that nothing would heal or fill it but the bread of life.[31]

Freedom under Jesus or bondage under the devil has been the old man's teaching, and of all forms of bondage none is more evil than under the Satan-directed Raybers of the secular apostolate. But the stranger's voice inside of young Tarwater at the still tells the drunken, rebellious disciple, on whom his mission has fallen like lead, that there is no Satan. "It ain't Jesus or the devil. It's Jesus or you."[32] Flannery O'Connor handles the symbolic "stranger" cleverly. He speaks Tarwater's thoughts in Tarwater's vernacular, but he goes beyond these in that he has more knowledge and sensitivity than Tarwater has. Tarwater could never tempt himself so well. The stranger is not merely Tarwater's suppressed rebellious self, he is a tempter from outside, the great universal tempter, Satan—yet put into the scene so skillfully that there is no need to be overt about the symbol.

When Tarwater recovers consciousness at the still, it is night. He creeps back to the shack at Powderhead, and, not knowing that a neighboring Negro has taken out old Tarwater's body and finished the burial, the boy sets fire to the floorboards from beneath the shanty, expecting to cremate his great-uncle above. As young Tarwater says on a later occasion, "You can't just say NO. . . . You got to do NO."[33] On the impetus of his fiery doing of NO, Tarwater flees Powderhead and hitches a ride into the city, where he goes to Rayber's house and announces to him the triumphant negative, " 'My great-uncle is dead and burnt. . . . I done your work for you,' and as he said the last a perceptible trace of scorn crossed his face."[34] It is clear to Tarwater at first glance that his Uncle Rayber is no doer himself. Rayber can't see without his glasses and can't hear without his hearing aid, and as Tarwater in the middle of the night watches him answer the door and hurriedly don the equipment without which he can't meet the world, the boy has the impression that this city uncle of his "ran by electricity."[35] The title of the book is taken from Matthew 11:12, "From the days of John the Baptist until now the kingdom of heaven suffereth violence, and the violent bear it away." Old Tarwater had this sort of violence, and young Tarwater has it even in his NO. Rayber, the secularist, obviously is not capable of it in any form.

Having established Rayber in suitably symbolic grotesqueness, Flannery O'Connor has somewhat insulated her readers from the dangers of liking him. This insulation is necessary, for Rayber represents a familiar and widely accepted modern ideal. Humane, kindly, sensible, believing in no Intelligence behind a universe where a "mistake of nature" produced his idiot son Bishop, Rayber, the humanist, is an appealing figure. When he once tried to drown Bishop as an act of euthanasia, he could not because of his overpowering love for the child. Rayber loves all humanity, and he believes in it. He plans to give Tarwater the secular "advantages," and undo the effects of the old man's superstitions.

The two figures between whom young Tarwater must choose are expertly contrasted. Rayber is a far better parody of humanism than the whining Enoch Emery, and old Tarwater is a better parody of the man of God than the confused Haze Motes. To the Catholic eye this basic dichotomy had been for a long time operating in the modern world. In the early years of the century Péguy accused on the one hand the clerks of the intellect, by whom he meant the masters of the Sorbonne whom he regarded as blind to spiritual reality, and on the other hand the clerks of the spirit, whom he accused of being blind to the needs of the body. In Flannery O'Connor's America, blindness to the needs of the body had given way to the fixations of materialism. For many even the social idealism once represented by such men as John A. Ryan had become a matter of bathtubs and refrigerators, free lunches and full employment, schooling and vocational testing—Rayber's special field.

Rayber spreads the net of secularism diligently for Tarwater. He buys books for the boy,[36] he takes him to movies and shows him the city. Tarwater is escorted to supermarkets, the

post office, and the railroad yards.[37] But all these wonders re-
bound from his rock-hard personality with scarcely a trace. On
his head at all times is his hat, which at Powderhead he never
took off and which he keeps on constantly in Rayber's house and
out, a symbol of his early training, as Haze Motes' hats, which
he always pounded into the exact uncompromising flat-brimmed
assertiveness of the hat his preacher-grandfather wore, were also
a symbol.

One night Tarwater steals out of Rayber's house. Rayber follows and finds him first outside of a bakery gazing with inexplic-
able hunger at a loaf of bread (he is, we know, remembering
the bread of life) and then at a Revival, where a child-evangelist
is preaching that "Jesus is love."[38] This is a fresh spur to Rayber's indignation, for in the child-evangelist he sees another
child deceived, as he and Tarwater in their formative years were
deceived—only Rayber has got over his trauma, while Tarwater
is still struggling with his. After the scene with the child-
evangelist (who, when she sees Rayber's head peering in the
window, cries out that she is beholding a man who belongs to
the devil) Rayber's determination to save Tarwater from the
horrors of religion increases. He takes the boy away to a lake-
side resort where he plans to continue Tarwater's education by
lecturing him on evolution and having him meet "his ancestor,
the fish."[39] He buys the boy a present, a combination bottle
opener and corkscrew; and for this Tarwater offers grudging
thanks. He reflects that his uncle's gift can open all sorts of
things. As the corkscrew symbolizes, Tarwater is surrendering
somewhat to Rayber's world. Rayber, too, preaches salvation,
although it is his own kind. Like old Tarwater, he seeks disci-
ples—for his own creed. As the perceptive Tarwater tells Rayber, the old man's seed fell in Rayber too. " 'It ain't a thing you
can do about it. It fell on bad ground but it fell in deep. With
me,' he said proudly, 'it fell on rock and the wind carried
it away.' "[40]

At this time the "wind" carrying it away is the voice of the "stranger," which has returned to Tarwater's consciousness from the moment he looked at the lake and was reminded of Bishop and the mission old Tarwater gave him to baptize the boy. " 'I wasn't going to baptize him,' " Tarwater tells his reflected face in the water. " 'I'd drown him first.' " " 'Drown him then,' " the face appears to say. The voice then takes up. " 'If you baptize once, you'll be doing it the rest of your life. If it's an idiot this time, the next time it's liable to be a nigger.' "[41] The "stranger" goes on. " 'You think there's a trap laid all about you by the Lord. There ain't any trap. There ain't anything except what you've laid for yourself. . . . And me. I'll never desert you.' "[42] Clearly, freedom either in the "trap" of the Lord or at the beck of the stranger is limited—and in Flannery O'Connor's portrayal this is all the freedom Tarwater has, a choice between alternative services. " 'I never ast for that lake to be set down in front of me.' "[43] What Tarwater finally does in his final and most conclusive NO is to row Bishop out on the lake and there at sunset he drowns him. But, as the child goes under, Tarwater unwillingly mutters the words of baptism. He has, therefore, said both no and yes.

Hitchhiking again, Tarwater is picked up by a truck driver who offers him a sandwich. The boy cannot eat bread because of its association in his mind with the bread of life, but, in spite of this, he is satisfied by his achievement. With the drowning of Bishop he believes he has found true freedom, regardless of the words that "spilled in the water."[44] He will return to Powderhead and "begin to live his life as he had elected it."[45] The corkscrew glitters "as if it promised to open great things for him."[46]

Flannery O'Connor has reached a difficult place in her story. Euthanasia, the drowning of Bishop, was Rayber's wish. An answer to God's call, the baptism of Bishop, was old Tarwater's command. Tarwater has partly surrendered to each. But the principle of his surrender has been opposition. He opposed old Tarwater by drowning Bishop. He opposed Rayber by baptizing the boy. The one opposition, meanwhile, in which young Tarwater has been unwavering is his opposition to God—to Christ and the bread of life. Now Flannery O'Connor needs a reversal for Tarwater as she once needed one for Haze Motes. Her method this time is infinitely more skillful. She will use Tarwater's trait of opposition and show him surrendering to God as a result of opposition to the devil. In order to do this, she prepares now to bring the devil, her symbolic "stranger," on the scene in person. It is the most telling scene of this kind in all the Catholic novels. It makes Bernanos' device of the horse trader in *Under the Sun of Satan* look clumsy. Flannery O'Connor's art is deeply sophisticated, particularly when she turns most strongly to symbolism.

After the truck ride ends, another man picks Tarwater up, to whom Tarwater confides that he lives alone and says, " 'Nobody tells me what to do.' "[47] This man is described as "the stranger," and he is the embodiment of the diabolic "stranger" who has been speaking for so long within Tarwater's consciousness. During the ride in the stranger's car, the stranger drugs the boy, stops his car, carries Tarwater into the woods, strips him and ravishes him. The stranger emerges with two trophies, Tarwater's corkscrew, the key to the material world given him by Rayber, and Tarwater's hat, the never-abandoned symbol of his spiritual self as he was shaped by the old man. Both sides of Tarwater have been overcome by the enemy.

Recovering consciousness, Tarwater in a horror of revulsion sets fire to all the ground he thinks the stranger may have touched. He dresses convulsively, hastens on foot to Powderhead, and there as he stands looking down into the clearing he hears the voice a last time.

Go down and take it, his friend whispered. It's ours. We've won it. Ever since you first begun to dig the grave, I've stood by you, never left your side, and now we can take it over together, just you and me. You're not ever going to be alone again.

The boy shuddered convulsively. The presence was as pervasive as an odor, a warm sweet body of air encircling him, a violent shadow hanging around his shoulders.[48]

Tarwater fires the woods again "until he had made a rising wall of fire between him and the grinning presence."[49] Going down into the clearing he finds as if by a miracle his great-uncle's grave, with the cross over it the Negro had set. He stands transfixed. Out of his knowledge of evil has come such a terrible opposition to it that in his spiritual hunger he feels "he could have eaten all the loaves and fishes after they were multiplied."[50]

He felt his hunger no longer as a pain but as a tide. He felt it rising in himself through time and darkness, rising through the centuries, and he knew that it rose in a line of men whose lives were chosen to sustain it, who would wander in the world, strangers from that violent country where the silence is never broken except to shout the truth. He felt it building from the blood of Abel to his own, rising and engulfing him. It seemed in one instant to lift and turn him. He whirled toward the treeline. There, rising and spreading in the night, a red-gold tree of fire ascended as if it would consume the darkness in one tremendous burst of flame. The boy's breath went out to meet it. He knew that this was the fire that had encircled Daniel, that had raised Elijah from the earth, that had spoken to Moses and would the instant speak to him. He threw himself to the ground and with his face against the dirt of the grave, he heard the comand. GO WARN THE CHILDREN OF GOD OF THE TERRIBLE SPEED OF MERCY. The words were as silent as seeds opening one at a time in his blood.[51]

The conversion of Tarwater is more explicit than the conversion of Haze Motes, but it is as much the result of the sudden and overwhelming action of God's grace. Tarwater has been prepared by God's allowing him to fall into the hands of the "stranger," and the boy's revulsion makes his conversion understandable. However, supernatural forces, not Tarwater's will, have determined Tarwater's redemption. But one should note how marvelously Flannery O'Connor has expressed her vision. The book ends with an epiphany. God "appears" to Tarwater as he once appeared to Moses—in fire. Yet there is no strain on the reader's credulity. Not only have we been aware from the beginning that we are reading a parable, so that the demands we make of realism are minimized; but Flannery O'Connor gives us in any case all the realism we can require, both on the actual and symbolic levels. The tree does not spring into flame miraculously. The fire spreads from the one the boy himself set —when he kindled it under the pressure of grace, which rose from his hatred of evil when he knew it as it was.

Tarwater's surrender to God is complete. He will take up his vocation as old Tarwater's successor. He takes a handful of dirt from his great-uncle's grave and smears it on his forehead. Wearing the sign of penitence, he leaves Powderhead, "his face set toward the dark city, where the children of God lay sleeping."[52]

Tarwater's aim was to live his life as he "elected it."[53] The biblical verb is significant. In Flannery O'Connor's world *we* cannot *elect* our lives; they are *elected* for us by God. Tarwater, like Haze, could not in the end, fight his vocation. In the symbolism of *The Violent Bear It Away*, a soul that seeks to avoid the path God has appointed for it will fall into the power of evil, as Tarwater fell into the power of the stranger. There is no more ground for objecting to the fact that Flannery O'Connor's heroes have limited freedom than there is in objecting to the Fates that govern the characters of Sophocles. We may not believe in the Fates, and we may give more weight to free will than Miss O'Connor does, but this cannot alter the fact that she was not only a great artist but a Catholic typical of her time and place. She took derivatives of American Catholic Puritanism and in them found magnificent dramatic themes. It is a superb accomplishment, one of the finest in recent years in the American novel.[54]

Flannery O'Connor and J. F. Powers both have the freshness that Europeans so admire in American fiction. Flannery O'Connor is indisputably the more accomplished artist. Nevertheless, I do not believe she can be ranked with Greene or Bernanos. Her brief life gave her time for only two novels, both of which express essentially the same idea. On the other hand, Bernanos has a rich variety of themes and Greene is a master novelist with an even wider spectrum. Another fact we must notice is that in the American Catholic novels we never find secular figures as dark as the "villains" from the secular world we remember in Mauriac, Waugh, and Greene. The portrayals of Raymond Courrèges in Mauriac's *The Desert of Love*, the Malorthys in *Under the Sun of Satan*, Margot Beste-Chetwynde in *Decline and Fall*, and Colleoni in *Brighton Rock* display monsters of evil, and a connoisseur of "monsters" in modern fiction will greet them with a shudder of delight, for they are fearfully and wonderfully drawn. We do not shudder at Enoch or Rayber. Enoch makes us laugh; Rayber evokes indignation but also a tolerant smile. This fact reflects, I believe, the contrast between the European background and the American. As we saw, American Catholics never felt the same contempt and anger for the non-Catholic environment as developed in France after 1789 and in England after the industrial revolution.

Thus there is not in the American novels, even in those of Flannery O'Connor, the range that exists in the work of such writers as Bernanos and Greene. Nevertheless, I believe her fiction will live. One can never predict fashions in literary criticism, but it would seem that, though Powers, Waugh, and possibly even Mauriac may slip from recognition in years to come, Greene is certain to be remembered and a place is also assured Bernanos. The Harvard psychiatrist, Dr. Robert Coles, in an article in the *New York Times Book Review* for November 3,

1968, spoke of *The Diary of a Country Priest* as a work that thirty years after publication he still "reads and rereads," and regards as one of the memorable achievements of its time. What Dr. Coles feels in *The Diary* is, it seems to me, its vision of universal truths about the human condition, the power of whose drama strikes deeply no matter what the differences in belief. Greene achieves, I believe, a comparable effect in at least two of his books, *The Heart of the Matter* and *The Power and the Glory*. The same vision rests on Flannery O'Connor, and if it rests more lightly, her pungent wit and uncompromising approach have their own very special flavor. Meeting Flannery O'Connor is a little like meeting Francis Marion Tarwater on his mission to arouse the sleeping children of darkness. One is not likely to forget the encounter, whatever one's reaction to the message.

PART IV

Convergence and Confluence

CHAPTER XII

Assimilation
and Interpenetration

What should be most remembered about the Catholic novels, now that a cross-section of the best of them has been seen in relation to their religious and historical backgrounds? First it should be remembered, I believe, that we have been examining the appearance of an entirely new kind of fiction in French, English, and American literature. Insight into spiritual development had been an object of creative inquiry since earliest times —as witness the grail legends, the tale of Palamon and Arcite, and the story of *The Pearl*. But, as the Vicomte de Voguë pointed out in *Le Roman Russe* in 1886, the French schools of realism and naturalism had eroded emphasis on the spiritual, and the French novel could not compare to the Russian in the latter's dramatic use of metaphysics and values of the spirit. It is true that in France Standhal probed spiritual states and made spiritual progress or spiritual corruption an element of action, and in England the educated heart of Jane Austen's Emma or George Eliot's Dorothea were fascinating subjects for contemporary readers, while in America Hawthorne created his tormented Puritans. But metaphysics, ontology, and particularly the power of the historic Roman Catholic apocalyptic "matrix" of heaven, hell, and purgatory as deeper realities framing, enclosing, and terminating ostensible "reality" were never the touchstone of novels until the time of Bernanos and Greene. And all the long complex development from the time of Barbey d'Aurevilly was required before the work of Greene and Bernanos became possible. The work in aesthetics of Maritain, Claudel, and Mauriac was necessary to establish the critical premises of such a radically new form. Maritain made his distinction between an "individual," a human being as a social or political unit, and a "person," a man or woman with a soul to save or lose. Claudel asserted the possibility of dramas concerned with ontological problems and developed such dramas for the stage. Meanwhile Mauriac claimed that the "romanticism" of stories about "individuals" was exhausted and declared that writers should examine the "eternal Tartuffe" or the "eternal Harpagon" to create a gallery of spiritual "types," as in his own fiction he proceeded to do.

Second, it should be remembered how deeply Roman Catholic the novels are. Historic Roman Catholic theological and philosophical ideas furnished the mainsprings of dramatic action. As the Roman Catholic communities emerged from isolation, altered Catholic thinking offered sources of controversy. And, finally, thinking typical of specific Catholic communities provided background and themes. In the Catholic novels, a man or woman may offer his or her life for others, as the Abbé Donissan does in *Under the Sun of Satan*, a pattern as old in Catholic theology as the dogma that Christ gave up his life to save mankind. Or a man may be a "whiskey priest" and yet a true minister of Christ, as is Graham Greene's protagonist in *The Power and the Glory*, a shocking concept in the 1930s to the average Catholic but twenty years later regarded as an orthodox, acceptable, and even traditional development of Catholic thought, with premises as old as the realization that the efficacy of a sacrament is independent of the merits of the offi-

ciant. Or a man could fight a vocation to serve God, only to suc-
cumb to the pressure of grace, as does Tarwater in *The Violent
Bear It Away*—the boy, Tarwater, serving as a symbol of all
people who vainly oppose their God-given destinies, as such
destinies were envisioned by American Catholics under Jansenist or Irish Puritan influences. Whether the theme was theological, or was an instance of "development," or was simply a
product of the traditional thinking characteristic of one of the
Roman Catholic communities, the Catholic novels made a distinct contribution to the history of modern fiction. We mentioned
how at the end of the nineteenth century the Vicomte de Voguë
believed that the novel in France had exhausted its possibilities
as a literary form because of the repeated emphasis on external
action by the dominant schools of realists and naturalists. The
appearance of the Catholic novels not only weakened those
schools in France but also revitalized the novel by contributing
to the demonstration of the dramatic potential of stories whose
chief action was internal.

We should also remember, I believe, the typical orientation
of the Catholic novelists toward their subject matter, an orientation that contributed to growth and change within the Catholic
communities. From the beginning the orientation of the Catholic
writers manifested itself as opposition, either to the secular environment or to conditions in the Catholic community or to both.
We saw that, while the early Catholic novelists usually focused
on criticism of the environment, most of the later novelists focused on criticism of the Catholic community. And we saw, with
Greene and Bernanos, that such criticism was not only symp-
tomatic of changing Catholic views but actually speeded the
alteration of Catholic thinking in such a way as to hasten the
convergence of the once separatist communities with the secular
and Protestant environments surrounding them.

We noted, too, that this dynamic of development which
passed from criticism of the environment to criticism of the

Catholic community brought a change in the quality of Catholic fiction. The separatist work of the European Catholic novelists who emphasized conditions in the secular environment—Huysmans, Belloc, Chesterton, and Evelyn Waugh—could not be compared in literary quality to the work of later writers whose emphasis was on criticism of their own Catholic communities—Mauriac, Bernanos, and Graham Greene. We recall Cardinal Newman's observation that "doctrines and views which relate to man are not placed in a void but in the crowded world." Doctrines and views that mattered most to Roman Catholic writers were Roman Catholic doctrines and views. These were the writer's own; they were, so to speak, nearer the quick of his own heart and intellect. This nearness explains why criticism of the community led to the most compelling fiction and also to the most compelling historical influence. It is criticism of the community that is most fruitful for the developing tradition so vitally alive within the dynamic of Roman Catholicism. Just as the self-reflexive power is the source of spiritual growth for each human soul, so it is the source of growth for the Church.

As was indicated by our historical surveys, the decades from the mid-1920s to the mid-1950s were the period of swiftest convergence between the Catholic communities and their surrounding environments. It was also the period when a new aesthetic was being developed, when emphasis was shifting from criticism of non-Catholics to criticism of the Catholic communities, and when most of the best Catholic novels were being written. The most important and least debatable conclusion is that a period of swift and intense convergence is highly stimulating to the dynamic of creative development.

There is no space in this chapter to discuss at any length the literatures of other cultural communities which are in convergence with surrounding environments, but perhaps it may be noted at least parenthetically that similar phenomena of renascence are observable elsewhere—in India and Japan, for example. These two once relatively isolated communities have been opening themselves rapidly to influences from the West during the last century, and particularly during the last seventy years. We should add that both the Japanese and the Indian literary movements seem from the beginning to have focused more on criticism of their own communities than on criticism of the West. When there is Japanese or Indian criticism of the Western environment, it is directed at the nature of the changes brought into the native community by the intrusion of foreign ways rather than at the foreign environment itself. Also, the Japanese and Indian literary movements, which even in their early stages deal primarily with their own communities, appear to be in fuller flower from the beginning than was the case with the Catholic novelists. Natsume Soseki's *Kokoro* (1914) compares favorably with the work of most Japanese writers working today. Similarly in India the best work of M. R. Anand can be read quite comfortably even in such company as R. K. Narayan's masterpiece, *The Man-Eater of Malgudi* (1962), particularly if one turns to Anand's zestful and humane short stories such as "The Barbers' Trade Union" (1936). The more even development in India and Japan compared to the contrast between the early Catholic novelists and the later ones tends to support the finding that the literature produced by a cultural community in a period of convergence profits more from dealing with its own community than from attacking the environment.

As confirmation from our survey, we may look back briefly to some of the novels we analyzed. One of the most searing criticisms of the French Catholic community was, as we saw, François Mauriac's *Vipers' Tangle*. In Mauriac's story, the old miser, Louis, who is Mauriac's portrait of the type of "eternal Harpagon," is more sensitive to spiritual values of brotherhood and charity than most members of his Catholic family. Popular Catholic belief at the time Mauriac was writing (1932) still held to the nineteenth-century convention that Catholics had special "passports" to sanctity. In company with the "eternal Harpagon," Mauriac also examines what he called the type of "eternal Tartuffe," and Louis' wife, Isa, is a subtle and savage portrait of hypocritical and self-deceiving "religious devotion." *Vipers' Tangle* was an indignant refutation of the idea of Huysmans, Barbey d'Aurevilly, and most Catholics of the nineteenth century, that "good Catholics" were automatically good people, and pagans were either wicked or degenerate.

The secular view of the moral state of ostensibly "religious" people was, of course, quite different from the view accepted by nineteenth-century Catholics. To French secularists a man's religion or lack of it had never been a mark of the "goodness" or "badness" of his character. Secularists were also apt to be suspicious of the sincerity of "religious" people, particularly the "religious" bourgeoisie, as one may see in the popular acceptance of Moliere's portrait of the original Tartuffe as early as the seventeenth century and of Bickerstaff's eighteenth-century adaptation for the English stage, in which Tartuffe appears as Dr. Cantwell. In writing *Vipers' Tangle* Mauriac was assimilating perceptions that had long been recognized by the secular environment and long denied by most of the Catholic community. Newman says that "doctrines and views" placed as they are "in the crowded world" grow by "assimilation," and that the vitality of the assimilating organism is demonstrated by its power to take these "external materials" into "its own substance." Assimilation thus is profitable. It always involves, however, a shock to the assimilating organism, and it is a shock that is moving even to watch. As we saw, *Vipers' Tangle* remains one of Mauriac's most compelling books.

The New Story of Mouchette by Bernanos was also an attack on popular misconceptions within the Catholic community, but it illustrates more than "assimilation." It illustrates also what may be called the "next step" after "assimilation": "interpenetration." We were actually examining this process which

Newman called "interpenetration" when we discussed the "universality" of Bernanos' *New Story of Mouchette*, but we did not then use Newman's term because we were not yet able to review *The New Story* in comparison with the other Catholic novels, and so could not see its place among them as we are ready to see it now.

The first thing to recall about *The New Story of Mouchette* is that, unlike most of Bernanos' books, it belongs to that type of Catholic fiction (*The Desert of Love, Decline and Fall, England Made Me*, "The Eye," *The Violent Bear It Away*, and others) which does not use Catholic characters. The entire action of *The New Story* takes place in a "dead parish." When Bernanos was writing this book (1936), most Catholics tended to believe that the aspirations and values characteristic of Roman Catholics could operate only in a "Catholic" setting, or at least where a Roman Catholic was present. Bernanos' demonstration of Mouchette's longing for purity in love was the center of the action, as was her rejection of an environment where not only love but even mutual concern were nonexistent. We remember the man who came along the road at the end of the book. If he had noticed Mouchette, if he had spoken, perhaps she would not have died. But he passed as all people in that dead land passed each other—without concern. In showing the persistence of Mouchette's longing for love, and her terrible isolation in this community where love was impossible, Bernanos was drawing on values of love and brotherhood that Catholics believed were most specifically their own. Catholics assumed they were shared to some degree by other Christians, but "pagans," and particularly people from such brutalized backgrounds as Mouchette's were generally regarded as not holding them, at least not to the same degree. But Bernanos shows Mouchette holding them so strongly that without them her life is unbearable. Thus far *The New Story of Mouchette* indicates "assimilation" by the Catholic community of a new recognition, an assimilation that continued and developed, as one may see from the documents issued by the Second Vatican Council, particularly the *Pastoral Constitution on the Church in the Modern World* (1965). Bernanos, in making Mouchette real to Catholics, symbolized for them all the millions of Mouchettes, and today his story forces a Catholic audience to recognize their existence. Assimilation was not so much the work of the mind of Bernanos where the story was conceived, as the result of the coming into being of the thousands of dead parishes in France. Bernanos was recognizing facts; his mind was simply the means of transmitting a truth. "Assimilation" of ideas from "the crowded world" usually takes place in precisely this way.

But there is more than assimilation in *The New Story of Mouchette*. In 1936 most non-Catholics were as apt as Catholics to suppose that people in communities as primitive as Mouchette's had few spiritual needs and no means of expressing them. The meaning of Mouchette's suicide, which is in effect her murder by the callousness of those around her, was as shocking to most secularists as to most Catholics. Bernanos' story was part of the development of the modern Catholic attitude toward the deprived, an attitude that began to grow in the time of Lamennais and de Coux. His story, however, also demonstrated recognitions that since 1936 have become more and more widely accepted in the secular world. Newman wrote that after development takes place by "assimilation," it makes way for itself by "interpenetration." As the Catholic recognitions illustrated by *The New Story* entered into the non-Catholic environment, where similar recognitions had also been forming, the altered forms of Catholic thinking were reinforced by the similarly altered thinking of many non-Catholics, who in turn were often strengthened in their changing views by the discovery of their new and unexpected Catholic allies. Thus Newman's term of "interpenetration" describes very well the process by which "doctrines and views" make their "way" in the "crowded world."

When we examined *The New Story* in the chapter on Mauriac and Bernanos, we saw that Bernanos' novel was "Catholic" in the old meaning of that word as "universal." Bernanos was addressing all people everywhere as well as all Catholics, and he was also demonstrating that all people have similar longings and similar spiritual values. Even the most ignorant and those so poor that their living conditions are scarcely above the animal level share the longings that "religious" people or "educated" people had supposed were particularly their own. Bernanos demonstrated that these values are not generated by education or religion but exist wherever there are human beings. The fact is obvious to us in the 1970s. We receive *The New Story* quite easily today. Indeed, in 1969 it was made into a successful movie. But in the 1930s such "universality" as this was revolutionary.

The New Story of Mouchette was so "new" that it took a long time for the altered thinking it represented to be assimilated by the Catholic community, and even longer for it to penetrate the environment. In the 1940s many people and most Catholics had heard of *The Diary of a Country Priest* but few had heard of *Mouchette*. It is not surprising, therefore, to find Graham Greene undertaking much the same sort of task in 1948 with *The Heart of the Matter*.

The New Story of Mouchette concerned an "innocent" suicide. Greene used the same theme. Twelve years after *The New Story* Catholic popular belief still held that self-murder was an offense that led automatically to damnation. Greene's *The Heart of the Matter* made it clear to the reader that Scobie's suicide, which was motivated by his sense of responsibility for others, did not shut him off from God's mercy. To most Catholics this was a shocking idea. As we saw in the section on Graham Greene, Scobie's fate was vigorously disputed. What made the dispute particularly compelling, however, was that Greene complicated Bernanos' theme by adding another, and the second theme was even more shocking to Catholics—and to all people everywhere at that time.

Scobie's suicide was not "innocent" in the same way as Mouchette's but was caused by Scobie's "corruption by pity," a most debatable issue both then and today. Scobie was a man obsessed by his sense of responsibility. In no case did he trust God, but he himself took up the burden of care for the people around him. As we observed, the sense of responsibility for others had been the central preoccupation of Greene's generation. We saw that in books which preceded *The Heart of the Matter* Greene so thoroughly accepted the ideal that each human being is responsible for his fellow human beings that responsibility was his most frequently used theme. But the meaning of *The Heart of the Matter* is that the sense of responsibility, particularly in the guise of "pity" can corrupt. And Greene's contention that a man must do the best he can for others but that there are limits beyond which he must cease his own efforts and place his trust in the universe—in ultimate good, in God, is as hotly debatable today as it was when Greene made it his subject twenty years ago. Greene was reassessing a belief which was not only widespread among Roman Catholics but which was probably common to all but a minority of thinking people in the decades following the 1930s. Trust in God was a principle that had survived precariously where it had survived at all. It retained more strength among Protestants, particularly among so-called Fundamentalists, than among Catholics, whose adherence to "Catholic action" rested on pragmatic effort, and often on precisely the sort of "pity" Greene attacked. As for the secularists, they gave their allegiance in those years to such various forms of social action and "solidarity" as the United Fronts. Not trust in the universe, but active and pragmatic mutual help, or aid for the wretched of the earth were the most widely accepted secular principles.

Thus in attacking "responsibility" Greene was attacking both a Catholic belief widespread since at least the time of Oxanam, Lamennais, and de Coux, and also a cardinal tenet of the entire Western world. *The Heart of the Matter*, therefore, represented "interpenetration," as did *The New Story of Mouchette*. While *The Heart of the Matter* was attempting to "assimilate" into Catholic thinking a point of view radically at odds with that thinking, it was also attempting to "interpenetrate" the secular environment, whose habits of thought were equally at variance. *The New Story of Mouchette* represents a step in assimilation and interpenetration that succeeded. The theme Greene illustrated in the life and death of Scobie, however, has not yet become a part either of Catholic thinking or of the thinking of most secularists. Interpenetration cannot prevail if there is slight or impaired response, or if no incipient or concomitant recognition exists in the environment. Where the theme of Bernanos' *Nouvelle Histoire* eventually met such a response, the theme of Greene's *Heart of the Matter* has not yet done so, at least not to any great extent.

There are signs, however, that Greene's theme may one day prove to have been prophetic. Since 1948 there has been a perceptible change in the attitude of the West. The French have withdrawn from Algeria, the British are withdrawing from the last areas of their former empire, and the increasing American reluctance toward involvement in Asia may indicate that the Western world has begun to be ready for Greene's belief that just as no man can morally carry the burdens of everyone around him, so no member of the Western community of nations can any longer be a keeper of mankind's conscience, but must trust to the evolution of the race, in which each community follows its own destiny.

But whether or not Greene's point of view is ever fully accepted, one fact is clear: Greene defined his beliefs in opposition to beliefs current in his time. We saw why and how this tendency to take positions of opposition grew in the French and English Catholic communities after 1789 and after the industrial revolution until with the Catholic novelists positions of spiritual opposition became their major source of drama. In the climate of awareness and self-awareness that grew as cultural convergence intensified, the Catholic novelists fell into radical opposition as their natural stance. And opposition became the "spark" of the creativity which produced the Catholic novels.

CHAPTER XIII

Abrasiveness and the
Creative Spark

Catholics in America never had the cultural security to lash out at non-Catholics as Catholics did in England and France. America produced no writers like Huysmans or Chesterton, who assumed that the surrounding environment contrasted to the environment of the Catholic community in being either degenerate or mad. The strain of really impassioned hatred of secularism that survived as a minor note even in *The Heart of the Matter* with the portrait of Scobie's wife's degenerate suitor, Wilson, or in Bernanos' *Under the Sun of Satan* with the depiction of the Malorthys, never appeared in the United States. As we noted briefly in the section on the American novels, the absence of this strain makes the novels written here seem less varied and rich than those produced in Europe. The two American Catholic novelists we discussed, Flannery O'Connor and J. F. Powers, represented the two tendencies we had seen in the work of the European Catholic novelists, criticism of the secular environment and criticism of "religious" people, but in criticism of the environment the approach was milder than the European. When Powers or Flannery O'Connor criticized non-Catholics, or nonreligious people, the criticism had nothing to do with non-Catholicism or anti-Catholicism. Powers tended to attack some general characteristic: inhumanity as in "The Old Bird" or racial prejudice as in "The Trouble." Flannery O'Connor tended to attack broadly prevalent patterns of human behavior, such as meliorism (Rayber in *The Violent Bear It Away*) or the need to dominate (Mr. Head in "The Artificial Nigger"). For all of his grotesqueness, Rayber was not a repellent personality, as Wilson was in *The Heart of the Matter*. And Powers' stories such as "The Eye" had a self-conscious social significance, a sentimentality that would have made Powers a different kind of writer if he had pursued this kind of work. He might have developed a tenderness and romanticism that would have been appealing and might perhaps have become as moving as the work of Saroyan or of some other recent American sentimentalist, but I cannot believe this would have been a fortunate development. In any case, it did not occur—or at this writing has not yet occurred—and when Powers turned to scrutinize his own Catholic community a vein of iron came into his work that was not present when he treated universal subjects. In his criticisms of the Catholic community he became capable of dissecting character to depths he had not reached before. This fact confirms the finding that criticism of the Catholic community was most stimulating to Catholic writers.

At first glance, Flannery O'Connor seems an exception to this rule. Seldom does she bring Catholics on the scene. The Catholic family in "A Temple of the Holy Ghost," the priest in "A Displaced Person," and old Father Finn in "An Enduring Chill" are rare examples of Catholics being given roles in Flannery O'Connor's casts of characters. But the symbolic meaning of the story rather than the characters was central in Flannery O'Connor's fiction, and her symbolism was profoundly Catholic. It expressed the problems of human beings who were called by God to serve him, but who either opposed or distorted that call. This conflict has been a compelling concern for Roman

Catholics in all periods, but the opposition between religious "vocation" and the rejection of religious vocation for a secular orientation has never been more current or more pressing among Catholics than it is today. In this sense, Flannery O'Connor's work must be termed "Catholic" and also "modern Catholic" with the same emphasis as *The New Story of Mouchette*. But the calling by God and the response to that call have also been as deeply a Protestant concern as a Catholic one. Many Protestants would consider them particularly characteristic because of the Protestant emphasis on the personal encounter between each human being and his God. Furthermore, there has never been a period in Protestantism when the conflict, distinction, and coincidence between secular and religious orientations have been more central than at present, when pragmatic amelioration of poverty and ignorance is regarded by many as the greatest "religious" challenge of our time, a conclusion with which Flannery O'Connor emphatically did not agree. Her disagreement is, however, a minority position at present. *The Violent Bear It Away*, like *The Heart of the Matter*, represents an effort to assimilate into Catholic thinking elements which have not yet been successfully assimilated, and to penetrate Protestant and secular thinking with a point of view that is still opposed by the great majority. *The Violent Bear It Away* has a great deal in common with *The Heart of the Matter*. Much of the interest with which *The Violent Bear It Away* has been read grows out of the very fact that its point of view was and is probably rejected by ninety percent of its readers. Yet one may assume that readers are at least moved to doubt their own position, they are stirred to reassessment and are reached by the argument. Otherwise they would not trouble to read or discuss. And few novels have roused more discussion among their readers than *The Heart of the Matter* or *The Violent Bear It Away*. Spiritual growth within the Catholic tradition has often rested on obstinate and compelling statements of what is temporarily a minority position. I believe that these books represent particularly vital forces in the shape of growth to come.

We have found three kinds of writing being produced by the Catholic novelists: separatist writing whose chief preoccupation was criticism of the non-Catholic environment; assimilative writing based on criticism of the Catholic community and recognition of the attitudes of the surrounding world; and also the writing we have described as representing interpenetration. It would be fallacious, however, to suppose that these three kinds correspond to an ascending hierarchy of literary excellence, and that just as self-criticism produced better drama than criticism of the environment, so themes seeking interpenetration produced better drama than writing based on the Catholic community. "The Eye" seeks interpenetration, and its quality as literature is notably lower than *Morte d'Urban*, which deals almost exclusively with the Catholic community.

Before concluding this study we should distinguish between the historical significance of the fiction we have examined and that fiction's achievement of literary excellence. Have we discovered any fact of historical significance beyond our central finding that "a period of swift and intense convergence is stimulating to literary activity"?

It is obvious from our study that a mistake has been made by the many people who believe that the Catholic community in the late 1960s fell suddenly into a state of chaos and confusion. A definite development, convergence with the secular environment, had been taking place for at least seventy years—since the time of Huysmans. It is necessary to remember that this convergence was not all on one side. If the Catholics cleared away many of the corruptions of their faith that had repelled secularists, so also did secularists abandon many of their own superstitions. Catholics were no longer forced into opposition by the secular belief in scientific determinism which repelled Claudel and Maritain. There was also erosion in the secular belief that the profit system was a source of automatic "progress," and that the poor and ignorant could be ignored because ultimately the benefits trickling down to their level would eliminate the conditions from which they suffered. A recognition that material advances can go with spiritual and moral impoverishment also grew strongly among most thinking secularists from 1920 to the present. The secular world's recognition that the gap between the privileged and the deprived was widening instead of narrowing, its growth of concern for this world's Mouchettes, its loss of confidence in "profits" as automatic for all, its abandon of the belief that "education" was the one necessary measure of moral health, did away with sources of much of the indignation that had moved Mauriac, Bernanos, Chesterton, and Belloc. If Catholics approached the modern world, it was because the modern world finally arrived at recognitions that made possible an approach by a people oriented to values of the spirit. In the 1960s convergence between thinking Catholics and thinking people in the secular world became, for many practical purposes, an overwhelming confluence.

It was observed at the beginning of this essay that the Catholic novels of the highest quality virtually ceased to appear after the mid-1960s. The period of most intense creativity tapered off about the time of the Second Vatican Council. In the present era of confluence, Graham Greene's new novels cannot compare to *The Power and the Glory*, written during the time of convergence. Muriel Spark is not the equal of Evelyn Waugh, and Jean Montaurier is a pale shadow of Georges Bernanos. And it is significant that Flannery O'Connor's novels, the latest in the great tradition, depend for drama on an intransigeant refusal to compromise the values of the spirit.

The period of creativity that produced the Catholic novels had a characteristic which during the 1960s was largely lost. That characteristic was abrasiveness, an overlapping with the secular world in which the Catholic community was always so

conscious of its difference from the outer environment that friction never ceased, even if, as in the United States, friction was
caused rather by the entry of typically American secular values
into American Catholicism than by Catholic attack on the environment itself. The source of the friction between Catholicism
and secularism was always the same: from 1789 until at least
the end of the 1950s Catholics emphasized the primacy of spiritual values, while the secularists, in contrast, emphasized the
necessity for material progress, whether through scientific en-
deavor, economic advance, or political action. The abrasiveness
was mild at first because contact between the secular environment and the Catholic community was for a long time inhibited
by traditional Catholic separatism, but as convergence increased
so did abrasiveness. In the beginning European Catholic writers
simply saw their own communities as "good," the secular environments as in error or "bad," and Catholic novels lacked the
intensity that comes from critical self-scrutiny; but, as time went
on and Catholics emphasized more and more the values of the
spirit in opposition to the values pressed upon them by secularism, sensitive Catholic writers, such as Mauriac, were so closely
in contact with secularism that they recognized the justice of the
secular environment's accusations: that Catholics themselves did
not observe the spiritual values they professed. This period was
the one of most vital creativity, as the Catholic novelists were
forced into agonizing reappraisal of their own communities.
Nevertheless, at the same time, they did not cease their opposition to the secular environment, and the friction between secularism and the convictions of a people oriented primarily to
spiritual values sparked the greatest of the Catholic novels. The
determinism of Zola and the long line of naturalists was answered by the works of Bernanos, in which free human beings
shaped their own destinies. The skepticism of Anatole France
and the ontological bitterness of Thomas Hardy were contra-
dicted by Mauriac's novels of grace and redemption and

Greene's evocations of the mystery of God's mercy. Meanwhile, in the United States, the tendency of American Catholics to adopt the secular community's values of social meliorism without spiritual reservations gave rise to Flannery O'Connor's brilliant satires, in which social meliorists were depicted as blind victims of illusion, who did not understand that without spiritual dedication social meliorism was powerless to reach even those it sought to help. J. F. Powers had already exposed the spiritual bankruptcy of the "golfing priests" and the "regular fellows," who had abandoned spiritual values to go over to secularism on secularism's most superficial terms.

All this came about in the period of convergence, a period in which contact between the secular environment and the Catholic communities, while close and frequent, found each resolutely maintaining its own identity.

When the secular environment and the Catholic communities entered into confluence, however, abrasiveness lessened. The secular world, having softened its emphasis on pragmatism, became more receptive to values of the spirit. The Catholic communities, with a long overdue opening of the heart to all men of good will, recognized the change—but often recognized it so unreservedly that many Catholics lost nearly all sense of separatism and with it much of their sense of spiritual dedication. At the same time, the Catholic communities, after their long absorption of secular criticism and of the necessity Péguy had seen so long ago for the "clerks of the spirit" to pay attention to the needs of the body, had fallen into that state described by Newman in which the assimilating organism is endangered by repletion. So much assimilation had taken place that there was a crisis of identity. Catholics, no longer so critical of secularism, became by an unfortunate corollary often also no longer critical of the inroads of secularism into Catholicism's own essence. It became difficult for many Catholics to discern what Catholics advocated that was not also advocated by most men of good will. Flannery O'Connor was the last to protest—against meliorism—and she was virtually a solitary voice. For great numbers of Catholics, confluence by the mid-1960s became so complete that they were no longer sure what the true Catholic essence was. The primary and defiant Catholic emphasis upon the spirit, which for so many generations had generated the creative spark between the Catholic communities and the secular environment, virtually ceased.

In this period Catholic novels appeared with less and less frequency. Their vigor diminished, and their assertions were frail echoes of what they once had been. Just as we found isolation once inhibiting to literary excellence, so assimilation, if it becomes confluence, obviously also exercises an inhibiting influence. True assimilation in Newman's sense should not bring impoverishment of identity, but the reverse. The process is seen to have fulfilled its purpose only when the assimilating organism has overcome repletion and increased, not decreased, its own characteristic being. The period of highest creativity in the case of the Catholic novels was the period between the time of isolation and the period of confluence. In the period of isolation, Barbey d'Aurevilly, Huysmans, Belloc, and Chesterton were determined to mark out the insulated separatism of the Catholic communities. By the mid-1960s the opposite was true, and Catholics were emphasizing the beliefs and goals they had in common with modern secularism rather than beliefs and goals which were in opposition. Obviously, the period between these two extremes was the one of highest creativity.

The unavoidable conclusion is that neither confluence nor isolation are productive of the flowering that produced the Catholic novels and the accompanying spiritual growth within the vital, centuries-old Catholic tradition. It would seem that the Catholic community should have *both* contact with the secular world *and* a keen sense of its own essence, particularly of its historically characteristic emphasis on the spirit. Without the abrasiveness of such a distinction from the secular environment, the spark of creative growth cannot be struck. Creativity's manifestations diminish. It seems probable that they will continue to diminish until such time as Catholics reestablish their identity and maintain their distinctness from the modern world at least as emphatically as their association with it. The part immersed in the whole must be more itself by virtue of union, not less, if convergence is finally to achieve its real function.

CHAPTER XIV

The Catholic Novel and Historical Criticism

In distinguishing between the cultural aspects of the novels discussed in this study and their achievements as literature, there is one general assertion that should be made. It would have been folly to have tried to examine these works without historical knowledge of the Catholic tradition in which they were produced. One cannot fully appreciate, or even fully understand Mauriac unless one has some comprehension of French Jansenism and of the nature of the French bourgeoisie after 1789. Comprehension of Bernanos and his "dreams past all measure" is impossible unless one knows how French rightist idealism cherished its code of spiritual values and reacted to the coming of the industrial age. To understand Waugh's point of view of extreme detachment and Greene's ease with foreign backgrounds, one must take into account the individualism of English Catholics from the time of the Reformation. Similarly, it is impossible to appreciate fully the satires of J. F. Powers without knowing the Americanist ideas that developed in the time of Father Isaac Hecker and depended on the whole ideal of pragmatism the American Church had shown since the days of Carroll. Nor can one grasp all the nuances of Flannery

O'Connor's work unless one knows something about Jansenism in America and Irish American Puritanism with its resemblance to Protestant Fundamentalism.

It would seem imperative that literary studies abandon their present lack of emphasis on historical background. It should be obvious that today individuals, particularly sensitive and creative individuals, are subject to cultural overlappings, interpenetrations, and abrasions which generate tremendous discharges of energy. In the study of modern literature the cultural multiplicity of the modern world is of enormous importance. This study has covered only the Catholic novel. There is also a "Negro novel" and a "Jewish novel." There are the literatures of other nations, other cultural communities, many of them alien to the traditions of the Western world, and these literatures are being newly translated into many languages. It is imperative to comprehend how diverse and complex cultural backgrounds are today, how culture affects art, and how the conflicts, overlappings, and abrasiveness of different cultures affect the processes of creativity. In the case of Japanese literature, no one can even begin to appreciate Soseki's *Kokoro* who does not know something of the tensions in Japan under Soseki's Emperor Meiji. In the case of Indian literature, no one can comprehend the depth of Khushwant Singh's fine novel, *The Last Train to Pakistan*, unless one not only knows something about the postcolonial partition of India but understands at least enough about the beliefs of the Sikhs to realize the religious and ethical significance of giving up one's life in combat for others. Nor can one appreciate the serious bearing of Narayan's delightful comedy, *The Man-Eater of Malgudi*, unless one has some understanding of Hinduism and the idea that a *rakshasa* or demon can be safely left to go his own way because ultimately he will not need to be combated but will destroy himself—a theme in which a perceptive reader may feel Narayan's attitude reflects somewhat the spirit of India's stance in the 1950s toward Communism and the Western world. It is even more difficult to evaluate Negro literature without some knowledge of the Negro background, or Jewish literature without understanding the present state of the world's Jewish communities. Negroes are torn between forces of convergence and forces of separatism. Jews are divided over the issue of a separatist Zionism and the increasing assimilation of once separated Jewish communities in most nations of the world. Neither Negroes nor Jews have arrived at a state of confluence, but have been instead in the condition of tension between separation and convergence that in the case of the Catholic tradition was most productive of development and growth.

We saw with the Catholic novels that the form was sterile, producing works of second and third rate aesthetic and intellectual appeal, until the Catholic artists transformed the established and chronic Catholic spirit of opposition to the secular world into opposition to their own tradition also, and began their criticism of their own community. We also saw how by so doing they entered the growing, changing, suffering spirit of development that was shaping Catholicism in those crucial years. When the Catholic novelists turned to scrutinize what was most sensitively their own, they touched for the first time the developing thought of a great creative tradition, they became part, so to speak, of one of the vast tides of the creative spirit that moves below and within man's history through the ages; they reached and were gripped by a part of the eternal creative urge shaping man by shaping man's beliefs. There is something ecstatic in the creative power that surges in the prophetic force of *The New Story of Mouchette*. It is present in *The Power and the Glory, The Heart of the Matter, Vipers' Tangle*, and *The Violent Bear It Away*, books touched with the anguish of changes deep in Catholicism as it defined and redefined itself in abrasive contact with the secular world. From the time of Christ until the present day, within Catholicism a vast idea is stirring and developing. Through a "seizure" of this idea, a seizure which is yet a surrender to it at the same time as a carrying of it to greater heights, the creative force of one of man's great tides of spiritual growth, a living tide, moving far beneath the surface of things, entered the world of conscious articulation. The Catholic novels' power as aesthetic experience and their power as intellectual influence sprang from this fact. They became part of the vaster "articulation" that underlies all. And every act that similarly touches and draws from tides of vitally living and creative traditions does this. One may wonder whether every piece of literature worthy of the name does not similarly belong to a tradition and draw from depths far below man's conscious heritage. A work, for example, that may seem superficially to belong merely to the "English tradition," or the "French tradition," or the "Japanese tradition," or the "Indian tradition," or, more specifically to Sikhism or Hinduism or some other religious or cultural substratification, may draw its unusual power from being in touch, as were the best of the Catholic novels, with one of the deep creative tides which are moving man he knows not where, but whose shaping is in his own free hands and his own free heart.

CHAPTER I French Catholics after 1789

1 Adrien Dansette, *Histoire religieuse de la France contemporaine* (Paris: Flammarion, 1965), p. 194.
2 *Ibid.*, p. 207.
3 *Ibid.*, p. 153.
4 The Loi Falloux in 1850 extended the domain of the religious orders in the field of education. A state diploma was required of secular teachers in secondary schools, but members of religious orders could teach on the strength of their training in their orders. *Ibid.*, p. 285.
5 *Ibid.*, p. 263.
6 *Ibid.*, p. 278.
7 *Ibid.*, p. 274.
8 Henri Daniel-Rops, *The Church in an Age of Revolution, 1789-1870,* translated by John Warrington (London: Dent, 1965).
9 Dansette, pp. 496, 507 f.
10 *Ibid.*, p. 359.
11 *Ibid.*, p. 270.
12 *Ibid.*, p. 271.
13 *Ibid.*, p. 497.
14 *Ibid.*, p. 500.
15 Pius IX, *Syllabus of Errors,* in *Dogmatic Canons and Decrees* (New York: Devin-Adair, 1912), pp. 185-209.
16 *Ibid.*, I, art. 10.
17 *Ibid.*, III.
18 *Ibid.*, VI, art. 39.
19 *Ibid.*, VII, art. 64.
20 *Ibid.*, VIII, art. 58.
21 *Ibid.*, VII, art. 58.
22 *Ibid.*, VIII, art. 67.
23 *Ibid.*, IX, art. 76.
24 *Ibid.*, X.

25   *Ibid.*, X, art. 80.
26   *Ibid.*
27   *Ibid.*, III, art. 15.
28   Dansette, p. 355.
29   *Ibid.*, pp. 796 f.

CHAPTER II   Aestheticians and Precursors

1   "Le Dessous de cartes d'une partie de whist," the first of the stories in the collection to be entitled *Les Diaboliques*. It was refused in January of 1850 by the *Revue des Deux Mondes* but accepted for the spring issue of *Mode*, a worldly, legitimist, "society" periodical. The major novels, *Une vieille Maîtresse* (1851), *L'Ensorcelée* (1852), *Le Chevalier des Touches* (1864), *Un Prêtre marié* (1865), followed the same pattern in portraying human beings in the grip of evil greater than could be accounted for by the sum of human actions, but there is no effort to explore psychological or ontological hypotheses.

2   In 1865, in the preface to a new edition of *Une vieille Maîtresse*, Barbey d'Aurevilly wrote, "Peindre ce qui est, peindre la réalité humaine, crime ou vertu. . . . Les Artistes sont, catholiquement, au-dessous des Ascètes, mais ils ne sont pas des Ascètes, ils sont des Artistes. . . . En peignant la réalité telle qu'elle est . . . en lui insufflant la vie, il a été assez morale comme celà." Jacques Henri Bornecque, "Introduction" to *Les Diaboliques* by Jules Barbey d'Aurevilly (Paris: Garnier, 1963), p. cxxx.

3   Bornecque cites some interesting examples, p. xiv.

4   Charles Péguy, *Cahiers de la Quinzaine, Oeuvres en prose de Charles Péguy* (Paris: Pléiade, 1959), p. 118.

5   Joris-Karl Huysmans, *Là-bas* (Paris: Plon, 1891), p. 144.

6   Robert Baldick, *The Life of Joris-Karl Huysmans* (Oxford, England: Clarendon Press, 1955), pp. 150 f. Boullan was the lapsed priest and served Huysmans as a model for the relatively beneficent Johannes. After Boullan's death Huysmans found a document, the *Cahier rose*, among his papers. In it was a confession of the murder. A nun, Adèle Chevalier, was associated with Boullan in his practices.

7   Marjorie Villiers, *Charles Péguy, A Study in Integrity* (New York: Harper and Row, 1965), pp. 107 f. Frenchmen had good reasons to suppose that the Affair could lead to dangerous international repercussions. General Mercier led the anti-Dreyfus party to suppose that "he held some secret document which would prove Dreyfus' guilt irrefutable. . . . The military judges, when questioning Paléologue, who represented the French Foreign Office, . . . seemed to be haunted by the belief that documents had been returned to the German Embassy and that, if this had not been done, war would have been inevitable" (*ibid.*, p. 116). Therefore, asserting the innocence of Dreyfus was an act of courage. But Péguy and those who agreed with him were sure of their belief in Dreyfus, moved not only by Picquart's evidence but by the anti-Semitism of conservatives. Not only *La Libre Parole* of Edouard Drumont and

Veuillot's *L'Univers* but *La Croix*, a publication belonging to the ultracon-
servative religious order, the Assumptionists, did their utmost against the Jews
throughout the Affair. The Jew as antipatriot, as international profit-seeker
was the center of the anti-Jewish myth, and it had a hold on more groups in
Europe than merely the Catholics—as Germany was to prove.

8   Bernanos was aware of the incipient conflict between *Action française* and the
Church much earlier than is generally supposed, and he had chosen his side.
In 1925 he wrote to Henri Massis that at seventeen he believed completely in
the "ordre que je croyais total" of Maurras. "Mais j'ai compris très tot qu'on
ne peut confondre l'adhésion de l'intelligence avec la foi—et je suis qu'un
homme de foi." Letter of September 25 in a collection of unpublished correspondence in process of being edited by Sister Meredith Murray, Rosary College, River Forest, Illinois.

9   For the account of *Action française* I am drawing on Hannah Arendt, *The
Origins of Totalitarianism* (New York: Harcourt, Brace and World, 1966);
Ernst Nolte, *The Three Faces of Fascism* (New York: Holt, Rinehart and
Winston, 1966); and Dansette, *Histoire religieuse de la France contemporaine.*

10 See Gordon Wright, *Rural Revolution in France: The Peasantry in the Twentieth Century* (Stanford, Calif.: Stanford University Press, 1964), pp. 103 f.

11 Dansette, p. 159.

12 Gilbert Keith Chesterton, *Orthodoxy* (New York: Dodd, Mead, 1936), p. 185.

13 Charles Péguy and Marcel Baudouin, "Jeanne d'Arc," in *Charles Péguy,
Oeuvres poétiques complètes* (Paris: Gallimard, 1957), p. 38. See also Charles
Péguy, "Le Mystère de la charité de Jeanne d'Arc," *ibid.*, p. 426. It is significant that almost exactly the same lines as Péguy wrote with Baudouin in 1897
are repeated in the long play of 1909-1910, when the work was published in
the *Cahiers de la Quinzaine* from October to August.

14 See the declaration that prefaces the first issue of NRF November 15, 1908:
"Les écrivains qui réunit aujourd'hui la *Nouvelle Revue Française* appartien-
nent à la generation qui dans la chronologie littéraire suivit immédiatement le
symbolisme. . . ." A group conscious of its newness and distinctness from the
past was pointing out its existence and setting itself apart.

15 François Mauriac, "Concerning the Claudel-Gide Correspondence," in *Letters
on Art and Literature*, translated by Mario A. Pei (New York: Philosophical
Library, 1953), p. 78.

16 Robert Mallet, editor, *The Correspondence between Paul Claudel and André
Gide, 1899-1926*, translated by John Russell (London: Secker and Warburg,
1952), letter of March 7, 1914, p. 203.

17 I have taken this account, including the description of Bergson's theory of the
"durée" as it affected his young hearers, from Raïssa Maritain's *Les grandes
Amitiés et Les Aventures de grace* (Paris: Desclée de Brouwer, 1948),
pp. 91 f.

18 The influence of Bloy on Maritain did not give the latter either an unduly
dark view of the world or an expectation of the Apocalypse. As Maritain's
relations with Bergson were to indicate, Maritain always thought for himself.

19 *Théonas, ou les entretiens d'un sage et de deux philosophes sur diverses
matières inégalement, actuelles* (Paris: Nouvelle Librairie Nationale, 1921),

quoted by Charles A. Fecher, *The Philosophy of Jacques Maritain* (Westminster, Md.: Newman Press, 1953), p. 340. See Fecher, pp. 337 f., for the effect on students of Thomism as taught in France before Maritain.

20   Paul Claudel, *L'Art poétique* (Paris: Mercure de France, 1913), p. 45.

21   Jacques Rivière and Paul Claudel, "Correspondence," *Nouvelle Revue Française*, XII (September 1925), 300.

22   Jacques Rivière, "De la Foi," *Nouvelle Revue Française*, No. 47 (November 1912), p. 781; No. 48 (December 1912), p. 970. No volume numbers are given for the NRF until Rivière took over as editor in 1919.

23   Jacques Maritain, *Art and Scholasticism and The Frontiers of Poetry*, translated by Joseph W. Evans (New York: Scribner's, 1962). *Art and Scholasticism* was completed in 1920 and *The Frontiers of Poetry* in 1927. It is my impression from the context that the notes in this edition were enlarged in 1927.

24   *Ibid.*, p. 57. Bernanos showed his fidelity to this idea when he wrote, "On ne peut le nier: l'art a un autre but que lui-meme. Sa perpetuelle recherche de l'expression n'est que l'image affaiblie, ou comme le symbole, de sa perpetuelle recherche de l'Étre." He wrote this in 1926 in the "Letter to Fréderic Lefevre" that forms the first chapter of *Le Crépuscule des vieux* (Paris: Gallimard, 1956), p. 13. Date of letter ascertained from the correspondence being edited by Sister Meredith Murray.

25   Maritain, *Art and Scholasticism*, p. 59.

26   *Ibid.*, p. 46.

27   *Ibid.*, "Notes," p. 221.

28   Jacques Maritain, *Creative Intuition in Art and Poetry*, The A. W. Mellon Lectures in the Fine Arts (New York: Pantheon, 1953), p. 239.

29   By accidental irony (or deliberate balancing on the part of the judges) the last French winner of the Nobel Prize before Mauriac in 1952 was André Gide in 1947.

30   François Mauriac, "Chronique dramatique," *Nouvelle Revue Française*, XXIV (February 1925), 220.

31   Rivière said characteristically in *Moralisme et littérature*, which he wrote with Ramon Fernandez, that while the advances of romanticism in introducing the individual into literature must be valued and retained, the intensity of the classicists in treating universal traits of character should be incorporated, and he cited Racine as a model. Jacques Rivière and Ramon Fernandez, *Moralisme et littérature* (Paris: Éditions Corréa, 1932), p. 83. Also, the clarity of classicism appealed to Rivière. He declared that he was grateful to Dadaism for carrying the tendencies of nineteenth-century poetry into the "neant linguistique" which proved his need of returning to the clarity of traditional French expression. Jacques Rivière, *Nouvelles Études* (Paris: Gallimard, 1947), p. 308.

32   François Mauriac, "Chronique dramatique," *Nouvelle Revue Française*, XXIV (May 1925), 925.

33   François Mauriac, "On Writing Today," in *Second Thoughts, Reflections on Literature and on Life* (New York: World, 1961), p. 16.

34   *Ibid.*

35 *Ibid.*, p. 35.
36 See Mauriac, "After the Death of Georges Bernanos," in *Letters on Art and Literature*, p. 7.
37 Georges Bernanos, *Nous autres français* (Paris: Gallimard, 1939), p. 31.
38 Georges Bernanos, *Les Enfants humiliés* (Paris: Gallimard, 1949), p. 86.
39 Bernanos says of Donissan. "J'avais besoin d'une espèce de héros de la vie intérieure." Letter to Jean Guiraud, Bar-le-Duc, end of May 1926. From the unpublished correspondence being edited by Sister Meredith Murray.
40 The areas of France that clung to orthodoxy showed their characteristics very early. When priests were asked to swear allegiance to the Revolutionary Constitution, the great number who agreed (forty-five to forty-eight percent) came from the central provinces, the chief ports, and the cities. For a century and a half, Brittany, Flanders, Artois, and the Massif Central were the most Catholic (and Royalist) sections, while Burgundy, Champagne, and the plains of Ile-de-France were the mainstay of the Republic. Dansette, pp. 72 f.
41 Bernanos, *Les Enfants humiliés*, p. 199.
42 André Gide, *Journal, 1889-1919* (Paris: Gallimard, 1951), p. 186.

CHAPTER III   François Mauriac

1 Cecil Jenkins, *Mauriac* (London: Oliver and Boyd, 1965), p. 5.
2 François Mauriac, *Le Désert de l'amour* (Paris: Grasset, 1925), p. 31.
3 *Ibid.*, p. 198.
4 *Ibid.*, p. 201.
5 *Ibid.*, p. 243.
6 The article in which Sartre made his famous objection, "God is not an artist and neither is M. Mauriac," is reprinted in *Situations I* (Paris: Gallimard, 1947).
7 As Graham Greene points out, there is no reason why it should be felt that every writer in the modern period is somehow obligated to tailor his style to the Jamesian ideal of nonintrusion, an ideal which has in fact been carried too far. "François Mauriac," in *The Lost Childhood, and Other Essays* (New York: Viking, 1952), p. 70.
8 François Mauriac, *Le Noeud de vipères* (Paris: Grasset, 1933), p. 87.
9 *Ibid.*, p. 29.
10 *Ibid.*, p. 93.
11 *Ibid.*, p. 126.
12 *Ibid.*, p. 109.
13 *Ibid.*, pp. 128, 129.
14 *Ibid.*, p. 39.
15 *Ibid.*, p. 148.
16 *Ibid.*, p. 158.
17 After Louis' death, his eldest son writes a letter that expresses his ideas on investments. One gathers that under his guidance the family may not long keep the fortune it has garnered.
18 *Ibid.*, p. 201.

CHAPTER IV   Georges Bernanos

1   Georges Bernanos, *Journal d'un curé de campagne*, in *Oeuvres romanesques* (Paris: Gallimard, 1961), p. 1139. The translation is by Pamela Morris, *The Diary of a Country Priest* (New York: Macmillan, 1948), pp. 138, 139.
2   Bernanos, *The Diary of a Country Priest*, p. 167.
3   *Ibid.*, p. 162.
4   *Ibid.*, p. 157.
5   *Ibid.*, p. 165.
6   *Ibid.*, p. 170.
7   I, 14, 8; I-II, 72, 3, i.
8   Bernanos, *The Diary of a Country Priest*, p. 173.
9   A serious mistranslation occurs here. In the Morris translation Dufréty's final letter refers to the "lady who shares my life" (p. 298). In the original the verb reads, "qui partageait alors ma vie," clearly showing the important fact that she shares his life no longer (p. 1259).
10   Gaëton Picon, "Préface" to *Oeuvres romanesques de Georges Bernanos* (Paris: Gallimard, 1961), p. xxi.
11   Bernanos, *The Diary of a Country Priest*, p. 199.
12   *Ibid.*, p. 40.
13   *Ibid.*, p. 65.
14   *Ibid.*, p. 234.
15   *Ibid.*, p. 237.
16   *Ibid.*, p. 239.
17   If any reader has a sense that the chivalric ideal Bernanos embodies in M. Olivier has some resemblance to fascism, he should remember that this ideal had a long history in Europe before fascists came on the scene. All royalists and most conservatives in France shared it. Fascism found it in existence and attempted to exploit it. There can be no doubt that the furious hatred that Bernanos felt for the whole fascist phenomenon had its roots partly in the fact that he regarded it as a sort of blasphemy. See his bitter attack in *Les grands Cimetières sous la lune* (Paris: Plon, 1938).
18   Bernanos, *The Diary of a Country Priest*, p. 237.
19   Albert Béguin, *Bernanos par lui-même* (Paris: Éditions du Seuil, 1959), p. 80.
20   Henri Debluë, *Les Romans de Georges Bernanos* (Neufchâtel: La Baconnière, 1965), p. 218.
21   Georges Bernanos, *Under the Sun of Satan*, translated by Harry L. Binsse (New York: Pantheon, 1949), p. 125. This is a careful and scrupulously exact translation. The Morris translation of this work, *The Star of Satan* (New York: Macmillan, 1940), is not at all satisfactory.
22   Bernanos, *Under the Sun of Satan*, p. 144.
23   *Ibid.*, p. 145.
24   *Ibid.*, p. 147.
25   *Ibid.*, p. 148.
26   *Ibid.*, p. 154.
27   *Ibid.*, p. 189.
28   *Ibid.*, p. 235.
29   *Ibid.*, p. 253.

CHAPTER V   England after the Reformation

1 Unlike the French Catholic writer, who depends heavily on French history and local color, an Englishman may develop a story in Rome, Africa, or Mexico as naturally as in England. For example, Frederick Rolfe's *Hadrian VII* is chiefly set in Rome, Evelyn Waugh's *Black Mischief* in Abyssinia, and Graham Greene's *The Power and the Glory* in Mexico. Greene makes particularly good use of the exotic interest of foreign environments.

2 E. I. Watkin, *Roman Catholicism in England* (London: Oxford University Press, 1957), p. 101.

3 *Ibid.*, p. 111.

4 Tobias Smollett, *Roderick Random* (New York: J. M. Dent, 1927), pp. 160 f.

5 Lawrence Sterne, *Tristram Shandy* (New York: Holt, Rinehart and Winston, 1962), p. 90.

6 Margaret M. Maison, *The Victorian Vision, Studies in the Religious Novel* (New York: Sheed and Ward, 1961), p. 169.

7 M. P. Carthy, *Catholicism in English-Speaking Lands* (New York: Hawthorn, 1964), p. 33.

8 Evelyn Waugh, *Edmund Campion* (London: Longmans, 1937), p. 212.

9 See G. Culkin, "England," in *New Catholic Encyclopedia* (New York: McGraw-Hill, 1967), V, 369.

10 Waugh, *Edmund Campion*, p. 45.

11 Herbert Thurston, S.J., and Donald Attwater, editors, *Butler's Lives of the Saints* (New York: Kenedy, 1943), I, 682.

12 Watkin, p. 209.

13 Wilfrid Ward, *William George Ward and the Catholic Revival* (London: Macmillan, 1893), pp. 320-52.

14 Maisie Ward, *Gilbert Keith Chesterton* (New York: Sheed and Ward, 1943), pp. 181 f.

15 See discussion of *Emmanuel Burden* below.

16 Robert Speaight, *The Life of Eric Gill* (New York: Kenedy, 1966), pp. 39 f.

17 See Ronald Knox, "Studies in the Literature of Sherlock Holmes," in *Essays in Satire* (London: Sheed and Ward, 1928), pp. 148 f.

18 Meriol Trevor, *Newman, The Pillar of the Cloud* (Garden City, N. Y.: Doubleday, 1962), pp. 587 f.

19 Meriol Trevor, *Newman, Light in Winter* (Garden City, N. Y.: Doubleday, 1963), pp. 204 f.

20 Newman was as quiet about his opposition as Ward was ostentatious in his partisanship. See Trevor, *Light in Winter*, pp. 473 f., and Wilfrid Ward, pp. 249 f.

21 Ralph M. Wiltgen, *The Rhine Flows into the Tiber* (New York: Hawthorn, 1967), p. 17.

22 Wilfrid Ward, p. 261.

CHAPTER VI   The Precursors and Minor Writers

1 Frederick Rolfe, *Hadrian VII* (New York: Knopf, 1937), p. 8.
2 Ronald Knox, *A Spiritual Aeneid* (London: Longmans, 1918), p. 32.
3 Gilbert Keith Chesterton, "The Ballad of the White Horse," *The Collected Poems of G. K. Chesterton* (London: Palmer, 1927), s83, l. 242.
4 Hilaire Belloc, *Emmanuel Burden* (London: Methuen, 1904), p. 13.
5 *Ibid.*, p. 309.

CHAPTER VII   Evelyn Waugh

1 Frank Kermode, "Mr. Waugh's Critics," *Puzzles and Epiphanies* (London: Routledge and Kegan Paul, 1962), p. 167.
2 John Dryden, "The Origin and Progress of Satire," prefixed to his translation of Juvenal and Perseus in 1693, quoted by William K. Wimsatt and Cleanth Brooks, *Literary Criticism* (New York: Random House, 1957), p. 207.
3 Frances Donaldson, *Evelyn Waugh, Portrait of a Country Neighbor* (London: Weidenfeld and Nicolson, 1967), p. 32.
4 Evelyn Waugh, *Decline and Fall* (Boston: Little, Brown, 1946), p. 159.
5 J. F. Powers, Lecture at the University of Chicago, Spring 1966.
6 Waugh, *Decline and Fall*, p. 183.
7 Evelyn Waugh, *Vile Bodies* (Boston: Little, Brown, 1930), p. 284.
8 Evelyn Waugh, "Come Inside," *The Road to Damascus*, edited by John A. O'Brien (Garden City, N. Y.: Doubleday, 1949), p. 18.
9 Edmund Wilson, "Never Apologise, Never Explain," *Classics and Commercials* (New York: Farrar, Straus and Cudahy, 1950), p. 143.
10 Evelyn Waugh, *A Handful of Dust* (London: Chapman and Hall, 1934), p. 222.
11 Stephen Spender, *The Creative Element: A Study of Vision, Despair and Orthodoxy Among Some Modern Writers* (New York: British Book Center, 1954), pp. 167-68.
12 The category of "apologue" as applied here to *A Handful of Dust* relies upon the typology of the novel as developed by Dr. Sheldon Sacks in his book *Fiction and the Shape of Belief* (Berkeley and Los Angeles: University of California Press, 1964) and on his lectures at the University of Chicago in 1968.
13 Evelyn Waugh, *Brideshead Revisited* (Boston: Little, Brown, 1945), p. 340.
14 *Ibid.*, p. 350.

CHAPTER VIII   Graham Greene

1 Graham Greene, "François Mauriac," in *The Lost Childhood, and Other Essays*, p. 70.
2 Graham Greene, *The Heart of the Matter* (New York: Viking, 1964), p. 199.
3 Graham Greene, *Brighton Rock* (New York: Viking, 1961), p. 357.
4 John Atkins, *Graham Greene* (London: Calder and Boyars, 1966), p. 79.

5 Steiner compares Greene's prose to Lawrence Durrell's: "a gold-spun and jeweled Byzantine mosaic next to a black-and-white photograph." See George Steiner, *Language and Silence* (New York: Atheneum, 1967), p. 282. Steiner praises Greene as one of the few exceptions to the "deep, tacit break" that "has occurred between the novelist and the natural spinner of tales," *ibid.*, p. 267.

6 François Mauriac, "Préface" to *Graham Greene* by Victor de Pange (Paris: Éditions Universitaires, 1953), p. 11.

7 Greene, "François Mauriac," in *The Lost Childhood, and Other Essays*, p. 71.

8 Morton Dauwen Zabel, *Craft and Character: Texts, Method, and Vocation in Modern Fiction* (New York: Viking, 1957), p. 280.

9 David Pryce-Jones, *Graham Greene* (London: Bodley Head, 1961), p. 62.

10 I am thinking especially of the arguments of the French critic, de Pange, building on the earlier works of Jacques Madaule, that Greene was not converted to Catholicism but to an English Calvinist form of the doctrine of predestination. I believe this argument is absolutely untenable. See Victor de Pange, "Graham Greene and Jacques Madaule," *Graham Greene* (Paris: Éditions Universitaires, 1953).

11 Greene, *Brighton Rock*, p. 128.

12 *Ibid.*, p. 155.

13 *Ibid.*, p. 179.

14 *Ibid.*, p. 243.

15 *Ibid.*, p. 260.

16 *Ibid.*, p. 331.

17 *Ibid.*, p. 329.

18 *Ibid.*, p. 332.

19 *Ibid.*, p. 357.

20 Graham Greene, "Introduction," *The Power and the Glory* (New York: Viking, 1965), p. 5.

21 When the priest is in jail and the lieutenant, not recognizing him, thinks he is simply a drunken vagrant, he gives him five pesos—the "price of a mass," the priest thinks; and he says in astonishment, "You're a good man." Greene, *The Power and the Glory*, p. 189.

22 *Ibid.*, p. 157.

23 Greene's most recent portrait of the same type is the Negro, Dr. Magiot, the Haitian Communist in *The Comedians* (New York: Viking, 1966).

24 George Orwell, *Encounter*, No. 100, p. 65. Quoted by Pryce-Jones, *Graham Greene*, p. 11.

25 Greene, *The Heart of the Matter*, p. 128.

26 *Ibid.*, p. 277.

27 *Ibid.*, p. 290.

28 *Ibid.*, p. 173.

29 *Ibid.*

30 Greene, *Brighton Rock*, p. 348.

31 Greene, *The Heart of the Matter*, pp. 298-99.

32 Flannery O'Connor's *Wise Blood* was published in 1949, the year after *The Heart of the Matter*.

CHAPTER IX   Catholicism in the United States

1   John Tracy Ellis, *American Catholicism* (Chicago: University of Chicago Press, 1956), p. 33.
2   Theodore Maynard, *The Story of American Catholicism* (Garden City, N. Y.: Doubleday, 1960), I, 132. See also Ellis, *American Catholicism*, pp. 36, 72.
3   Maynard, I, 183.
4   Quoted by Maynard, I, 92.
5   John Tracy Ellis, *The Life of James Cardinal Gibbons* (Milwaukee: Bruce, 1952), I, 80.
6   *Ibid.,* I, 93.
7   Maynard, I, 256.
8   *Ibid.,* I, 255.
9   Ellis, *American Catholicism*, p. 33.
10   Ellis, *Life of Cardinal Gibbons*, I, 178.
11   *Ibid.,* I, 817.
12   *Ibid.,* I, 101.
13   *Ibid.,* I, 150.
14   Louis B. Binsse was consul general for the papal states at this time. He had purely temporal powers. Pius IX hoped for some official representation of the Church with the United States government. See Vincent F. Holden, *The Yankee Paul, Isaac Thomas Hecker* (Milwaukee: Bruce, 1958), p. 245.
15   Ellis, *Life of Cardinal Gibbons*, II, 15.
16   See James Cardinal Gibbons, *A Retrospect of Fifty Years* (Baltimore: J. Murphy, 1916), pp. 187 f.
17   Ellis, *Life of Cardinal Gibbons*, I, 499 f.
18   The combination of fields is significant. Proper treatment of labor was regarded as a moral question from the time of *Rerum Novarum*. In the "Conclusion" of the encyclical Leo XIII said, ". . . Religion alone, as We said at the beginning, can destroy the evil at its root. . . . the primary thing needful is to return to real Christianity, in the absence of which all the plans and devices of the wisest will be of little avail." Leo XIII, *Rerum Novarum*, in *Seven Great Encyclicals* (Glen Rock, N. J.: Paulist Press, 1963), p. 29.
19   Letter from Stephen C. Mason to Gibbons, February 25, 1919, quoted by Ellis in his *Life of Cardinal Gibbons*, I, 541. Ellis' effort to find Gibbons' reply was unsuccessful.
20   The Hecker family prospered later. Isaac's brothers developed a highly successful flour and farina business. See Holden, p. 158.
21   This feeling was more pronounced after the experience at Alcott's Fruitlands. See *ibid.,* pp. 60 f.
22   Walter Elliott, *The Life of Father Hecker* (New York: Columbus Press, 1891), p. 429; Holden, pp. 367 f.
23   In 1850, at the height of Nativism, Hecker wrote to Brownson, "the American people will never believe, or be convinced that we love our country, so long as we do not show genuine patriotic feeling for its interests and destiny." Holden, p. 195. In 1854 Nativist principles as listed in a Know-Nothing "manual" included "repeal of all Naturalization laws, none but Native Amer-

icans for office," and "the sending back of all Foreign Paupers landed on our shores." See John Denig, *The Know-Nothing Manual* (Harrisburg, Pa.: Printed for the author, 1855), p. 20.

24 Walter J. Ong, *American Catholic Crossroads* (New York: Macmillan, 1959), p. 48.

25 Ellis, *Life of Cardinal Gibbons*, II, 11.

26 *Ibid.*, I, 324.

27 See Charles Maignen, *Études sur l'Américanism: le Père Hecker est-il un saint?* (Rome: Desclée, Lefebre, 1899), pp. 9 f.

28 Elliott, pp. 119 f., 183 f.

29 While still at Brook Farm he wrote, "What I do must be Christ in me doing and *not me. . . .*" Holden, p. 54.

30 As a political party Nativism lost its strength in 1855, when Know-Nothingism split on the slavery issue, with the Southern forces left in control. But anti-Catholicism remained very much alive, rising to new heights with the tide of immigration. Anti-Catholicism always found its strongest fuel in the issue of patriotism. During the Second World War the anti-Catholic magazine *Menace* reached a peak of 1,500,000 circulation. In protesting their own patriotism Catholics were simply refuting their opponents. Maynard, II, 187.

31 Quoted by Dorothy Dohen, *Nationalism and American Catholicism* (New York: Sheed and Ward, 1967), p. 110.

32 Ellis, *Life of Cardinal Gibbons*, I, 432.

33 J. F. Powers, "The Wrong Forks," in *Prince of Darkness* (Garden City, N. Y.: Doubleday, 1958), pp. 99 f.

34 *Ibid.*, p. 98.

35 Maynard, I, 104.

36 Augustus Thébaud, *Three Quarters of a Century: A Retrospect* (New York: Catholic Historical Society, 1904), p. 270.

37 Holden, pp. 94, 118.

38 Quoted by Emmet Larkin, "Church and State in Ireland in the Nineteenth Century," in *Church History*, XXXI (September 1962), 90.

39 *Ibid.*, 93.

40 Ellis, *Life of Cardinal Gibbons*, I, 423.

41 Samuel F. B. Morse made much of the "pliable conscience of the Jesuit," which he saw controlling United States Catholics. An "army" of Jesuits was in command of America. Keeping themselves invisible, they were commanded by Gregory XVI, who in turn was commanded by Metternich and Austria. The object was to do away with American rights and liberties by flooding the country with immigrants, who were "but obedient instruments in the hands of their more knowing masters." See Samuel F. B. Morse, *Foreign Conspiracy Against the Liberties of the United States* (New York: Leavitt, Lord, 1835), pp. 6 f.

CHAPTER X   J. F. Powers

1   Powers, *Prince of Darkness*, p. 94.
2   *Ibid.*, p. 100.
3   *Ibid.*, p. 179.
4   Ellis, *Life of Cardinal Gibbons*, I, 54.
5   Powers, *Prince of Darkness*, p. 173.
6   *Ibid.*, p. 173.
7   *Ibid.*, p. 170.
8   *Ibid.*, p. 188.
9   *Ibid.*, p. 191.
10 *Ibid.*, p. 189.
11 J. F. Powers, *Morte d'Urban* (Garden City, N. Y.: Doubleday, 1962), p. 81.
12 I do not mean to imply that the Clementines specifically satirize the Paulists. I think Powers has in mind other orders of missioners who have sprung up in imitation.
13 *Ibid.*, p. 301.
14 *Ibid.*, p. 161.

CHAPTER XI   Flannery O'Connor

1   Flannery O'Connor, *A Good Man Is Hard To Find and Other Stories* (New York: Harcourt, Brace, 1955), p. 102.
2   *Ibid.*, p. 121.
3   *Ibid.*, p. 123.
4   *Ibid.*, p. 127.
5   *Ibid.*, p. 128.
6   *Ibid.*, p. 103.
7   *Ibid.*, pp. 128, 129.
8   Flannery O'Connor, *Wise Blood*, in *3 by Flannery O'Connor* (New York: New American Library, 1964), p. 15.
9   *Ibid.*, p. 39.
10 *Ibid.*, p. 21.
11 *Ibid.*, p. 23.
12 *Ibid.*, p. 26.
13 *Ibid.*, p. 34.
14 *Ibid.*, p. 64.
15 *Ibid.*, p. 60.
16 *Ibid.*, p. 68.
17 *Ibid.*, p. 90.
18 *Ibid.*
19 *Ibid.*, p. 112.
20 See William W. O. E. Oesterly and Robert Henry Charles, "Enoch," *Encyclopaedia Britannica* (Chicago: Encyclopaedia Britannica, 1946), VIII, 615.
21 Robert Fitzgerald, "Introduction" to *Everything That Rises Must Converge* by Flannery O'Connor (New York: Farrar, Straus and Giroux, 1965), p. xv.

22   O'Connor, *Wise Blood*, p. 88.
23   *Ibid.*, p. 110.
24   Fitzgerald, p. xvi.
25   O'Connor, *Wise Blood*, p. 114.
26   *Ibid.*, p. 123.
27   *Ibid.*, p. 122.
28   See *ibid.*, p. 8.
29   Flannery O'Connor, *The Violent Bear It Away*, in *3 by Flannery O'Connor* (New York: New American Library, 1964), p. 330.
30   *Ibid.*, p. 345.
31   *Ibid.*, p. 315.
32   *Ibid.*, p. 326.
33   *Ibid.*, p. 390.
34   *Ibid.*, p. 355.
35   *Ibid.*
36   *Ibid.*, p. 363.
37   *Ibid.*, p. 369.
38   *Ibid.*, p. 382.
39   *Ibid.*, p. 409.
40   *Ibid.*, p. 416.
41   *Ibid.*, p. 401.
42   *Ibid.*, p. 402.
43   *Ibid.*, p. 397.
44   *Ibid.*, p. 428.
45   *Ibid.*, p. 433.
46   *Ibid.*, p. 436.
47   *Ibid.*, p. 439.
48   *Ibid.*, p. 444.
49   *Ibid.*, p. 445.
50   *Ibid.*, p. 446.
51   *Ibid.*, p. 447.
52   *Ibid.*
53   *Ibid.*, p. 433.
54   Flannery O'Connor has repeatedly protested her belief in freedom of the will. She has also protested that she does not believe in total depravity. A typical passage reads: "The Catholic novel . . . cannot see man as determined; it cannot see him as totally depraved. It will see him as incomplete in himself, as prone to evil, but as redeemable when his efforts are assisted by grace." Flannery O'Connor, "In the Protestant South," *Mystery and Manners*, edited by Sally and Robert Fitzgerald (New York: Farrar, Straus and Giroux, 1969), p. 197. If one looks carefully at this passage, one will feel it full of important reservations. Man is not "totally depraved," but he is "prone to evil." He is redeemable "when his own efforts are assisted by grace." Orthodoxy will insist that man is always assisted by grace, and that, while man is prone to evil, he also has impulses toward good. In an article in the same collection, Miss O'Connor insists that man is so free that "with his last breath he can say *No*." "Catholic Novelists and Their Readers," *ibid.*, p. 183. The fact re-

mains that in her two novels neither of the heroes does finally say No. Her own description of their state is that a character like Tarwater "appears to have a compulsion," which is "the mystery of God's will for him." "Tarwater is certainly free and meant to be; if he appears to have a compulsion to be a prophet, I can only insist that in this compulsion there is the mystery of God's will for him . . . and that it is not a compulsion in the clinical sense. As for Enoch, he is a moron and chiefly a comic character. I don't think it is important whether his compulsion is clinical or not." "On Her Own Work," *ibid.*, p. 117. Clearly, although Miss O'Connor's conscious beliefs were orthodox, the framework of "compulsion" within which she places characters shows a "freedom" that is drastically reduced. There is no need to insist on this point. It is obvious in the novels.

Abbott, Walter M., editor. *The Documents of Vatican II*. New York: Guild Press, 1966.

Allott, Kenneth, and Miriam Farris. *The Art of Graham Greene*. London: Hamish Hamilton, 1951.

Angers, Pierre. *Commentaire de L'Art poétique de Paul Claudel*. Paris: Mercure de France, 1949.

Arendt, Hannah. *The Origins of Totalitarianism*. New York: Harcourt, Brace and World, 1966.

Atkins, John. *Graham Greene*. London: Calder and Boyars, 1966.

Baldick, Robert. *The Life of Joris-Karl Huysmans*. Oxford, England: Clarendon Press, 1955.

Balthasar, Hans Urs von. *Le Chrétien Bernanos*. Translated by M. de Gandillac. Paris: Éditions du Seuil, 1956.

Barbey d'Aurevilly, Jules. *Le Chevalier des Touches*. New York: Century, 1932.

——— *Les Diaboliques*. Paris: Garnier, 1963.

——— *L'Ensorcelée*. Paris: Bernouard, 1926.

——— *Un Prêtre marié*. Paris: Bernouard, 1927.

——— *Une vieille Maîtresse*. Paris: Bernouard, 1927.

Barry, J. Coleman. *The Catholic Church and the German Americans*. Milwaukee: Bruce, 1953.

Bassan, Maurice. "Flannery O'Connor's Way: Shock with Moral Intent." *Renascence*, XV (Summer 1963), 195-99, 211.

Bedoyere, Michael de la. *The Life of Baron von Hügel*. New York: Scribner's, 1951.

Beecher, Lyman. *A Plea for the West*. New York: Leavitt, Lord, 1836.

Béguin, Albert. *Bernanos par lui-même.* Paris: Éditions du Seuil, 1959.

———— *Georges Bernanos, essais et témoignages réunis.* Neufchâtel: La Baconnière, 1949.

———— *Léon Bloy, l'impatient.* Fribourg: Egloff, 1944.

———— *Léon Bloy, mystique de la douleur.* Paris: Labergerie, 1948.

Belloc, Hilaire. *The Cruise of the Nona.* Boston: Houghton, Mifflin, 1925.

———— *Emmanuel Burden.* London: Methuen, 1904.

———— *Essays of a Catholic Layman.* London: Sheed and Ward, 1931.

———— *How the Reformation Happened.* London: J. Cape, 1928.

Benson, Robert Hugh. *Light Invisible.* London: Burns Oates, 1921.

———— *Lord of the World.* New York: Dodd, Mead, 1908.

Bernanos, Georges. *Le Chemin de la croix des âmes.* Paris: Gallimard, 1948.

———— *Le Crépuscule des vieux.* Paris: Gallimard, 1956.

———— *Les Enfants humiliés.* Paris: Gallimard, 1949.

———— *Français si vous savez.* Paris: Gallimard, 1961.

———— *La grande Peur des bien-pensants.* Paris: Grasset, 1931.

———— *Les grands Cimetières sous la lune.* Paris: Plon, 1938.

———— *Nous autres français.* Paris: Gallimard, 1939.

———— *Oeuvres romanesques.* Paris: Gallimard, 1961.

   Madame Dargent

   Une Nuit

   Dialogue d'ombres

   Sous le Soleil de Satan

   L'Imposture

   La Joie

   Un Crime

   Un mauvais Rêve

   Journal d'un curé de campagne

   Nouvelle Histoire de Mouchette

   Monsieur Ouine

   Dialogues des Carmélites

———— Unpublished correspondence being edited by Sister Meredith Murray, Rosary College, River Forest, Illinois.

Blanchard, Paul. *American Freedom and Catholic Power.* Boston: Beacon, 1958.

Bloy, Léon. *Le Désespéré*. Paris: Mercure de France, 1923.

———— *La Femme pauvre*. Paris: Mercure de France, 1921.

Blumenthal, Guda. *The Poetic Imagination of Georges Bernanos*. Baltimore: Johns Hopkins Press, 1965.

Bornecque, Jacques Henri. "Introduction" to *Les Diaboliques* by Jules Barbey d'Aurevilly. Paris: Garnier, 1963.

Bourget, Paul. *Le Disciple*. Paris: Plon, 1939.

Bradbury, Malcolm. *Evelyn Waugh*. London: Oliver and Boyd, 1964.

Bush, William. *Souffrance et expiation dans la pensée de Bernanos*. Paris: Minard, 1961.

Canu, Jean. *Barbey d'Aurevilly*. Paris: Laffont, 1945.

Carens, James Francis. *The Satiric Art of Evelyn Waugh*. Seattle: University of Washington Press, 1966.

Carthy, M. P. *Catholicism in English-Speaking Lands*. New York: Hawthorn, 1964.

Chaigne, Louis. *Paul Claudel, the Man and the Mystic*. New York: Appleton-Century-Crofts, 1961.

Chesterton, Gilbert Keith. *The Autobiography of G. K. Chesterton*. New York: Sheed and Ward, 1936.

———— *The Ball and the Cross*. New York: John Lane, 1909.

———— *The Collected Poems of G. K. Chesterton*. London: Palmer, 1927.

———— *Heretics*. New York: John Lane, 1905.

———— *The Innocence of Father Brown*. London: Cassell, 1911.

———— *The Man Who Was Thursday*. Bristol, England: Arrowsmith, 1912.

———— *Orthodoxy*. New York: Dodd, Mead, 1936.

Claudel, Paul. *L'Annonce faite à Marie*. Paris: NRF, 1923.

———— *L'Art poétique*. Paris: Mercure de France, 1913.

———— *L'Otage*. Paris: Gallimard, 1938.

———— *Partage de midi*. Paris: Gallimard, 1949.

———— *Le Soulier de satin*. Paris: Gallimard, 1954.

Colla, Pierre. *L'Univers tragique de Barbey d'Aurevilly*. Bruxelles: Renaissance du Livre, 1965.

Corbishly, Thomas, and Robert Speaight. *Ronald Knox*. New York: Sheed and Ward, 1965.

Cormeau, Lilly. *L'Art de François Mauriac*. Paris: Grasset, 1951.

Cross, Robert. *The Emergence of Liberal Catholicism in America*. Cambridge, Mass.: Harvard University Press, 1958.

Culkin, G. "England." *New Catholic Encyclopedia*. New York: McGraw-Hill, 1967. V, 353-69.

Daniel-Rops, Henri. *The Church in an Age of Revolution, 1789-1870*. Translated by John Warrington. London: Dent, 1965.

Dansette, Adrien. *Histoire religieuse de la France contemporaine*. Paris: Flammarion, 1965.

Deblue, Henri. *Les Romans de Georges Bernanos*. Neufchâtel: La Baconnière, 1965.

Delhet, Jean. *Beginnings of the Catholic Church in the United States*. Washington, D.C.: Salve Regina Press, 1922.

Denig, John. *The Know-Nothing Manual, or, Book for America*. Harrisburg, Pa.: Printed for the author, 1855.

Desmond, Humphrey. *The Know-Nothing Party*. Washington, D.C.: New Century, 1904.

Digby, Kenelm. *The Broad Stone of Honour*. London: Quaritch, 1876.

Dohen, Dorothy. *Nationalism and American Catholicism*. New York: Sheed and Ward, 1967.

Donaldson, Frances. *Evelyn Waugh, Portrait of a Country Neighbor*. London: Weidenfeld and Nicolson, 1967.

Dowell, Bob. "Grace in the Fiction of Flannery O'Connor." *College English*, XXVII (December 1965), 235-39.

Drake, Robert. *Flannery O'Connor, A Critical Essay*. Grand Rapids, Mich.: Eerdman, 1966.

Du Bois, Charles. *François Mauriac et le problème du romancier catholique*. Paris: Éditions Corrêa, 1933.

Elliott, Walter. *The Life of Father Hecker*. New York: Columbus Press, 1891.

Ellis, John Tracy. *American Catholicism*. Chicago: University of Chicago Press, 1956.

———— *The Life of James Cardinal Gibbons*. Milwaukee: Bruce, 1952.

———— *Perspectives in American Catholicism*. Baltimore: Helicon, 1963.

Esprit, VIII (Winter 1964). Entire issue devoted to Flannery O'Connor.

Estang, Luc. *Présence de Bernanos*. Paris: Plon, 1947.

Esteve, Michel. "Biographie de Georges Bernanos." *Oeuvres roman-esques de Georges Bernanos*. Paris: Gallimard, 1961.

———— *Le Sens de l'amour dans les romans de Bernanos*. Paris: Lettres Modernes, 1959.

Evans, Robert O., editor. *Graham Greene*. Lexington: University of Kentucky Press, 1963.

Fecher, Charles A. *The Philosophy of Jacques Maritain*. Westminster. Md.: Newman Press, 1953.

Fitzgerald, Robert. "The Countryside and the True Country." *Sewanee Review*, LXX (Summer 1962), 380-94.

———— "Introduction" to *Everything That Rises Must Converge* by Flannery O'Connor. New York: Farrar, Straus and Giroux, 1965.

Fowlie, Wallace. *Jacob's Night, The Religious Renascence in France*. New York: Sheed and Ward, 1947.

Friedman, Melvin J., and Lewis A. Lawson, editors. *The Added Dimension, The Art and Mind of Flannery O'Connor*. New York: Fordham University Press, 1966.

Gaucher, Guy. *Georges Bernanos ou l'invincible espérance*. Paris: Gallimard, 1962.

———— *Le Thème de la mort dans les romans de Bernanos*. Paris: Lettres Modernes, 1955.

Gibbons, James Cardinal. "Defence of the Knights of Labor." *Documents of American Catholic History*. Edited by John Tracy Ellis. Chicago: Regnery, 1967. II, 444-45.

———— *A Retrospect of Fifty Years*. Baltimore: J. Murphy, 1916.

———— "The Roman Sermon of the American Cardinal on Church and State in the United States." *Documents of American Catholic History*. Edited by John Tracy Ellis. Chicago: Regnery, 1967. II, 461-63.

Gide, André. *Journal, 1889-1919*. Paris: Gallimard, 1951.

Gillespie, Jessie Lynn. *Le Tragique dans l'oeuvre de Georges Bernanos*. Geneva: Droz, 1960.

Gordon, Caroline, and others. "Diverse Readings of Flannery O'Connor." *Sewanee Review*, LXXVI (Spring 1968), 263-356.

"Grant's Proposal and Blaine's Amendment To Prevent Public Funds for Religious Schools." *Documents of American Catholic History*. Edited by John Tracy Ellis. Chicago: Regnery, 1967. I, 395-96.

Greenblatt, Stephen Jay. *Three Modern Satirists: Waugh, Orwell, and Huxley.* New Haven: Yale University Press, 1965.

Greene, Graham. *Brighton Rock.* New York: Viking, 1961.

———— *A Burnt-Out Case.* New York: Viking, 1961.

———— *The Comedians.* New York: Viking, 1966.

———— *The Confidential Agent.* New York: Viking, 1939.

———— *The End of the Affair.* New York: Viking, 1951.

———— *England Made Me.* Garden City, N. Y.: Doubleday, 1935.

———— *A Gun for Sale.* London: Heinemann, 1936.

———— *The Heart of the Matter.* New York: Viking, 1964.

———— *In Search of a Character.* New York: Viking, 1962.

———— *In Search of Reality.* New York: Viking, 1963.

———— *It's a Battlefield.* New York: Viking, 1962.

———— *Journey Without Maps.* London: Heinemann, 1936.

———— *The Lawless Roads.* London: Longmans, 1939.

———— *The Living Room.* New York: Viking, 1954.

———— *Loser Take All.* New York: Viking, 1957.

———— *The Lost Childhood, and Other Essays.* New York: Viking, 1952.

———— *The Man Within.* Garden City, N. Y.: Doubleday, 1929.

———— *The Ministry of Fear.* New York: Viking, 1943.

———— *The Name of Action.* Garden City, N. Y.: Doubleday, 1933.

———— *Orient Express.* Garden City, N. Y.: Doubleday, 1934.

———— *Our Man in Havana.* New York: Viking, 1958.

———— *The Potting Shed.* London: Heinemann, 1957.

———— *The Power and the Glory.* New York: Viking, 1965.

———— *The Quiet American.* New York: Viking, 1956.

———— *The Third Man.* New York: Viking, 1950.

———— *Twenty-One Stories.* London: Heinemann, 1954.

Guilday, Peter Keenan. *The Life and Times of John England.* New York: America Press, 1927.

Gurian, Waldemar, and M. A. Fitzsimons, editors. *The Catholic Church in World Affairs.* Notre Dame, Ind.: University of Notre Dame Press, 1954.

Hagopian, John V. *J. F. Powers.* New York: Twayne, 1968.

Hales, E. E. Y. *The Catholic Church in the Modern World.* Garden City, N. Y.: Doubleday, 1960.

———— *Pope John and His Revolution*. Garden City, N. Y.: Doubleday, 1965.

Hebblethwaite, Peter. *Bernanos, An Introduction*. New York: Hillary House, 1965.

Heppenstall, Rayner. *The Double Image, Mutations of Christian Mythology in the Work of Four French Catholic Writers of To-day and Yesterday*. London: Secker and Warburg, 1947.

Holden, Vincent F. *The Yankee Paul, Isaac Thomas Hecker*. Milwaukee: Bruce, 1958.

Hollis, Christopher. *Evelyn Waugh*. London: Longmans, 1954.

Hourdin, Georges. *Mauriac, romancier chrétien*. Paris: Éditions du Temps Present, 1945.

Hudson, Winthrop S. *Religion in America*. New York: Scribner's, 1965.

Huysmans, Joris-Karl. *À rebours*. Paris: Fasquille, 1961.

———— *En Route*. Paris: Plon, 1965.

———— *L'Oblat*. Paris: Plon, 1960.

Ireland, John. "Views on Socialism." *Documents of American Catholic History*. Edited by John Tracy Ellis. Chicago: Regnery, 1967. II, 489-92.

Jarrett-Kerr, Martin. *François Mauriac*. Cambridge, England: Bowes and Bowes, 1954.

Jenkins, Cecil. *Mauriac*. London: Oliver and Boyd, 1965.

John XXIII. *Mater et Magistra*. Glen Rock, N. J.: Paulist Press, 1962.

———— *Pacem in Terris*. Glen Rock, N. J.: Paulist Press, 1963.

Kinsman, Frederick. *Americanism and Catholicism*. New York: Longmans, Green, 1924.

Knox, Ronald. *Essays in Satire*. London: Sheed and Ward, 1928.

———— *A Spiritual Aeneid*. London: Longmans, 1918.

Kunkel, Francis. *The Labyrinthine Ways of Graham Greene*. New York: Sheed and Ward, 1959.

Lally, Francis. *The Catholic Church in a Changing America*. Boston: Little, Brown, 1962.

Larkin, Emmet. "Church and State in Ireland in the Nineteenth Century." *Church History*, XXXI (September 1962), 87-94.

Lawson, Lewis. "Flannery O'Connor and the Grotesque." *Renascence*, XVII (Spring 1965), 137-47.

Lefevre, Frederic. *Georges Bernanos*. Paris: Tour d'Ivoire, 1926.

Leo XIII. *Longinqua Oceani. Documents of American Catholic History.* Edited by John Tracy Ellis. Chicago: Regnery, 1967. II, 499-504.

———— *Rerum Novarum,* in *Seven Great Encyclicals.* Glen Rock, N. J.: Paulist Press, 1963.

———— *Testem Benevolentiae. Documents of American Catholic History.* Edited by John Tracy Ellis. Chicago: Regnery, 1967. II, 537-43.

Loewenisch, Walter von. *Modern Catholicism.* Translated by Reginald H. Fuller. New York: St. Martin's, 1959.

McAvoy, T. T. *The Americanist Heresy in Roman Catholicism.* Notre Dame, Ind.: University of Notre Dame Press, 1963.

McCarthy, Desmond. *Priests and People in Ireland.* Dublin: Hodges, Figgis, 1902.

MacEoin, Gary. *What Happened at Rome, The Council and Its Implications for the Modern World.* New York: Holt, Rinehart and Winston, 1966.

Madaule, Jacques. *Graham Greene.* Paris: Éditions du Temps Present, 1949.

Maignen, Charles. *Études sur l'Américanism: le Père Hecker est-il un saint?* Rome: Desclée, Lefebre, 1899.

Maison, Margaret M. *The Victorian Vision, Studies in the Religious Novel.* New York: Sheed and Ward, 1961.

Majault, Joseph. *Mauriac et l'art du roman.* Paris: Laffont, 1946.

Malin, Irving. *New American Gothic.* Carbondale, Ill.: Southern Illinois University Press, 1962.

Mallet, Robert, editor. *The Correspondence between Paul Claudel and André Gide, 1899-1926.* Translated by John Russell. London: Secker and Warburg, 1952.

Mandell, C. Creighton, and Edward Shanks. *Hilaire Belloc, the Man and His Work.* London: Longmans, 1916.

Maritain, Jacques. *Art and Scholasticism and The Frontiers of Poetry.* Translated by Joseph W. Evans. New York: Scribner's, 1962.

———— *Creative Intuition in Art and Poetry.* The A. W. Mellon Lectures in the Fine Arts, National Gallery of Art, Washington, D. C. New York: Pantheon, 1953.

———— *Le Paysan de la Garonne.* Paris: Desclée de Brouwer, 1966.

———— *True Humanism.* New York: Scribner's, 1954.

Maritain, Raïssa. *Les grandes Amitiés et Les Aventures de grace*. Paris: Desclée de Brouwer, 1948.

Mauriac, François. *L'Agneau*. Paris: Flammarion, 1954.

———— *Les Anges noirs*. Paris: Grasset, 1936.

———— *Le Baiser au lépreux*. Paris: Grasset, 1922.

———— *Bloc-notes*. Paris: Flammarion, 1958.

———— *Ce qui était perdu*. Paris: Grasset, 1930.

———— *La Chair et le sang*. Paris: Emile Paul, 1920.

———— *Les Chemins de la mer*. Paris: Grasset, 1939.

———— "Chronique dramatique." *Nouvelle Revue Française*, XXIV (February 1925), 220-21; (May 1925), 925.

———— *Le Désert de l'amour*. Paris: Grasset, 1925.

———— *L'Enfant chargé de chaines*. Paris: Grasset, 1913.

———— *La Fin de la nuit*. Paris: Grasset, 1935.

———— *Le Fleuve de feu*. Paris: Grasset, 1923.

———— *Genitrix*. Paris: Grasset, 1923.

———— *Journal*. Paris: Grasset, 1934.

———— *Journal d'un homme de trente ans*. Paris: Egloff, 1948.

———— *Letters on Art and Literature*. Translated by Mario A. Pei. New York: Philosophical Library, 1953.

———— *Le Mal*. Paris: Grasset, 1935.

———— *Mémoires intérieurs*. Paris: Flammarion, 1959.

———— *Le Mystère Frontenac*. Paris: Grasset, 1933.

———— *Le Noeud de vipères*. Paris: Grasset, 1933.

———— *La Pharisienne*. Paris: Grasset, 1941.

———— "Préface" to *Graham Greene* by Victor de Pange. Paris: Éditions Universitaires, 1953.

———— *Préseánces*. Paris: Emile Paul, 1921.

———— *Problèmes du catholicisme français*. Paris: Julliard, 1954.

———— *La Robe prétexte*. Paris: Grasset, 1928.

———— *Le Romancier et ses personnages*. Paris: Éditions Corrêa, 1933.

———— *Le Sagouin*. Paris: Grasset, 1951.

———— *Second Thoughts, Reflections on Literature and on Life*. New York: World, 1961.

———— *Souffrance et bonheur du chrétien*. Paris: Grasset, 1931.

———— *Thérèse Desqueroux*. Paris: Grasset, 1927.

Maynard, Theodore. *The Story of American Catholicism*. Garden City, N. Y.: Doubleday, 1960.

Moloney, Michael F. *François Mauriac, A Critical Study*. Denver: Swallow, 1958.

Morse, Samuel F. B. *Foreign Conspiracy Against the Liberties of the United States*. New York: Leavitt, Lord, 1835.

Mueller, William R. *The Prophetic Voice in Modern Fiction*. Garden City, N. Y.: Doubleday, 1959.

Naughton, Helen Thomas. *Jacques Rivière*. Paris and The Hague: Mouton, 1966.

Newman, John Henry. *Apologia pro Vita Sua*. New York: America Press, 1942.

———— *An Essay on the Development of Christian Doctrine*. Garden City, N. Y.: Doubleday, 1960.

———— *Loss and Gain*. London: Longmans, 1898.

Nolte, Ernst. *The Three Faces of Fascism*. New York: Holt, Rinehart and Winston, 1966.

Novak, Michael. *The Open Church*. New York: Macmillan, 1964.

O'Brien, Conor Cruise. *Maria Cross, Imaginative Patterns in a Group of Modern Catholic Writers*. New York: Oxford University Press, 1952.

O'Connor, Flannery. "The Capture." *Mademoiselle*, XXXIII (November 1948), 148-49, 195-96, 198-201.

———— "The Church and the Fiction Writer." *America*, XCVI (March 30, 1957), 733-35.

———— *Everything That Rises Must Converge*. New York: Farrar, Straus and Giroux, 1965.

———— "The Fiction Writer and His Country." *The Living Novel, A Symposium*. Edited by Granville Hicks. New York: Macmillan, 1957.

———— "The Geranium." *Accent*, VI (Summer 1946), 245-53.

———— *A Good Man Is Hard To Find and Other Stories*. New York: Harcourt, Brace, 1955.

———— *Mystery and Manners*. Edited by Sally and Robert Fitzgerald. New York: Farrar, Straus and Giroux, 1969.

———— "The Novelist and Free Will." *Fresco*, II (Winter 1963), 26-29.

———— "The Partridge Festival." *The Critic*, XIII (February-March 1961), 82-85.

———— *The Violent Bear It Away*, in *3 by Flannery O'Connor*. New York: New American Library, 1964.

———— "Why Do the Heathens Rage?" *Esquire*, LX (July 1963), 60-61.

———— *Wise Blood*, in *3 by Flannery O'Connor*. New York: New American Library, 1964.

Ong, Walter J. *American Catholic Crossroads*. New York: Macmillan, 1959.

———— *Frontiers of American Catholicism*. New York: Macmillan, 1957.

Palante, Alain. *Mauriac, le roman et la vie*. Paris: Le Portulan, 1946.

Pange, Victor de. *Graham Greene*. Paris: Éditions Universitaires, 1953.

Péguy, Charles. *Cahiers de la Quinzaine. Oeuvres en prose de Charles Péguy*. Paris: Pléiade, 1959.

———— "Le Mystère de la charité de Jeanne d'Arc," in *Charles Péguy, Oeuvres poétiques complètes*. Paris: Gallimard, 1957.

Péguy, Charles, and Marcel Baudouin. "Jeanne d'Arc," in *Charles Péguy, Oeuvres poétiques complètes*. Paris: Gallimard, 1957.

Pell, Elsie. *François Mauriac, In Search of the Infinite*. New York: Philosophical Library, 1947.

Picon, Gaëton. "Préface" to *Oeuvres romanesques de Georges Bernanos*. Paris: Gallimard, 1961.

Pius IX. *Syllabus of Errors*, in *Dogmatic Canons and Decrees*. New York: Devin-Adair, 1912.

Pius XI. *Quadragesimo Anno*, in *Seven Great Encyclicals*. Glen Rock, N. J.: Paulist Press, 1963.

Powers, J. F. "The Author as a Responsible Storyteller." National Book Award Address. *New York Times Book Review*, May 12, 1963, p. 2.

———— "Keystone." *The New Yorker*, XXXIX (May 18, 1963), 42-46, 48, 50, 53, 56, 59-60, 62, 65-67, 72, 75-76, 78, 81.

———— "Moonshot." *The Nation*, CXCII (March 3, 1962), 195-96, 204.

———— *Morte d'Urban*. Garden City, N. Y.: Doubleday, 1962.

———— *The Presence of Grace*. Garden City, N. Y.: Doubleday, 1957.

———— *Prince of Darkness*. Garden City, N. Y.: Doubleday, 1958.

Pryce-Jones, David. *Graham Greene*. London: Bodley Head, 1961.

Quinn, Sister M. Bernetta. "View from a Rock: The Fiction of Flannery O'Connor and J. F. Powers." *Critique*, II (Fall 1958), 19-27.

Rivière, Jacques. "De la Foi." *Nouvelle Revue Française*, No. 47 (November 1912), 781-93; No. 48 (December 1912), 970-80.

―――― *Nouvelles Études*. Paris: Gallimard, 1947.

Rivière, Jacques, and Paul Claudel. "Correspondence." *Nouvelle Revue Française*, XII (August 1925), 131-45; (September 1925), 290-304.

Rivière, Jacques, and Ramon Fernandez. *Moralisme et littérature*. Paris: Éditions Corrêa, 1932.

Roemer, Theodore. *The Catholic Church in the United States*. St. Louis: Herder, 1950.

Rolfe, Frederick. *Hadrian VII*. New York: Knopf, 1937.

Rubin, Louis D., Jr. *The Faraway Country: Writers of the Modern South*. Seattle: University of Washington Press, 1963.

Ryan, John A. *The Bishops' Program of Social Reconstruction. Documents of American Catholic History*. Chicago: Regnery, 1967. II, 589-95.

Sacks, Sheldon. *Fiction and the Shape of Belief*. Berkeley and Los Angeles: University of California Press, 1964.

Scott, Nathan A. *Craters of the Spirit*. Washington, D. C.: Corpus Books, 1968.

Scott, Walter. "Introduction" to *Le Chevalier des Touches* by Joris-Karl Huysmans. New York: Century, 1932.

Sécretain, Roger. *Péguy, Soldat de la Liberté*. New York: Brentano's; Montreal: Valiquette, 1941.

Sisk, John P. "The Complex Moral Vision of J. F. Powers." *Critique*, II (Fall 1958), 28-40.

Spark, Muriel. *The Ballad of Peckham Rye*. London: Macmillan, 1960.

―――― *The Comforters*. Philadelphia: Lippincott, 1957.

―――― *Memento Mori*. London: Macmillan, 1959.

―――― *The Prime of Miss Jean Brodie*. Philadelphia: Lippincott, 1962.

Speaight, Robert. *The Life of Eric Gill*. New York: Kenedy, 1966.

―――― *The Life of Hilaire Belloc*. London: Hollis and Carter, 1957.

Spender, Stephen. *The Creative Element: A Study of Vision, Despair and Orthodoxy Among Some Modern Writers*. New York: British Book Center, 1954.

Stanford, Derek. *Muriel Spark*. London: Centaur, 1963.

Steiner, George. *Language and Silence*. New York: Atheneum, 1967.

Stopp, Frederick J. *Evelyn Waugh, Portrait of an Artist*. London: Chapman and Hall, 1958.

Stratford, Philip. *Faith and Fiction, Creative Process in Greene and Mauriac*. Notre Dame, Ind.: University of Notre Dame Press, 1964.

Symons, A. J. A. *The Quest for Corvo*. New York: Macmillan, 1934.

Thébaud, Augustus. *Three Quarters of a Century: A Retrospect*. New York: Catholic Historical Society, 1904.

Trevor, Meriol. *Newman, Light in Winter*. Garden City, N. Y.: Doubleday, 1963.

———— *Newman, The Pillar of the Cloud*. Garden City, N. Y.: Doubleday, 1962.

Villiers, Marjorie. *Charles Péguy, A Study in Integrity*. New York: Harper and Row, 1965.

Vitis, A. A. de. *Roman Holiday, The Catholic Novels of Evelyn Waugh*. London: Vision Press, 1958.

Ward, Maisie. *Gilbert Keith Chesterton*. New York: Sheed and Ward, 1943.

Ward, Wilfrid. *William George Ward and the Catholic Revival*. London: Macmillan, 1893.

Watkin, E. I. *Roman Catholicism in England*. London: Oxford University Press, 1957.

Watrin, François Philibert. "The Banishment of the Jesuits from Louisiana and the Illinois Country." *Documents of American Catholic History*. Edited by John Tracy Ellis. Chicago: Regnery, 1967. I, 84-85.

Waugh, Evelyn. *Black Mischief*. Boston: Little, Brown, 1946.

———— *Brideshead Revisited*. Boston: Little, Brown, 1945.

———— "Come Inside." *The Road to Damascus*. Edited by John A. O'Brien. Garden City, N. Y.: Doubleday, 1949.

———— *Edmund Campion*. London: Longmans, 1937.

———— *A Handful of Dust*. London: Chapman and Hall, 1934.

———— *A Little Learning, The First Volume of an Autobiography*. London: Chapman and Hall, 1964.

———— *Love Among the Ruins*. London: Chapman and Hall, 1953.

———— *The Loved One*. Boston: Little, Brown, 1948.

———— *Monsignor Ronald Knox*. Boston: Little, Brown, 1949.

Waugh, Evelyn. *The Ordeal of Gilbert Pinfold*. London: Chapman and Hall, 1957.

———— *Put Out More Flags*. Boston: Little, Brown, 1955.

———— *Scoop*. Boston: Little, Brown, 1949.

———— "Some Scenes of Clerical Life." *Commonweal*, LXIII (March 30, 1956), 667-69.

———— *Sword of Honour*. Boston: Little, Brown, 1966.

———— *Vile Bodies*. Boston: Little, Brown, 1930.

Wilson, Edmund. *Classics and Commercials*. New York: Farrar, Straus and Cudahy, 1950.

Wiltgen, Ralph M. *The Rhine Flows into the Tiber*. New York: Hawthorn, 1967.

Wimsatt, William K., and Cleanth Brooks. *Literary Criticism*. New York: Random House, 1957.

Wiseman, Nicholas. *Fabiola*. London: Burns and Lambert, 1855.

Wright, Gordon. *Rural Revolution in France: The Peasantry in the Twentieth Century*. Stanford, Calif.: Stanford University Press, 1964.

Yarrow, P. *La Pensée politique et religieuse de Barbey d'Aurevilly*. Geneva: Droz, 1961.

Zabel, Morton Dauwen. *Craft and Character: Texts, Method, and Vocation in Modern Fiction*. New York: Viking, 1957.

———————

About this book

The Vital Tradition was designed by William Nicoll of Edit, Inc. It was set in the composing room of Loyola University Press. The text is 12 on 14 Bodoni Book; the reduced matter, 10 on 12; and the notes, 8 on 10. The display type is Bodoni Book (Mono 875).

It was printed by Photopress, Inc., on Warren's 60-pound English Finish paper and bound by The Engdahl Company in Bancroft cloth.